SOUTHERN LITERARY STUDIES

FRED HOBSON, EDITOR

Lovers and Beloveds

SEXUAL OTHERNESS IN
SOUTHERN FICTION, 1936–1961

GARY RICHARDS

LOUISIANA STATE UNIVERSITY PRESS
BATON ROUGE

Copyright © 2005 by Louisiana State University Press
Manufactured in the United States of America
FIRST PRINTING

DESIGNER: Barbara Neely Bourgoyne
TYPEFACE: Adobe Caslon
TYPESETTER: G&S Typesetters
PRINTER AND BINDER: Thomson-Shore, Inc.

Library of Congress Cataloging-in-Publication Data

Richards, Gary, 1969–
    Lovers and beloveds : sexual otherness in Southern fiction, 1936–1961 /
Gary Richards.
        p.   cm. — (Southern literary studies)
    Includes bibliographical references and index.
    ISBN 0-8071-3051-6 (cloth : alk. paper)
    1. American fiction—Southern States—History and criticism.
2. Homosexuality and literature—Southern States—History—20th century.
3. American fiction—20th century—History and criticism.   4. Erotic stories,
American—History and criticism.   5. Love stories, American—History and
criticism.   6. Difference (Psychology) in literature.   7. Sexual orientation in
literature.   8. Homosexuality in literature.   9. Lesbians in literature.   10. Gay
men in literature.   I. Title.   II. Series.
PS374.H63R53 2005
813'.509353—dc22

                                                            2004023918

Chapters 1 and 2, respectively, appeared previously in slightly different form as
"'With a Special Emphasis': The Dynamics of (Re)Claiming a Queer Southern
Renaissance," *Mississippi Quarterly* 55, no. 2 (Spring 2002): 209–29; and "Writing
the Fairy *Huckleberry Finn*: William Goyen's and Truman Capote's Genderings
of Male Homosexuality," *Journal of Homosexuality* 34, nos. 3–4 (1998): 67–86.
Used by permission.

for ROSELLAN FOUTY RICHARDS
and FRED RICHARDS, JR.

Contents

Acknowledgments

THIS PROJECT HAS REACHED COMPLETION only with the assistance and kindness of a number of people. I am especially grateful to members of Vanderbilt's Department of English for their support in the earliest phases of the project. Thadious Davis, Teresa Goddu, Cecelia Tichi, Valerie Traub, and the late Nancy Walker offered valuable advice and encouragement. Michael Kreyling in particular provided expert guidance, and his professional model and friendship remain pieces of my good fortune. My work also benefited from the support provided by a coterie of friends in Nashville, and I thank Erik Bledsoe, Suzanne Bost, June Ellis, Gregg Hecimovich, Bridget Heneghan, Dan Hipp, Phil Nel, Risa Nystrom, Phil Phillips, Alison Piepmeier, Jonathan Rogers, Adriane Stewart, Craig Watson, and Karin Westman for their friendship. I am particularly indebted to Eliza McGraw, whose insights about southern culture and literature have gratified me as few other elements of my intellectual exchanges have, and to Roger Moore, whose honed analyses have amused, irked, and sustained me for longer than he cares to admit.

Since coming to the University of New Orleans, I have had the opportunity to refine my ideas within an equally supportive environment. Both the College of Liberal Arts and the Department of English have provided generous financial resources. Students in my American, southern, and African American literature classes have consistently engaged with and challenged my thinking about region and sexuality. Kathy Amende, Rachelle Defillo, Josh Galjour, Marty Harris, Mia Legaux, and Janella Usher stand apart, however, not only for allowing me to witness their intellectual growth but also for becoming valued friends. Shane Breaux has extended so much generous hospitality, sometimes in quite literally dark days, that even Caroline would smile her appreciation. My colleagues in the Department of English have also offered ongoing encouragement, and Anne Boyd, John Cooke, Inge Fink, John Hazlett, and Tony Whitt in particular have touched me with their kindness. But my greatest debt is to Roz Foy and Catherine Loomis, colleagues and friends who, perhaps, can never know how much they have come to mean to me and how crucial they have been to the completion of this project.

Colleagues at meetings of the Twentieth-Century Literature Conference, the Society for the Study of Southern Literature, and the Modern Language Association have listened to my ideas and kindly offered useful feedback. I particularly thank the Saint George Tucker Society for enriching the project with an early acknowledgment of its ideas and the rigorous scrutiny of them by David Carlton, Elizabeth Fox-Genovese, Eugene Genovese, and Anne Wyatt-Brown. At that session, Fred Hobson also expressed his interest in the project, and his support has since been unflagging. His careful engagement with the manuscript, like that of the other reader, strengthened the project immeasurably, and because of him, I have the good fortune to have LSU Press oversee the publication of the project. I thank John Easterly, Cynthia Williams, and the other folks at the Press for their assistance and patience.

My family has been a constant presence in this project, enabling and impacting it in ways that have not always been easy. Although my maternal grandmother died during the writing of this book, she pervades it, having introduced me to the pleasures of southern narrative. Also in the course of the project, my brother proved himself a friend as well as a sibling. But this book is dedicated to my parents, who continue to sustain me, even when my thanks is insufficient.

Lovers and Beloveds

Introduction

IN *EPISTEMOLOGY OF THE CLOSET* Eve Sedgwick sets
herself the task of scrutinizing the relation of gay/lesbian studies to current
debates about literary canons, and, although she ultimately deems the relation tortuous, she argues for the absolute centrality of gay/lesbian inquiry.
According to Sedgwick,

> We can't possibly know in advance about the Harlem Renaissance, any more
> than we can about the New England Renaissance or the English or Italian Re-
> naissance, where the limits of a revelatory inquiry are to be set, once we begin to
> ask—as it is now beginning to be asked about each of these Renaissances—
> where and how the power in them of gay desires, people, discourses, prohibi-
> tions, and energies were manifest. We know enough already, however, to know
> with certainty that in each of these Renaissances they were central. (No doubt
> that's how we will learn to recognize a renaissance when we see one.)[1]

Although perhaps remaining more skeptical than Sedgwick about the knowability of a renaissance and the intimated homosexist presumption that a
renaissance is contingent upon "gay desires, people, discourses, prohibitions,
and energies," I nevertheless take her observation as a guiding principle for
this book and attempt to interrogate one of the ostensible renaissances that
she neglects to include, the literary production that has come to be designated as the Southern Renaissance. This study argues that, despite the canonization of this literature by several generations of literary historians either
largely unconcerned with or openly hostile to gay/lesbian inquiry, this body
of work reveals a dazzling and complex array of representations in which

sexuality in general and same-sex desire in particular help to constitute the mid-twentieth-century southern social matrix as understood by writers of this era and region.

This study does not, however, seek to isolate same-sex desire from other components of sexuality or to hold sexuality as extricable from biological sex, gender, race, and class. The study instead attempts to consider these elements crucial to the constitution of identity as always in relation to one another. Therefore, although representations of same-sex desire and activity are consistent sites of entry into this matrix, miscegenation, racialized misogyny, incest, and gender transitivity are at varying moments central to inquiry. It is to this broader set of sexual markers, expressions, and acts—those that are as integrally contingent upon sex, gender, race, and class as object choice—that the term *sexual otherness* of the study's subtitle refers.

In my terminology I have also attempted to use *same-sex desire, homoeroticism,* and, less frequently, *homosexual desire* synonymously with one another but not with *homosexuality,* just as I have tried to differentiate—even as I find these terms problematic—*gay desire* and *lesbian desire* from *gayness* and *lesbianism.* In each case, the latter terms, as suggested above, designate complex identities that are crucially structured by same-sex desire but are by no means constituted exclusively by it. Moreover, as the texts under scrutiny here reveal as a whole, same-sex desire can circulate—albeit anxiously—separate from homosexual identity, even amid mid-twentieth-century (and twenty-first-century) tendencies to collapse these concepts. I have similarly tried to differentiate *heteroeroticism* and *heterosexual desire* from *heterosexuality.* I also remain uneasy with and, except in the discussion of *To Kill a Mockingbird,* have not significantly deployed the term *queer* in its contemporary usage, even as scholars have proven the usefulness of the term. It, among other things, risks sacrificing the centrality of desire and same-sex desire in particular. Moreover, not all same-sex desire is queer; that is, this desire need not be contingent upon, as McCullers critic Rachel Adams phrases it, an "opposition to normative behaviors and social distinctions" and an impossibility of being "assimilated into the dominant social order." Finally, despite queer theory's enabling efforts to counter "a range of normalizing regimes" and call "into question the knowledge/power system from which identity-based categories are derived," *queer* ironically threatens to reinforce a binarism of normative/queer and thus the notion that there is a stable, finite, knowable normativity, one valorized by those within the arena of performances and demonized by those outside it with designations such as "the tyranny of the normal."[2]

To further my arguments about the complexities of desire and sexuality in the midcentury southern social matrix, I interpret the fiction of six southern writers: Truman Capote, William Goyen, Richard Wright, Lillian Smith, Harper Lee, and Carson McCullers. These writers' differences are multiple, perhaps self-evidently so in some cases. Wright stands alone in the group as an African American amid persons of European ancestry. He, Capote, and Goyen are men; Smith, Lee, and McCullers are women. Smith, born in 1897, is a full generation older than Lee, born in 1926, with the other four persons' years of birth falling between these dates. Although all six writers were born in the Deep South, they spent their childhoods in often markedly different subregions: Capote and Lee in southern Alabama, Goyen in southeastern Texas, Wright primarily in the Delta of Mississippi, Smith in northern Florida, and McCullers in middle Georgia. Only Smith and Lee remained in the South throughout the majority of their lives, although these women too spent significant periods away from the region. The other four writers fled to various locations outside Dixie—the desert Southwest, San Francisco, Chicago, New York, Paris—and returned to the South only periodically and often reluctantly, as McCullers put it, to renew their sense of horror. Finally, only Lee is still alive, Wright having died in 1960, Smith in 1966, McCullers in 1967, Goyen in 1983, and Capote in 1984.

Despite these differences, fiction of these writers shares at least two preoccupations: representing the South and representing sexual otherness. This literary production does not, however, always negotiate these concerns simultaneously. Although one hesitates to claim that any of these persons' fiction or work in other genres ever fails to include sexuality, there are texts relatively unconcerned with same-sex desire, such as Wright's *Black Boy* (1945) and Smith's *Memory of a Large Christmas* (1962), as well as those that represent neither the South nor southernness directly and centrally, such as Capote's *In Cold Blood* (1966) and Wright's *Native Son* (1940). These texts are crucial to a fuller understanding of these writers, but this study privileges those works simultaneously concerned with same-sex desire and southern identity: Capote's *Other Voices, Other Rooms* (1948), Goyen's *The House of Breath* (1950), Wright's "Big Boy Leaves Home" (1936) and *The Long Dream* (1958), Smith's *Strange Fruit* (1944) and, to a lesser degree, *One Hour* (1959), Lee's *To Kill a Mockingbird* (1960), and McCullers's *The Heart Is a Lonely*

Hunter (1940), *Reflections in a Golden Eye* (1941), *The Ballad of the Sad Café* (1943), *The Member of the Wedding* (1946), and *Clock Without Hands* (1961). Sexual otherness as negotiated within specifically southern contexts is of paramount importance in each of these texts, and same-sex desire is in turn central to their configurations of sexual otherness.

Although somewhat less directly, this study also argues that, just as this fiction makes clear the centrality of texts inflected by homoeroticism to mid-twentieth-century southern literary production, it also clarifies the concurrent centrality of southern writing to this era's gay/lesbian literary production. The proliferation of gay and lesbian fiction in the United States during the last quarter century has not been unanticipated, even if certain of its historically contingent themes and forms have. And yet these contemporary texts have not emerged only in the wake of earlier gay and lesbian literary production associated with the urban environments of San Francisco, New York, and Paris. Just as the publication of Gore Vidal's *The City and the Pillar* (1948) and *The Season of Comfort* (1949), James Barr's *Quatrefoil* (1950), and James Baldwin's *Giovanni's Room* (1956) ushered in subsequent representations of same-sex desire in mainstream American fiction, so too did southern texts such as *Strange Fruit*, *To Kill a Mockingbird*, and *Other Voices, Other Rooms*. Quite simply, southern writers at midcentury—like those today—proved themselves as central to American gay/lesbian literary production as did those of any of the nation's other regions.

There are many arguments this study does not make or seek to make either overtly or implicitly. It does not hold, for instance, that this catalogue of fiction is exhaustive of midcentury southern literary production preoccupied with same-sex desire. To the contrary, numerous exceptions exist and fall largely into two categories. There are those texts written outside the study's decades of focus: the 1940s and 1950s. Although these bracketing dates are not inviolable—"Big Boy Leaves Home" was first published in 1936, *To Kill a Mockingbird* appeared in 1960, and *Clock Without Hands* in 1961—the forms and themes of the texts focused on in this study are in keeping with dominant discourses structuring same-sex desire at midcentury. In contrast, the forms and themes of a work like *The Young and Evil* (1933), Charles Henri Ford and Parker Tyler's novel of gay southerners living in New York City, remain indicative of discourses from an earlier and, in this case, more permissive era.[3] Similarly, although written only a decade or so after *To Kill a Mockingbird* and *Clock Without Hands*, Rita Mae Brown's outspoken *Rubyfruit Jungle* (1973) and Edward Swift's campy *Splendora* (1978) reveal how significantly gay- and lesbian-focused southern fiction evolved away from earlier forms and themes in the 1960s' currents of civil rights, feminism, the so-called sexual revolution, and gay activism typified by the 1969 Stonewall riots.

There are also those works that are in keeping with these midcentury forms, themes, and sensibilities but which, because of constraints in time and space, this study cannot address: William Faulkner's *Light in August* (1932) and *Absalom, Absalom!* (1936), Calder Willingham's *End as a Man* (1947), Hubert Creekmore's *The Welcome* (1948), Thomas Hal Phillips's *The Bitterweed Path* (1949), and Truman Capote's *The Grass Harp* (1951), to name but a few. Moreover, works taking up southern themes and settings appear frequently among the scores of sensational—if often homophobic—pulp novels dealing with homosexuality produced during and after World War II.[4] In contrast to the novels examined in this study, these texts have received either an exorbitant amount of analysis, as is the case with Faulkner's novels, or practically none, as is the case with the rest.[5] When one considers work outside the genre of fiction, these novels and short stories are within an even larger field of southern texts negotiating sexual otherness at midcentury: William Alexander Percy's memoir, *Lanterns on the Levee* (1941); Lillian Hellman's play *The Children's Hour* (1934); and, perhaps most important, Tennessee Williams's midcareer plays, such as *A Streetcar Named Desire* (1947), *Cat on a Hot Tin Roof* (1955), and *Suddenly Last Summer* (1958).

Despite the pervasiveness of overt or, more typically, encoded same-sex desire in southern literary production, this study does not seek to characterize such production as systematically and exclusively queer, much less systematically and exclusively gay and/or lesbian centered. The literature of the so-called Southern Renaissance may have a lavender tint, but it is not shockingly pink. Regardless of regional specificity, any text is open for gay/lesbian inquiry, and I agree with Sedgwick that "no one *can* know *in advance* where the limits of a gay-centered inquiry are to be drawn, or where a gay theorizing of and through even the hegemonic high culture of the Euro-American tradition may need or be able to lead."[6] Yet, just as one should not presume an absence in an uninterrogated text, one also should not presume a presence. The rewards of gay/lesbian inquiry are varied and often meager if one expects always to detect and make public the presence of homoeroticism. Moreover, an essentialization of this literary production as de facto queer risks not only eradicating texts' nuances of sexuality—and especially heterosexuality—but also jeopardizing the legitimacy of gay/lesbian inquiry. Because it remains one of the more recent critical approaches and faces, at best, guarded acceptance within conservative southern literary studies, gay/lesbian inquiry of southern texts seems at present most efficacious when it addresses with diligence and finesse the considerable work to be done with specific texts concerned with same-sex desire rather than when this inquiry posits sweeping claims about the queerness of all midcentury southern literary production.

This study also does not argue that the work of these six writers constitutes a coherent, traceable gay literary tradition, as some critics have sought to delineate. For understandable political reasons, Mab Segrest, for instance, has argued for a southern lesbian tradition composed of Angelina Weld Grimké, Carson McCullers, Lillian Smith, Rita Mae Brown, Judy Grahn, Barbara Smith, Dorothy Allison, Adrienne Rich, and Minnie Bruce Pratt, to name but its most noted writers. Segrest can stabilize this precarious configuration, however, only by reducing these women's complex sexual identities to lesbianism, inflating their often tangential relations to the South, and minimizing the radical differences that mark both these writers and their texts. She seemingly holds a comparably uncomplicated vision of broader southern women's writing, deeming its texts either to internalize patriarchal scriptings of women as grotesque and isolated from one another, as is the case, she asserts, with the fiction of Carson McCullers and Flannery O'Connor, or to celebrate female community. It is the latter that Segrest attempts to mold into a coherent tradition, including writers as diverse as Kate Chopin, Lillian Smith, Alice Walker, Eudora Welty, and June Arnold.[7] Unlike Segrest's essays, this study works against the erection of a univocal southern gay/lesbian canon and seeks to delineate no "great tradition" of southern gay/lesbian-inflected texts. To the contrary, despite the limits imposed by the broad culture-bound discourses surrounding homosexuality in the 1940s and 1950s, these six writers' representations of same-sex desire are contradictory and disruptive of critical continuities.

Finally, while this study periodically draws upon biographical information about these writers, it makes no stronger arguments about these persons' sexualities than that their fiction consistently displays a keen preoccupation with issues of sexuality and same-sex desire in particular. It is true that Lillian Smith and Truman Capote were self-avowedly homosexual and seem to have understood their identities as crucially structured by same-sex desire. Capote was anything but silent regarding his gayness, baldly—and egotistically—concluding, for instance, a famous late autobiographical piece, "But I'm not a saint yet. I'm an alcoholic. I'm a drug addict. I'm homosexual. I'm a genius. Of course, I can be all four of these dubious things and still be a saint. But I shonuf ain't no saint yet, nawsuh."[8] Smith was not nearly so forthcoming about her lesbianism during her lifetime, but her posthumously published letters reveal both the physicality and depth of emotion that marked her relationship with Paula Snelling for over forty years.[9] In contrast to Smith and Capote, Richard Wright appears to have assumed an anxious heterosexual identity both inside and outside marriage, as did Carson McCullers to a large degree. And yet, according to McCullers's autobiography and biographies, those frequently informed by unsympathetic treatments of lesbianism, gayness, and/or bisexuality, she also negotiated intense desire for other women, although in all likelihood she never acted upon this desire physically. This biographical research also suggests that, regardless of what actual sexual identity—or identities—McCullers understood herself to have, her readers often assumed her queerness.[10] In the absence of significant public information about them, the sexualities of William Goyen and Harper Lee remain open for speculation. Unlike with Capote, Smith, Wright, and McCullers, there is no substantial biography of either Goyen or Lee. Although a sampling of Goyen's letters has been published, Robert Phillips's editing minimizes revelations about Goyen's sexuality.[11] To label these four persons' sexual identities as gay, lesbian, or bisexual thus seems premature, problematically simplistic, or flatly wrong. This study therefore focuses primarily on representations of same-sex desire in these writers' texts rather than on any documented or supposed personal experiences or self-proclaimed or imposed identities.

I

Freaks with a Voice

AN ANALYSIS OF FICTION by these six writers—Truman
Capote, William Goyen, Richard Wright, Lillian Smith, Harper Lee,
and Carson McCullers—demands something of a return to those well-
rehearsed questions that have been problematically posited as fundamental
to southern literary studies dealing with texts produced at midcentury.
What was the Southern Renaissance? When did it begin and end? Which
were its energizing writers, texts, critics, and readers; which were its deplet-
ing ones, and by whose standards? What was it a renaissance of, if anything?
These questions are hardly new, having persisted with maddening regularity since the publication of H. L. Mencken's catalyzing 1917 essay "The
Sahara of the Bozart." He frankly declared that, in contrast to a highly
romanticized antebellum South, the modern region was "almost as sterile,
artistically, intellectually, culturally, as the Sahara Desert." With characteristic hyperbole, he offers that, "when you come to critics, musical composers,
painters, sculptors, architects and the like, you will have to give it up, for
there is not even a bad one between the Potomac mud-flats and the Gulf.
Nor an historian. Nor a sociologist. Nor a philosopher. Nor a theologian.
Nor a scientist." "In all these fields," he definitively concludes this much-
cited passage, "the south is an awe-inspiring blank."[1]

Southern reactions to Mencken's essay varied, and many persons con-
curred with his sentiments. In *The Mind of the South*, for instance, W. J. Cash
nods to Mencken's "celebrated essay" and declares that, "while it all might
be very wicked, it still had an uncomfortable lot of truth in it."[2] The responses that proved most significant, however, were also among the most

hostile and arose from persons who not only ultimately formulated the cited litany of questions regarding the Southern Renaissance but arguably instigated modern southern literary studies: the Nashville Agrarians. Composed in part of former Fugitives and eventual New Critics, the Agrarians countered Mencken's claims after a decade of simmering to assert, as Donald Davidson did in the group's manifesto *I'll Take My Stand* (1930), that, to the contrary, the years following World War I featured significant southern "artists whose work reveals richness, repose, brilliance, continuity": James Branch Cabell, Ellen Glasgow, Paul Green, DuBose Heyward, T. S. Stribling. The problem, Davidson argued, was that these artists' tradition had been "discredited and made artistically inaccessible" by modern industrialism's near eradication of southern agrarianism, the traditional "culture of the soil," as John Crowe Ransom termed it in the volume's introduction. Although Davidson's decree is at best debatable, it nevertheless evinces the tactics that Agrarians continued—and their distant heirs continue—to amplify and use in response to Mencken's configurations of southern literary history and to the ongoing American "culture wars." The post–World War I South, so the leaders of the Agrarian movement asserted, did indeed give rise to a literary tradition whose "richness, repose, brilliance, [and] continuity" were recognizable and appreciable so long as one retained agrarian values. Moreover, according to Allen Tate, in the anxious negotiations of the loss of these values in the face of modern industrialization, this tradition ultimately produced the region's—and much of the nation's—best literature, that eventually labeled the Southern Renaissance.[3]

Especially within the last quarter of a century, other structuring terms and questions for southern literary studies have emerged to amplify, emend, and contradict this line of argument. The centrality of a conservative Agrarian legacy and its formulation of the Renaissance within these studies, however, has been slow in waning. As a result, mid-twentieth-century southern literature—and especially a handful of its texts and writers—even yet retains a significant degree of privilege. Consider, for instance, how the Renaissance is handled in *The History of Southern Literature* (1985), the compilation deemed by Michael Kreyling as that "skyscraper on the landscape of southern literary history." Although the volume's individual contributors partially reflect the diversity of contemporary southern literary studies, the editors—Louis D. Rubin, Jr.; Rayburn S. Moore; Lewis P. Simpson; Thomas Daniel Young; and Blyden Jackson, the quintet's only African

American—are a self-admittedly homogeneous group of men whose initial and pervading understandings of these studies were heavily influenced by Agrarian and New Critical thought. "All five of its senior editors," Rubin notes in the volume's introduction, "were born in the South of the 1910s and 1920s, grew up during the 1920s and 1930s, and did their graduate study during the 1940s and 1950s." As a result, "the senior editors of this history grew up while the leading figures of the Southern Renascence were writing and publishing the books that placed the onetime Sahara of the Bozart at the very center of American literary creativity." Moreover, these editors were "to varying degrees acquainted with many of the writers . . . , sometimes closely."[4]

Given the editors' close professional and personal ties to the first generation of Agrarians, *The History of Southern Literature* is, when taken as a whole, not surprisingly one of the latest significant deployments of Agrarian tactics to answer Mencken yet again. In the hands of Rubin and his fellow editors, the Renaissance remains the crux of southern literary production. "Considerably more pages in this book are devoted to the writings of the twentieth century than to those of earlier periods," Rubin asserts. "This is as it should be. Far more Southern writing has appeared in the present century than in all the previous years combined. Moreover, from a qualitative standpoint, the principal importance of much of the earlier literature lies in the extent to which it contributes to the development of the literary imagination that would flower in the twentieth-century Southern Literary Renascence." Writers coming to prominence after 1950 are equally de-emphasized, since the "sorting-out process of time has not yet produced an agreed-upon canon of important and less-important writings; to attempt to arrive at and enforce such a canon would be premature."[5] Rubin's presumptions about the need to enforce such a canon evince how firmly entrenched Agrarian and New Critical impulses to evaluate and rank remained five decades after *I'll Take My Stand*. Moreover, as has been repeatedly noted, the assurance with which these editors could offer for public consumption *the* history of southern literature betrayed the persisting centrality of the conservative Agrarian and New Critical legacy in southern literary studies as recently as twenty years ago.

Criticisms of this legacy have been multiple, and scholars have employed several strategies to engage it. Some have attempted to de-center the Renaissance's near tyranny over the rest of southern literary history by interrogating those periods left relatively neglected by *The History of Southern Literature* and the scholarship of which it is representative. Indeed, some of the most exciting work being done in southern literary studies involves the scrutiny of "forgotten" nineteenth-century texts, those that Rubin and likeminded others find valuable only insofar as these works contribute to the next century's literary production. Other critics seeking to engage assessments similar to Rubin's have read subversively within the established Renaissance canon to counter traditional arguments about these texts' affirmations of Agrarian values. As valuable as I find these approaches, I deploy a third strategy: to interrogate works produced during the years broadly understood as the Renaissance but that have been deliberately depreciated or excluded from the southern canon, and to probe the reasons for this exclusion.

Even among its champions, however, the largely conservative canon to which this study responds has not been universally agreed upon. That offered by Davidson in *I'll Take My Stand* was soon abandoned as other writers—often Fugitives, Agrarians, and/or New Critics themselves—rose to prominence and revealed themselves as "untainted" rather than "palpably tinged with latter-day abolitionism," as Davidson feared with the works of Cabell, Glasgow, Green, Heyward, and Stribling. By 1953, however, with the publication of *Southern Renascence: The Literature of the Modern South,* the canon that arose in place of Davidson's early formulation had been largely codified, and the Renaissance—or, rather, Renascence—had been designated as such. If these essays edited by Rubin and Robert D. Jacobs may be taken to reflect this new canon, it hesitantly retained Cabell and Glasgow— ("For my part, I do not advocate a Glasgow critical revival," asserts contributor John Edward Hardy. "The fact that her work does not lend itself to formalist criticism makes any such thing highly unlikely just now; and it is probably just as well.")—while tacking on the "smudged and inherently funny little car" Erskine Caldwell and adding, more enthusiastically, John Peale Bishop, Cleanth Brooks, Donald Davidson, William Faulkner, Caroline Gordon, Merrill Moore, Katherine Anne Porter, John Crowe Ransom, Allen Tate, Robert Penn Warren, Eudora Welty, Thomas Wolfe, and Stark Young. When Thomas Daniel Young rehearsed the major writers of the Renaissance thirty years later in *The History of Southern Literature,* the canon remained largely unchanged except for the removal of the disruptive presences of Glasgow, Cabell, Caldwell, and Young: "William Faulkner, Eudora Welty, Robert Penn Warren, John Crowe Ransom, Allen Tate, Thomas Wolfe, Caroline Gordon, Cleanth Brooks, and Andrew Lytle."[6]

To assert that this canon is simultaneously sexist, racist, and elitist is now, one hopes, unnecessary. The relative absence of women is as shocking as the absolute absence of persons of color, and the omission of popular writers such as Caldwell, Caroline Miller, Margaret Mitchell, and Marjorie Kinnan Rawlings is glaring, albeit understandable given lingering New Critical investments. Moreover, the canon's representations of Tennessee and Mississippi overshadow those of other subregions within a variegated South. What has yet to be forcefully pointed out, however, is the comparable absence in this canon of gay or lesbian persons and/or writers centrally concerned with same-sex desire. The scholarship responsible for creating and maintaining this canon grants extraordinarily little space to representations of this desire and instead more typically offers a series of its implicit dismissals as characterized by Sedgwick: "It didn't happen; it doesn't make any difference; it didn't mean anything; it doesn't have interpretive consequences. Stop asking just here; stop asking just now; we know in advance the kind of difference that could be made by the invocation of *this* difference; it makes no difference; it doesn't mean."[7]

Reasons for these dismissals are multiple and not necessarily contingent upon homophobia in the specific case of the Southern Renaissance's canonization, as Sedgwick's generic assertions risk implying. As mentioned, arising almost simultaneously with Agrarianism and perhaps most forcefully articulated by Agrarians and their sympathizers was a distinctively southern branch of formalism eventually designated as the New Criticism. Indeed, the theory's very name was given by one-time Agrarian John Crowe Ransom in his 1941 study *The New Criticism*. The theory's goal was to make the study of literature "more scientific, or precise and systematic," as Ransom explained in an earlier essay, by removing texts from sociohistorical contingencies and thus locating through formalist analysis a stability that was supposedly being lost to modernity: "The poet perpetuates in his poem an order of existence which in actual life is constantly crumbling beneath his touch. His poem celebrates the object which is real, individual, and qualitatively infinite. . . . The critic has to take the poem apart, or analyze it, for the sake of uncovering these features." Or, as acerbic Terry Eagleton offers, the "New Criticism was the ideology of an uprooted, defensive intelligentsia who reinvented in literature what they could not locate in reality. Poetry was the new religion, a nostalgic haven from the alienations of industrial capitalism."[8]

And yet, if this rigid insistence on supposedly apolitical formalist analysis largely delegitimizes acknowledgment of gay and lesbian representations, much less gay or lesbian identities of authors and readers, the New Criticism also seeks to delegitimize the scrutiny of all aspects of identity when divorced from formalist concerns. Thus, when considered strictly as literary theory and distanced from particular practitioners, the New Criticism cannot necessarily be labeled homophobic, even if to maintain such a distance is more easily said than done and thus betrays the difficulty of the task of practitioners. Indeed, analysis of these representations is acceptable so long as a text uses formalist dexterity to privilege culturally transgressive identities, such as those of women, African Americans, or gays and lesbians. Hence one encounters Tate's warm reception of Jean Toomer's depictions of African Americans in his deftly crafted *Cane* (1923) and Cleanth Brooks's matter-of-fact discussion of both Gail Hightower's and Joe Christmas's "latent homosexuality" in Faulkner's intricate *Light in August*.[9] Moreover, persons with New Critical investments frequently cultivated intimate friendships with gays and lesbians. For at least a portion of their lives, Tate and Caroline Gordon shared a warm friendship with gay poet Hart Crane, just as the novelist and theater critic Stark Young, whose homosexuality was widely known, was an integral contributor to the reactionary *I'll Take My Stand*.[10]

Despite sharing adherents, the New Criticism was not, however, synonymous with Agrarianism, and the latter's comparable neglect of same-sex desire did not arise from moves that were benign or at least explainable as such. Unlike unadulterated New Criticism and its fetish for form removed from its sociohistorical context, Agrarianism was anything but apolitical and instead valorized ideological and historical content. Such an appreciation was crucial to Agrarian political agendas in that an effective strategy was the production of self-consciously propagandistic texts that worked to reify myths of a blissful preindustrial, preurban South and to demonize modernization's threats posed to these myths. Although these works frequently displayed the formalist brilliance relished by Tate, Gordon, and Brooks, they more often than not exerted greatest influence through their inculcations of ideology, ones that were contingent upon the acknowledged importance of a text's content.

Among the foremost of these myths' elements was religious faith, and, although Agrarians debated the significance of institutional and denominational affiliations, these persons chiefly agreed on the importance of organized religion and mourned its waning. Tate's contribution to *I'll Take My Stand,* for instance, was a vague rumination on the South's lack of a "fitting" or "appropriate" religion, and Ransom's introduction to the volume rehearsed the significance of religious faith:

> Religion can hardly expect to flourish in an industrial society. Religion is our submission to the general intention of a nature that is fairly inscrutable; it is the sense of our role as creatures within it. But nature industrialized, transformed into cities and artificial habitations, manufactured into commodities, is no longer nature but a highly simplified picture of nature. We receive the illusion of having power over nature, and lose the sense of nature as something mysterious and contingent. The God of nature under these conditions is merely an amiable expression, a superfluity, and the philosophical understanding ordinarily carried in the religious experience is not there for us to have.

"The typical Southerner," Richard Weaver asserted in *Southern Renascence,* elaborating on Ransom's earlier claims, "is an authentically religious being if one means by religion not a neat set of moralities but a deep and even frightening intuition of man's radical dependence in this world." Yet the "authentic" religion was, of course, Christianity, and other Agrarians were far more direct in not only championing Christian faith but also positing the South as the site of "true" Christianity's last stronghold, often drawing upon vitriolic Confederate rhetoric to do so. Andrew Lytle's biography of Nathan Bedford Forrest, for instance, casts the Confederate general and leader in the early Ku Klux Klan as a hero who takes as his "most perfect image . . . Christ the man-god" and valiantly fights to save a Christian South from its godless northern foes.[11]

The letter—if perhaps not the spirit—of Christian law is as condemnatory of same-sex acts as it is sexist, elitist, and xenophobic. The Old Testament casts such acts and bestiality as equally offensive, asserting, "You shall not lie with a male as with a woman; it is an abomination. And you shall not lie with any beast and defile yourself with it, neither shall any woman give herself to a beast to lie with it; it is perversion" (Lev. 18:22–23 RSV). The punishment for such behavior is clear: "If a man lies with a male as with a woman, both of them have committed an abomination; they shall be put to death, their blood is upon them" (Lev. 20:13 RSV). The epistles of Saint Paul are comparably unambiguous in figuring same-sex acts as inciting the wrath of God. Since the world's creation, persons disrespectful of God have been given to "dishonorable passions. Their women exchanged natural relations for unnatural, and the men likewise gave up natural relations and were consumed with passion for one another, men committing shameless acts with men and receiving in their own persons the due penalty for their error" (Rom. 1:26–27 RSV). Insofar as Agrarian investments in traditional Christianity retained these and comparable other Mosaic and Pauline injunctions against acts that have come to be understood and designated as homosexual ones, there seems to have been little legitimate place for same-sex desire in the Christian South imagined by Agrarians.

Overt biblical condemnation was not, however, the only or even the most forceful element in Agrarianism's antagonistic stance toward homosexuality. To the contrary, Christianity's valorization of the patriarchal family also contributed significantly. For most contributors to *I'll Take My Stand* and their sympathizers, the Agrarian South centered on the cohesiveness of the nuclear and extended family, its biblical sanctions, and its perpetuation through heterosexuality. To disrupt this unit was to disrupt the entirety of the southern social order. Thus the work of Agrarians and other southern social conservatives, including those such as William Alexander Percy and Stark Young, who were themselves negotiating homosexual identities, as a rule cautioned against and/or decried the ongoing destabilization of the family in the face of modernity. Lyle Lanier's essay in *I'll Take My Stand,* for instance, bemoans "the decline of the family," since it "is the natural biological group, the normal milieu of shared experiences, community of interests, integration of personality." These "benefits," Lanier concludes, "we are fast surrendering to the industrial order, whose patterns of conduct are incompatible with the conditions necessary to the stability and integrity of family life."[12]

Lytle's essay in the same volume comparably delineates the "homebreaking" instigated by moves away from agrarian life, and his biography of Forrest idealizes the general's extended patriarchal family and even figures his troops as its surrogates during the Civil War. As Walter Sullivan explains in his preface to the biography, this unit was directly contingent upon Christianity in the understandings of Lytle and most other Agrarians:

Of most importance, without God the patriarch to serve as example, the sense of the family as a patriarchy is lost. Mutual respect among members of the family deteriorates. Each person begins to elevate his own personal interests above those of the group. Thus, order is destroyed with the failure of discipline. When the family ceases to exist as a patriarchy, the larger social and political patriarchies—community, state, country—that take the family as their foundation are lost as well. Thus begins the plunge into general chaos. So Andrew Lytle argued in 1930 when he was writing his life of Nathan Bedford Forrest.

To assert a gay or lesbian identity openly in the mid-twentieth-century South was implicitly to counter the heterosexuality on which this patriarchal family rested. To elevate one's own "personal interests" in this manner was thus ultimately to begin the collapse of civilization into "general chaos." Indeed, this collapse was already at hand for some conservatives. Richard Weaver demanded "the fruitful distinction between the sexes, with the recognition of respective spheres of influence," and, perhaps referring to gays and lesbians as well as to broader gender nonconformists, held that the "end of the era of 'long-haired men and short-haired women' would bring a renewal of well-being."[13]

Although Agrarian literary production, whether fiction, drama, poetry, or critical analysis, rarely condemned same-sex desire in an overt way, as Robert Penn Warren seems to do with Billie Constantidopeles in *At Heaven's Gate* (1942), the ensuing silence should not be taken to indicate a lack of anxiety about homosexuality.[14] To the contrary, Agrarians implemented a homophobic agenda that had as its primary tactic the subtle yet persistent exclusion of gays, lesbians, and other persons of nonnormative sexualities from the accepted Renaissance canon. Recall Rubin's and Young's rosters of these writers. The heterosexuality of no one on Young's list has been seriously questioned, and only that of James Branch Cabell and Stark Young on Rubin's list has. (One notes, though, that both authors disappear from the later list.) Even more telling, however, is Robert B. Heilman's articulation of this canon in "The Southern Temper," his essay that opens Rubin and Jacobs's *Southern Renascence*. As the title suggests, Heilman attempts to define an essentialized southern temper and argues for the centrality of, among other things, a sense of the concrete among Renaissance writers: "The sense of the concrete, as an attribute of the fiction writer, is so emphatically apparent in Faulkner, Warren, and Wolfe, so subtly and variously apparent in Porter, Welty, and Gordon, and so flamboyantly so in someone like Capote (who hardly belongs here at all) that everybody knows it's there. It is there, too, in the poetry of Ransom, Tate, and Warren."[15] Heilman frankly excludes Capote from the elite of southern literature yet leaves cryptic whether it is his personality or the content of his work that bars his inclusion in the group. Even more disconcerting, however, is the rhetorical strategy that Heilman uses in grouping these writers. He first catalogues a trio of men, all of whom are presumably heterosexual. A trio of women then follows, and Heilman concludes his sentence with the nod to "someone like Capote," someone who is neither man nor woman within the logic implied by the sentence's construction. Thus, without identifying Capote as gay, Heilman suggests that the problematic nexus of Capote's sex and sexuality is perhaps as crucial to his exclusion from the Renaissance canon as is his actual literary production.

Heilman is not alone in employing this sort of strategy. In the same volume Ray B. West, Jr., uses a similar move when treating Katherine Anne Porter's relationship to her contemporaries. In a discussion of these writers' creation and use of southern myth, West offers:

> Perhaps their most complete use is represented in the novels and short stories of William Faulkner, where the timeless world of eternal values of the Southern past is posted against the fluid and pragmatic present. In one way or another, these contrasts have got into most Southern writing, whether the poetry of Allen Tate, John Crowe Ransom, John Peale Bishop, Robert Penn Warren, and Donald Davidson, or into the prose fiction of Ellen Glasgow, Caroline Gordon, Stark Young, Eudora Welty, Peter Taylor, Carson McCullers, Tate, Warren, and Katherine Anne Porter. With a special emphasis, it is to be found in the writings of Truman Capote, Elizabeth Hardwick, William Goyen, Tennessee Williams, and Leroy Leatherman.[16]

In West's configuration of the Renaissance, Capote no longer stands alone in his isolation from the main canon, but he nevertheless finds company primarily in other men confirmed or suspected to be gay and/or associated with gay subcultures: Goyen, Williams, and Leatherman. Thus, as in Heilman's catalogue, gay writers and/or those preoccupied with representing same-sex desire usually find themselves relegated to the periphery of mid-century southern literary production. Moreover, like Heilman, West offers the vaguest of explanations for this relegation, asserting only that these writers negotiate southern myth with "a special emphasis."

This simultaneous valorization of agrarianism and subtle dismissal of sexual deviancy also appear in the era's reviews of southern fiction. Few are more striking than John Farrelly's 1948 piece for the *New Republic* discussing *Other Voices, Other Rooms* and Robert Penn Warren's collection of short stories *The Circus in the Attic*. Farrelly begins with the standard—if brief—articulation of agrarianism's central role in the South's literary production. "It is not too much to say that most good American fiction in recent years has come from the South," he asserts: "This is largely due to such obviously propitious circumstances as a complex, fantastic and usable past extending into continuous social traditions, a rich colloquialism of language and customs, and a predominantly agrarian, or at any rate rural, life. In this it is the main line of American literature, one of towns, villages and the country, since, as a people, we have always suspected city life, never learned to build livable cities, to control them, or subsist decently and comfortably—that is, 'urbanely'—in them." As the review continues, the non-Agrarian Capote merits only faint praise. His previously published stories "were unusually good," Farrelly asserts, "though not as remarkable as they first appeared; the bright note of the precocious and the exotic easily tarnishes, and a native and poetic sense for words occasionally slips into the mannered and ornate." *Other Voices, Other Rooms* is similarly disappointing because of its preoccupation with "perverse variations" and "freaks" and its elision of the "human element," all of which lead Farrelly to conclude that "Capote's present reputation is the sort concocted from fashionable ballyhoo which is too likely to exploit the 'glamorous' elements of his talents at the expense of his development." In contrast, Warren's stories offer for Farrelly a variety and range of character that is "proof of a strong inventive imagination," and Warren reveals himself a master in this use of "human emotion."[17]

By the mid-1950s, when Rubin and Jacobs were collecting the essays of *Southern Renascence,* it was clear that gay writers such as Capote and Williams were significant in national and even international circulations of literary southernness, a fact that perhaps culminated in Williams's Pulitzer prizes for *A Streetcar Named Desire* and *Cat on a Hot Tin Roof.* Indeed, Heilman's, West's, and Farrelly's anxious negotiations of these writers—if only to dismiss them—reflect this significance. Agrarians seem therefore to have instigated another tactic to minimize the presence of same-sex desire (and other disruptive elements of otherness and multiplicity) in twentieth-century southern literature: declare the Renaissance over at precisely the moment when southern writers were increasingly and more explicitly representing homosexuality. As with the members of its conservative canon, the Renaissance's end has been much debated and rarely agreed upon. However, the decade from the mid-1940s to the mid-1950s offers the most frequent dates. Tate, for instance, argues that the Renaissance ended in 1945, while *The History of Southern Literature* posits 1950 as the close, and Richard King asserts that "one might conveniently locate the end of the main phase of the Renaissance somewhere around 1955."[18] Regardless of the specific date, it remains true that the Renaissance is most usually figured to end just as Capote, Goyen, and Williams were establishing their significance and before McCullers was to represent gay desire most explicitly. The suggestion thus remains that, if and when Agrarian configurations of twentieth-century southern literature acknowledged same-sex desire, they quarantined this presence almost exclusively outside what they deemed the Renaissance proper.

Although the reasons for the Renaissance's end are, of course, far more multiple and complex than this quarantining of same-sex desire, even other theories that rehearse a distinctive shift in southern literary production on or about 1950 often draw obliquely upon discourses of sexuality. Consider King's psychoanalytic study of the region when he supports his argument for the Renaissance's end in 1955:

> This is not to say that Southerners stopped writing or that nothing of worth appeared after the mid-1950s. Far from it. But by this point the figures dealt with in my study were either dead or past their creative peaks. Though he won a Nobel Prize in 1949, Faulkner's powers as a novelist had waned considerably. Allen Tate and John Crowe Ransom had all but ceased writing poetry, while their critical and cultural essays appeared with decreasing frequency. W. J. Cash, William Alexander Percy, and Thomas Wolfe were dead; and James Agee was to succumb to a heart attack in 1955. . . . And though Robert Penn Warren's reputation as a poet waxed tremendously in the 1960s and 1970s, his fiction never regained the heights of *All the King's Men*. The apogee had been reached; the Renaissance had become a tradition.

King unwittingly suggests that his impulse to retain the date of the Renaissance's traditional end is crucially related to negotiations of the presence of same-sex desire in this work. After 1955, he offers, "the South was preoccupied with 'other voices, other rooms.'"[19] Thus, as with Heilman and

West, King respects the silence of the love that dare not speak its name but nevertheless alludes to it with Capote's title and hints the Renaissance ended at the moment when southern literary production began at least in part to centralize representations of same-sex desire.

Even the more recent scholarship of critics who have distanced themselves from the Agrarian legacy and have sought to broaden southern literature continues to neglect the same-sex desire of midcentury writers and their texts. As a rule, these writers have (until of late) merited discussion but only so long as their sexualities or sexual themes have been carefully muted. Perhaps because of the larger project's conservatism, essays in *The History of Southern Literature* not surprisingly avoid discussions of homosexuality in this fashion, even when treating authors and works where same-sex desire seems central. Thomas Bonner, Jr., characterizes Capote's *Other Voices, Other Rooms* as "an autobiographical novel" in which "Joel Knox seeks identity and love amid a house and setting surrounded by people leading meaningless lives." Bonner makes no mention of Joel's awakening to same-sex desire; of Capote's later, more explicitly sexual pieces that would be gathered together after his death as *Answered Prayers;* or of Capote's own homosexuality. The same-sex desire in the works of William Alexander Percy, Lillian Smith, and Reynolds Price also goes unmentioned, as do these authors' homosexuality, and the works of Carson McCullers and William Goyen are only vaguely designated as dealing with sexuality. Joseph R. Millichap nods to McCullers as a writer who occasionally deals with "bizarre sexuality," and Martha Cook asserts, in the only two mentions of Goyen in the entire work, that his characters are often "confused in their identity and sexuality."[20]

Contributors were no doubt pressed for space, but this tendency to omit or minimize sexual otherness persists even in more in-depth studies of the era. King's chapter on Smith, for instance, crucially brings her work into a serious consideration of midcentury southern literary production but simultaneously neglects her lesbianism and labels Laura Deen's same-sex desire in *Strange Fruit* as "her artistic, sensual impulses," adding parenthetically, "One could safely guess that Laura is a stand-in for Smith here." King comparably minimizes Percy's desire for other men, mentioning only in passing his "several fleeting and apparently unfilled homoerotic encounters." Similar neglect marks the early work of Fred Hobson. Although during the 1980s he was as crucial as King in expanding the Renaissance to include voices outside the narrow parameters offered by first-generation Agrarians, neither Hobson's *Tell About the South* (1983) nor his foreword to the 1985 reissue of *Strange Fruit* mentions Smith's lesbianism or its recurring presence in her work, identifying her relationship with Paula Snelling as that of friendship.[21]

Like the essays in *The History of Southern Literature,* this work by King and Hobson is representative of broader trends in southern literary studies at a specific moment, and I have not singled out these scholars as scapegoats to face accusation of this inquiry's relative insensitivity to issues of same-sex desire. Moreover, although their work does not centralize discussion of sexual otherness, it is hardly homophobic. Merely to mention Percy's desire for other men, as King does, is a daring act that continues to risk censorship and even legal action. And, as Hobson's recent career showcases, he, like so many scholars of his generation, has not remained inattentive to issues of same-sex desire but rather has been amazingly receptive to gay/lesbian inquiry. He has, for example, both integrated this inquiry into his scholarship, as with his treatment of Smith in *But Now I See,* his 1999 study of racially focused conversion narratives of southern whites, and has promoted this inquiry through the support of scholars engaged in projects like this very book.[22]

And yet *But Now I See* intimates a final way that the Agrarians' conservative legacy continues to impact southern literary studies and the negotiation of same-sex desire. Although Hobson notes the significance of Smith's lesbianism to her writing, his main focus in the study is emphatically race. As I have discussed elsewhere, this focus seems a problematic result of the southern canon reformation that has undermined reductive Agrarian paradigms. To compensate for decades in which issues of race in southern literary production were either ignored or, worse, handled from simplistic and/or racist perspectives, current scholarship now verges on belaboring these issues at the minimization or exclusion of others, as suggested by Norton's recent *Literature of the American South.* Although the anthology includes texts preoccupied with same-sex desire, such as selections by Dorothy Allison and Randall Kenan, the collection both reveals that a negotiation of racial difference seems the new touchstone for critical assessment and offers an adroitly manipulated metanarrative in which the South moves from the shame of slavery through the trials of Jim Crow to a halcyon present moment when the region has righted its racial wrongs or at least, in the case of the white South, become guiltily aware of past sins. The range of selections within this tripartite structure affirms the valorization of the late twentieth century, since these scant sixty years receive the lion's share of pages and include a proliferation of voices, all at the particular expense of the pre-1880 section, that covering approximately two centuries yet quarantined to less than a fourth of the anthology's pages.[23] Crucial though these interrogations of southern race are in challenging an inherited conservative canon, their saturation of critical discourses threatens to keep other aspects of identity, such as sexuality, marginalized.

Although the often awkward yoking of the New Criticism and Agrarianism has predominated in southern literary studies, leaving behind a tenacious legacy ranging from outright homophobia to benign critical neglect of same-sex desire, these critical investments have not been the only approaches to the South's mid-twentieth-century fiction. As "The Sahara of the Bozart" and other essays suggest, persons outside the South have often kept as keen an eye on the region and its literary production as did Ransom, Tate, Davidson, Brooks, Young, Heilman, and Rubin. Not surprisingly, there have been many differing voices in nonsouthern discussions of the South's literature, just as there have been in southern discussions, and yet one usually predominates at any given moment. Such seems to have been the case in the 1940s, 1950s, and 1960s. While first- and second-generation Agrarians and New Critics were codifying the Renaissance as a canon relatively devoid of transgressive sexualities, whether in its writers or their representations, many American artists and critics from outside the South tacitly agreed upon a comparably essentializing codification of the region's literary production. The crucial difference was that these persons posited southern literature at midcentury not only to contain the very same sexualities that the Agrarians argued were absent but also to consist of almost nothing but these representations. Moreover, this line of thought suggested that southern literature was unique among the various arenas of national literary production in featuring this sexual depravity. That is, this interpretive strategy quarantined the South as one of the few allowable sites of fictionalized deviancy, thus assuring nonsoutherners of their own relative normality. This move to impose order on mid-twentieth-century southern literary production thus paralleled that of the Agrarians and was comparably homophobic. In both strategies, American society is binaristically divided into North and South, and, depending on one's own regional affinities, sexual otherness is always *their* problem, *their* preoccupation, *their* identity, and *not* ours. Look, see; *their* literature proves it.

This strategy is a familiar one. Homosexuality has been and often continues to be understood as "someone else's problem," that which must be pointed out as desperately needing attending to at once, lest others presume it to be the accuser's own. Barbara Smith notes, for instance, that this strategy has frequently involved racialized identities, with persons of color often scripting same-sex desire as endemic to persons of European descent. "Homosexuality is a white problem or even a 'white disease,'" Smith rehearses. "This attitude is much too prevalent among people of color. Individuals who are militantly opposed to racism in all its forms still find lesbianism and male homosexuality something to snicker about or, worse, to despise."[24] And yet whites have repeatedly used the same rhetorical move to posit sexual deviancy as inherent in African Americans and other persons of color. In the 1920s and 1930s, for example, white New Yorkers pointed to black Harlem's lasciviousness and increasingly visible gays and lesbians to console themselves about homosexuality's exclusive predominance among African Americans. To do so, however, was to overlook the thousands of white gays and lesbians who flocked to the black neighborhoods because of the relative tolerance they offered.[25]

Like race, nationality and ethnicity have also provided elements of identity with which persons can, as historian George Chauncey has suggested, "differentiate and stigmatize subordinate groups by attributing 'immoral' or 'bizarre' sexual practices to them." Much as syphilis has historically been designated variably as the English, French, or Spanish disease, depending on the speaker's nationality and that nation's current political antipathies, homosexuality has often been quarantined to the populaces of some other nation or nations. For centuries, Chauncey observes, the "English tended to blame homosexuality on the French, and the French to blame it on the Italians, but the Americans blamed it rather more indiscriminately on European immigration as a whole" during the last decades of the nineteenth century and the first ones of the twentieth. Similar accusations went on among the immigrants themselves, with Jews most typically relegating male homosexuality to Italians. Italian same-sex activity was extensive in urban areas, as Chauncey's research shows, but to make this accusation in such exclusionary terms was, as in whites' characterizations of Harlem, to overlook the group's own homosexual activity within the subcultures of New York and other urban centers of the era.[26]

As suggested, the debates over the presence of sexual otherness in mid-twentieth-century southern literary production foregrounded regional identity more than either racial or national ones, although these two identities were not wholly absent. This particular process was not new, however, for it extended as far back as the construction of Edgar Allan Poe's gothic literary identity in the nineteenth century. Although of ambiguous regional identity, Poe and his work were frequently characterized as representative of a decadent South filled with drunkenness, murderous passions, paranoia, and necrophilia. The sectional hostilities that led to the Civil War and the accompanying vitriolic rhetoric did little to temper this construction of southern identity, and these understandings of southern literary production continued well into the twentieth century despite the spate of reconciliatory narratives during the last decades of the nineteenth century.

Ernest Hemingway's *Death in the Afternoon* (1932) provides a striking example of nonsoutherners' conflation of southern literature with sexual deviancy and homosexuality in particular at midcentury. One of the central chapters of Hemingway's discussion of Spanish bullfighting ends with the following dialogue:

> *Old lady:* Well, sir since we have stopped early to-day why do you not tell me a story?
> About what, Madame?
> . . . .
> *Old lady:* Do you know any of the kind of stories Mr. Faulkner writes?
> A few, Madame, but told baldly they might not please you.
> *Old lady:* Then do not tell them too baldly.
> Madame, I will tell you a couple and see how short and how far from bald I can make them. What sort of story would you like first?
> *Old lady:* Do you know any true stories about those unfortunate people?[27]

Within this exchange Hemingway never overtly identifies homosexuality, but both the Old Lady and Hemingway's textual surrogate realize that it is precisely this that is under discussion. Moreover, both of them assume that Faulkner's work is indeed preoccupied with "those unfortunate people" whose tales are so shocking that they must be handled carefully so as not to distress the elderly—if inquisitive—woman.

Before the Hemingway character complies and launches into a tale of two gay men in Paris, he cautions the Old Lady that such stories "in general lack drama as do all tales of abnormality" and thus also manages to call the young Faulkner's craftsmanship into question. The Old Lady agrees with Hemingway's assertion when he concludes the framed story rather anticlimactically: "The last time I saw the two they were sitting on the terrace of the Café des Deux Magots, wearing well-tailored clothes, looking clean cut as ever, except that the younger of the two, the one who had said he would rather kill himself than go back in that room, had had his hair hennaed." "This seems to me," the Old Lady replies, "a very feeble wow," her term for a story's usual dramatic conclusion. Hemingway tersely responds, "Madame, the whole subject is feeble and too hearty a wow would overbalance it." He—both Hemingway the author and Hemingway the textual surrogate— thus bolsters a final time the equation that this passage implies to readers: southern literature ("the kind of stories Mr. Faulkner writers") = gay- and lesbian-themed narratives ("stories about those unfortunate people," "tales of abnormality") = formalistically second- and third-rate narratives (those that "lack drama" and are "feeble").[28]

Such equations were by no means unique to the work of Hemingway or even that of other American novelists. The period's mainstream literary criticism also displayed similar configurations of southern literary production with consistent regularity. Few scholars' critical work, however, conflated gay and southern literary production more dramatically and insistently than that of Leslie Fiedler. *Love and Death in the American Novel* burst onto the literary scene in 1960, startling its readers with its sweeping assertions and unapologetic reconfigurations of the American canon to include works such as the novels of Charles Brockden Brown and Harriet Beecher Stowe. Most shocking, however, was Fiedler's essentializing thesis that the United States' literary production had "a desperate need to avoid the facts of wooing, marriage, and child-bearing" and had therefore privileged representations of interracial homosexuality. Again and again in "our favorite books," he asserts in his original preface, "a white and a colored American male flee from civilization into each other's arms": Natty Bumppo and Chingachgook, Gordon Pym and Dirk Peters, Ishmael and Queequeg, Huck Finn and Jim.[29]

Representations of this "innocent homosexuality" ("not homosexuality in any crude meaning of the word, but a passionless passion, simple, utterly satisfying, yet immune to lust—physical only as a handshake is physical, this side of copulation") have not, however, remained constant. According to Fiedler, although interracial male pairings are extraordinarily prevalent in nineteenth-century American fiction, they dwindle significantly on the whole in the twentieth century. In fact, he frequently strains to prove how contemporary texts usually taken to be homoerotically charged or permeated with sexual otherness are not really that way. For instance, Fiedler approvingly cites Paul Goodman's review of Jack Kerouac's *On the Road* (1957), one of the cornerstones of nonconformist Beat writing: "One is stunned by how conventional and law-fearing these lonely middle-class fellows are. They dutifully get legal marriages and divorces. The hint of a 'gang-bang' makes them impotent. They never masturbate or perform homosexual acts. . . . To disobey a cop is 'all hell.' Their idea of crime is the petty shoplifting of ten-year-olds stealing cigarettes or of teen-agers joyriding in other people's cars."[30] In Fiedler's opinion, Sal Paradise and Dean Moriarty are far less transgressive than Tom Sawyer and Huckleberry Finn and thus hardly deserve the iconic status of taboo-breakers accorded them in popular imagination.

But if representations of "innocent" male homosexuality primarily decline in twentieth-century American literary production, there remains one holdout, according to *Love and Death:* the literature of the South. Like so many persons, including Hemingway, Fiedler largely reduces this literature to Faulkner's work, that which is presumed to be inescapably gothic and therefore, according to Fiedler's conflations, homosexual. Faulkner is both the "mythopoeic genius" responsible for the fact that "the South has remained through the last three decades our preferred literary arena of terror" and the legitimate heir of American gothicism.[31] Only his literary production fully replicates that of Poe, Melville, and Twain to include both the homoeroticized interracial male pair—Gail Hightower and Joe Christmas, Henry Sutpen and Charles Bon—and the demonized women from whom the men's misogyny prompts them to flee.

According to Fiedler, insofar as white mid-twentieth-century southern writers—John Peale Bishop, Erskine Caldwell, Truman Capote, Carson McCullers, Flannery O'Connor, Katherine Anne Porter, Elizabeth Spencer, Robert Penn Warren, and Eudora Welty—labored in Faulkner's gothic shadow, their work all contributed to the deviancy of this era's southern literature. Unlike Faulkner, however, a majority of these supposed followers tended to represent not "innocent" but rather "crude" homosexuality. Using a logic akin to that of Robert Heilman and Ray West, Fiedler divides these followers into "the masculine Faulknerians" (the men Warren, Bishop, and Caldwell), "the feminizing Faulknerians" (the women Porter, Welty, McCullers, Spencer, and O'Connor), and the gay man Capote, "the heir of the feminizing Faulknerians." Despite the first group's sporadic power and popularity, it is the latter that has been "[m]uch more influential" and "taken a leading part" on the national scene. It is also their work that is "quite frankly homosexual" and displays "the true Magnolia Blossom or Southern homosexual style." Fiedler indeed holds these writers to be so significant that he posits them as the producers of all southern literature, arguing that post-World War II American fiction can be roughly divided into "the Jewish-heterosexual wing" and "the Southern-homosexual."[32]

In a discussion of reviews of Cash's *The Mind of the South*, Richard Gray sums up this phenomenon as revealed by Hemingway and Fiedler: "'What makes the mind of the South different is that it thinks it is,' observed a reviewer of Cash's book when it first appeared. If that has an element of truth in it, then so has a closely related point: that what may also make the mind of the South different is that Northerners persist in thinking it is as well." This northern thought, Gray clarifies, has "as its centre a sharply negative image of the South," one in which southerners are "inherently provincial" and "usually at odds with the rest of the nation." Gray thus closely echoes Flannery O'Connor, who asserted two decades earlier that "anything that comes out of the South is going to be called grotesque by the Northern reader."[33] He does not clarify, however, that nonsoutherners not only hold such opinions but also create and reinforce these stereotypes, as Hemingway and Fiedler have done with regards to southern sexual otherness and homosexuality in particular.

This quarantining of deviancy to the South should not, however, be considered a detriment to southern literary production. Instead, the work of Capote, Goyen, Wright, Smith, McCullers, and Lee, among others, suggests that this potentially pejorative designation ironically may have allowed these writers to create some of the nation's most intricately nuanced representations of sexuality as well as some of the earliest articulations of same-sex narratives before Stonewall. That is, because the quarantining of homo-sexuality to the South in the popular national imagination dictated to some degree that the region's writers must represent sexual otherness, their work could, in acts of strategic subversion, reconfigure these representations with depth and complexity. In short, these writers seem to have anticipated the call made by Sara Suleri in a different context: "On a very simplistic and pragmatic level, if we must be freaks, let us be freaks with a voice."[34]

2

Truman Capote, William Goyen, and the Gendering of Male Homosexuality

IF EVE SEDGWICK IS CORRECT, the flurry of scholarship dealing with same-sex desire and erotic interactions following the appearance of the introductory volume of Michel Foucault's *The History of Sexuality* has not been without cost. She maintains that, in its "historical search for a Great Paradigm Shift" in understandings of same-sex relations, this scholarship has tended to reify a knowable, stable contemporary homosexual identity, an identity she clearly holds as suspect. This work, she asserts, "has tended inadvertently to *re*familiarize, *re*naturalize, damagingly reify an entity that it could be doing much more to subject to analysis" by "counterposing against the alterity of the past a relatively unified homosexuality that 'we' *do* 'know today.'" Despite the significant work in several disciplines that checks this reification, there often still persists "the notion that 'homosexuality as we conceive of it today' itself composes a coherent definitional field rather than a space of overlapping, contradictory, and conflictual definitional forces."[1]

To substantiate this claim, Sedgwick contrasts two divergent understandings of the relationship between gender and homosexuality. Returning to Foucault's "act of polemical bravado," his offering of 1870 as the "birth of modern homosexuality," Sedgwick clarifies that Foucault posits contemporary homosexuality as being generally understood "in terms of gender inversion and gender transitivity." He famously asserts in *The History of Sexuality* that, unlike the earlier sodomite, the person whose forbidden sexual acts made him or her "a temporary aberration," the homosexual is "a personage, a past, a case history, and a childhood, in addition to being a type of life, a life form, and a morphology, with an indiscreet anatomy and possibly a mysterious physiology." Perhaps most crucially, homosexual *identity* is constituted "less by a type of sexual relations than by a certain quality of sexual sensibility, a certain way of inverting the masculine and the feminine in oneself."[2] That is, in Foucault's delineation of sexuality's history, the identity of the "modern" homosexual has generally been held, often as much by him- or herself as by others, to be constituted by the absence of gender attributes that society deems appropriate for that sex and the simultaneous manifestation of gender attributes socially appropriate only for the other sex.

In contrast to Foucault, who seemingly posits a homosexuality that has been considered consistent in its manifestations and knowability since 1870, David Halperin offers a more historically mutable sexuality, yet one that has also followed a unidirectional, supervening progression. He accepts Foucault's privileging of the mid-nineteenth century as the moment of an epistemic shift in understandings of sexuality in the West, the moment of "the formation of the great nineteenth-century experience of 'sexual inversion,' or sex-role reversal, in which some forms of sexual deviance are interpreted as, or conflated with, gender deviance." Halperin asserts, however, that mid-twentieth-century homosexuality—"the distinctive creation of the period after the Second World War"—emerged "out of inversion" and had as its "highest expression" the "'straight-acting and -appearing gay male,' a man distinct from other men in absolutely no other respect besides that of his 'sexuality.'" Thus, for Halperin, gender intransitivity rather than transitivity defines "modern homosexuality" as it generally would have been understood in the 1940s and 1950s.[3]

Sedgwick concludes that what must be acknowledged is the simultaneous existence of both of these paradigms and the slippage between—and perhaps even outside—the two. For her, "the most potent effects of modern homo/heterosexual definition tend to spring precisely from the inexplicitness or denial of the gaps *between* long-coexisting minoritizing and universalizing, or gender-transitive and gender-intransitive, understandings of same-sex relations." Indeed, Sedgwick's broadest project is self-admittedly "to show how issues of modern homo/heterosexual definition are structured, not by the supersession of one model and the consequent withering away of another, but instead by the relations enabled by the unrationalized coexistence of different models during the times they do coexist." In short, her "first aim is to denaturalize the present, rather than the past—in effect, to render less destructively presumable 'homosexuality as we know it to-day.'"[4] To anatomize "our" contemporary homosexuality, to question the ways in which it has already been defined through its fragmentation, to interrogate its performances within culturally and historically specific settings: this is the work called for but by no means completed in *Epistemology of the Closet*.

By juxtaposing two of the most prominent gay-themed southern novels at midcentury, this chapter seeks to contribute to the work called for by Sedgwick and show how these texts reveal contradictory understandings of relations of gender, same-sex desire, and sexual identity. In *Other Voices, Other Rooms* (1948), Truman Capote's first novel, the effeminate adolescent Joel Knox awakens to desire for his distant cousin within the gothic surroundings of a desolate and forsaken plantation. With amazing consistency, this narrative superimposes gender transitivity on male homoeroticism, simplistically holding the two to be mutually and exclusively indicative of one another and to constitute male homosexuality. In contrast, the lyric monologues of William Goyen's *The House of Breath* (1950) posit that same-sex desire may be as pronounced in the masculine man as in the effeminate and that this is, in fact, the more culturally valued gendering of male homosexuality.

With these contrasting models of understanding same-sex desire in mind, one easily detects in *Other Voices, Other Rooms* a presumption of gendered homosexuality resembling that which Foucault describes. At least in this early text, Capote holds male same-sex desire and gender transitivity to be mutually and exclusively indicative of one another and crucial to structuring an inescapable gay identity. Gay men are effeminate; effeminate men are gay. This understanding was, however, perhaps of little surprise to the novel's initial readers. When *Other Voices, Other Rooms* appeared, one suspected it was a text preoccupied with transgressive performances of gender even before reading the first pages. A glance at the back of the dust jacket revealed Harold Halma's soon-to-be-famous—or perhaps even infamous—photograph of the young Capote. Although it was Robert Linscott, senior editor at Random House, who chose the photograph, the decision was made only at Capote's urging. As biographer Gerald Clarke maintains, Capote was almost unerringly sure of what would seize the public's attention, and Halma's photograph was just that.[5]

Languidly sprawled on an ornately carved Victorian settee, Capote turns a provocative, pouting face to the camera. His left hand holds a cigarette, while his right hand lies draped across his crotch, almost in parody of Édouard Manet's *Olympia*. But whereas the prostitute is, although naked, rigidly alert and aggressive, almost all elements of Halma's photograph work to establish utter passivity: the resting hands, the inclined body, the head raised only with the support of the arm of the settee, the strong horizontals of the composition's central sections. Indeed, the photograph seems deliberately to counter the image of a similarly dressed Capote that appeared the previous year in *Life*. In that photograph, although effeminate Victoriana crowds the room, pressing in on Capote as in Halma's photograph, Capote nevertheless projects an active presence. His pose is rigid, with his head erect, hand poised, and eyes directly confrontational. Except for the replicated penetrative gaze, however, the later photograph removes all comparable activeness from Capote, presenting instead a brazen performance of one of the most frequently recurring gay types: the passive, effeminate, foppish gay man. Critics' struggles to capture in language this photograph and its effects began immediately and continue to document how inescapable the conveyed effeminacy is. Gloria Steinem offers that this "peculiarly riveting photograph" did not "encourage readers looking for depth. He [Capote] appeared as a kind of teen-age, marzipan Peter Lorre in a tattersall vest, reclining on a Victorian sofa, and peering myopically into the camera from under cornsilk bangs." Eric Norden comparably asserts, "Overshadowing the paens, however, and perhaps as responsible for the book's success as its luminous prose, was the photograph of Capote on the dust jacket. Gazing limpidly out of a thousand bookshop windows at a public alternately beguiled, outraged and amused was a portrait of Capote reclining on a couch, fastidiously attired in a tattersall vest and black bow tie, blond bangs dangling over his forehead, full lips moist and pouting." Clarke adds to this refrain that in the photograph Capote resembles a "slim, exotic-looking faun."[6]

It is this same representation of gayness that Capote exploits within the novel itself. Each male character struggling to negotiate desire for another man repeatedly—and almost exclusively—displays gendered performances deemed socially appropriate of women. Moreover, characters whose sexualities Capote arrests at the onset of puberty but nevertheless scripts as protogay display equally persistent gender deviancy. Like the Capote of Halma's photograph, the gay men and boys of *Other Voices, Other Rooms* are passive, foppish, and effeminate. Therefore, as in the broader cultural understanding of sexuality delineated by Foucault, Capote seems to hold gender transitivity and homosexuality as mutually constitutive.

Consider first Randolph, the novel's primary adult whose identity is centrally informed by same-sex desire. Remembering when he first sees his ostensible girlfriend Dolores with Pepe Alvarez, Randolph recalls his tentative acknowledgment of homoeroticism: "I looked at Pepe: his Indian skin seemed to hold all the light left in the air, his flat animal-shrewd eyes, bright as though with tears, regarded Dolores exclusively; and suddenly, with a mild shock, I realized it was not she of whom I was jealous, but him." Much as May Bartram recognizes John Marcher's potential sexual otherness in "The Beast in the Jungle," Dolores identifies and reassures Randolph of his gayness: "Afterwards, and though at first I was careful not to show the quality of my feelings, Dolores understood intuitively what had happened: 'Strange how long it takes us to discover ourselves; I've known since first I saw you.'" [7]

Just as Randolph's desire for other men is so crucial to his identity that Dolores can recognize it before even he does, Capote also suggests that once this desire has been recognized, it is inescapable, regardless of homophobic adversity. Dolores proves correct when she warns Randolph of Pepe, "I do not think, though, that he is the one for you; I've known too many Pepes: love him if you will, it will come to nothing" (147). Randolph's infatuation with Pepe is never reciprocated and ultimately prompts the boxer to destroy Randolph's art and verbally abuse and beat him. Nevertheless, after years of separation, this desire remains so strong that he still sends out daily letters to random places in hopes of contacting Pepe: "Mr Pepe Alvarez, c/o the postmaster, Monterrey, Mexico. Then Mr Pepe Alvarez, c/o the postmaster, Fukuoka, Japan. Again, again. Seven letters, all addressed to Mr Pepe Alvarez, in care of postmasters in: Camden, New Jersey; Lahore, India; Copenhagen, Denmark; Barcelona, Spain; Keokuk, Iowa" (111). Although the logic that structures Randolph's attempts to reach Pepe is absurd, the letter-writing nevertheless testifies to the depth of Randolph's desire for another man and the persistence of gay desire even in adversity, all of which suggests Capote's investment in the immutability of gay identity.

Randolph's erotic investments are not, however, confined to Pepe. Not unlike Tennessee Williams and his romantic involvement with the swarthy Pancho Rodriguez during the 1940s, Joel's cousin has an ongoing penchant for hypermasculine, often nonwhite men and thus provides support for Fiedler's controversial thesis about interracial male affections. Randolph treasures the photograph in which Pepe cuts "an amazing figure" with that delicate virility one finds among Hemingway's bullfighters and fishermen: "he was powerfully made and, even in so faded a print, very dark, almost Negroid; his eyes, narrow and sly and black, glittered beneath brows thick as mustaches, and his lips, fuller than any woman's, were caught in a cocky smile" (138). Other swarthy masculine men comparably fascinate Randolph. He incessantly paints and collects their images, and his curio cabinet features among its treasures "several plush-framed daintily painted miniatures of virile dandies with villainous mustaches" (87). Even more captivating for Randolph, however, are actual African American men, such as Zoo's lover Keg, whom Randolph consistently casts in homoerotic—and racist— terms, as in the telling of his near-fatal attack on Zoo. "This happened more than a decade ago, and in a cold, very cold November," Randolph recounts. "There was working for me at the time a strapping young buck, splendidly proportioned, and with skin the color of swamp honey" (77).

Although humorist Florence King may exaggerate for comic effect in her discussion of gay southern fiction typified by *Other Voices, Other Rooms,* she is nevertheless correct in implying that Capote's most central representation of gay desire is a white man's eroticization of a nonwhite hypermasculine body. "It's always summer in these books," King offers of this fiction, "thanks to Gonad Manqué's favorite wishful thinking equation: heat = sweat = blacks = sex = me." For King, mythic black male virility and sexual aggression remain at the fore of white gay southern writers' midcentury coming-of-age novels typified by Capote's. The youthful protagonist

> starts seeing all sorts of things guaranteed to nudge him into delayed adulthood—copulating couples, fellatio, weeping strangers, sodomy, a black named Raoul staring at a dead fish, fellatio, the town's eighty-year-old doyenne burying a jewelry box, sodomy, more weeping strangers busily castrating themselves, fellatio, a crushed flamingo, and of course, the town idiot busily masturbating.
>
> None of these incidents is ever related to any central event, nor to each other. They are allegories whose sole purpose is to make the little hero's testicles descend. Being a Southern lad who hangs out in woods, he has seen such things before, but now he really sees them because he has started to become Aware. He is Growing Up.[8]

For all its satire, King's point stands: Capote's representations of gay desire are restricted ones that are doubly deviant by cultural standards, transgressing the taboos of both same-sex desire and interracial desire.

That Randolph's objects of desire are invariably hypermasculine bodies highlights the contrasting representations of him as anything but manly. Indeed, Capote establishes Randolph's effeminacy to excess: "As he puckered his lips to blow a smoke ring, the pattern of this talcumed face was suddenly complete: it seemed composed now of nothing but circles: though not fat, it was round as a coin, smooth and hairless; two discs of rough pink colored his cheeks, and his nose had a broken look, as if once punched by a strong angry fist; curly, very blond, his fine hair fell in childish yellow ringlets across his forehead, and his wide-set, womanly eyes were like sky-blue marbles" (78–79). Like the foppish Capote of Halma's photograph, Randolph is soft and curvaceous rather than hard and linear. He is composed of "nothing but circles," the most phallic of his facial components seemingly broken. Even the shock of ringlets across his forehead and the "wide-set, womanly eyes" recall Capote's image on the novel's dust jacket.

Randolph's clothing does little to cover and therefore negate this unmasculine body. His wardrobe, much like Uncle Rondo's in "Why I Live at the P.O.," is composed of breezy kimonos and sandals, androgynous items with few connotations of masculinity: "Over his pyjamas he wore a seersucker kimono with butterfly sleeves, and his plumpish feet were encased in a pair of tooled-leather sandals: his exposed toenails had a manicured gloss. Up close, he had a delicate lemon scent, and his hairless face looked not much older than Joel's" (85). Even when the clothing is removed or inadvertently opened, it reveals an insistently feminized body: "Randolph, clutching the bedpost, heaved to his feet: the kimono swung out, exposing pink substantial thighs, hairless legs" (121). Like his face, Randolph's torso has virtually no hair, stock cultural designation of virility, and readers thus confront a body conspicuously lacking male secondary characteristics, those Randolph presumably finds so erotic in his "virile dandies with villainous mustaches."

As much as his bodily appearance and dress, Randolph's behavior reinforces his lack of conventional masculinity. His handwriting is the first hint of this effeminacy. When Joel shows Radclif the letter from Randolph "penned in ink the rusty color of dried blood" that formed "a maze of curlicues and dainty i's dotted with daintier o's" (8), the trucker snorts contemptuously to himself. Yet Randolph is himself as delicate as *Gone with the Wind*'s dithering Pittypat and other parodic stereotypes of southern femininity. Like them, Randolph giggles "in the prim, suffocated manner of an old maid" (77) and forces those around him to defer to his ostensibly fragile constitution. When Joel and Zoo transgress with their raucous laughter, a chastising Amy appears. Her concern is not, however, for Joel's invalid father, Edward Sansom, but rather for Randolph: "'If we aren't more careful,' stage-whispered Miss Amy, 'we're liable to find ourselves in serious difficulty. All this racket: Randolph will have a conniption'" (52–53).

Given Randolph's numerous associations with femininity, it is perhaps not surprising that he largely confines himself to the domestic sphere and cherishes the rituals of and labor invested therein. For instance, in his tale of Keg and Zoo, Randolph tells how, when Keg slits Zoo's throat "from ear to ear," he "ruined a roseleaf quilt my great-great aunt in Tennessee lost her eyesight stitching" (80). Rather than sexistly disregarding female labor and artistry, Randolph overvalues it, begrudging Zoo her life because it comes at the expense of his cherished quilt. In his own artistry he opts for the small, the delicate, the self-contained, and therefore that which is typically considered womanly. His paintings of the virile, mustachioed men are "plush-framed daintily painted miniatures" (87), and the gifts he makes for the house's other residents are trifling. Zoo explains, for instance, about her snuffbox: "Mister Randolph gimme it one Christmas way long ago. He make it hisself, makes lotsa pretty doodads long that line" (61–62). Such ornamental clutter fills Randolph's own room, creating for him an environment much like Capote's surroundings in the 1947 *Life* photograph. Joel "still could not quite take it in, for it was so unlike anything he'd ever known before: faded gold and tarnished silk reflecting in ornate mirrors, it all made him feel as though he'd eaten too much candy. Large as the room was, the barren space in it amounted to no more than one foot; carved tables, velvet chairs, candelabras, a German music box, books and paintings seemed to spill each into the other, as if the objects in a flood had floated through the windows and sunk here" (137). Randolph's life arguably culminates in his self-relegation to this domestic sphere. Because of his accidental shooting of Ed Sansom, Randolph assumes the traditionally feminine role of caretaker for his friend and functions as more of a nurse to Sansom than does even his own wife.

Rather than attempting to minimize this gender transitivity, Randolph exaggerates it through Wildean campiness. He is a "[s]ilver-tongued devil" ready with a quip, a flamboyant hand motion, and a dash of French for every occasion—not unlike Capote himself. Randolph presides over conversation at dinner with incessant witty chatter, floridly chastising the brooding Amy one moment for being, as "usual, out picking the little blue flower of forget-fulness" and nonchalantly excusing a belch the next: "'To begin at the be-ginning, then,' he said, and burped ('*Excusez-moi, s'il vous plait*. Blackeyed peas, you understand; most indigestible'). He patted his lips daintily" (76). This campiness culminates in his most blatant gender-transitive perform-ances, his cross-dressing as "the queer lady" with "white hair . . . like the wig of a character from history: a towering pale pompadour with fat dribbling curls" (67). Indeed, reviews of the novel almost invariably exaggerated the centrality of this cross-dressing, offering, for instance, that Capote's was a tale of a man "who loves dressing up in ladies' clothes, and whose womanly fingers are extremely deft with fine handicraft work."[9] And yet Capote does offer in the novel's sole gay man one so insistently gender transitive as to at-tempt to eradicate, if only momentarily, all traces of masculinity.

Although Joel's performances of gender are less socially violating than his cousin's, they are nevertheless sufficiently transitive to anticipate Joel's ul-timate gayness within the matrix of sex, sexuality, and gender that Capote presents. He consistently scripts his autobiographical protagonist as effem-inate, beginning in the novel's first pages. Radclif reflectively eyes the boy as the two travel to Skully's Landing. The trucker "had his notions of what a 'real' boy should look like, and this kid somehow offended them." Joel "was too pretty, too delicate and fair-skinned; each of his features was shaped with a sensitive accuracy, and a girlish tenderness softened his eyes, which were brown and very large." Moreover, such a body seems all the more ef-feminate when juxtaposed against Radclif's own, that of "a big balding six-footer with a rough, manly face" (4) whose truck displays a jumbled assort-ment of masculine paraphernalia: "a collection of yellowed newspapers, a slashed inner tube, greasy tools, an air pump, a flashlight and . . . a pistol. Alongside the pistol was an open carton of ammunition; bullets the bright copper of fresh pennies" (13). These physical differences from Radclif are not lost on Joel, and when he reaches Skully's Landing, he is overcome with anx-iety about his less-than-masculine body. At his most desperate moment, he imagines his father rejecting him because "that runt is an imposter; my son would be taller and stronger and handsomer and smarter-looking" (51–52).

Despite this anxiety, Joel's activities and mannerisms are no less effeminate than his appearance, and he repeatedly behaves as a stereotypical girl. He carries a change purse rather than a wallet, neatly organizes his possessions, devours Hollywood movie magazines, whimpers, blushes violently, and cries out of homesickness. Moreover, once he arrives at the Landing, Joel is, like Randolph, most at home in domestic spheres, leaving the comforting kitchen only under duress. As a result, other characters dismiss him as unmanly, as Idabel Thompkins's recurring orders to Joel reveal: "Go on home and cut out paper dolls, sissy-britches" (109).

Given that Capote's representations establish male same-sex desire and a lack of masculinity to be mutually constitutive of one another, it is not surprising that the novel culminates in the effeminate Joel's seeming acknowledgment of gay identity. His comfort with and resemblance to Randolph foreshadow precisely this recognition. Joel consistently feels "very much at ease with Randolph" (75), comes "near to speaking out his love" (211) for his cousin, and even literally mirrors him: "So he questioned the round innocent eyes [of Randolph], and saw his own boy-face focused as in double camera lenses" (86). The fateful trip with Randolph to the Cloud Hotel allows Joel to articulate this love, and the novel closes with his metaphoric acceptance of the gay identity he shares with his cousin. From Randolph's window the "queer lady" "beckoned to him [Joel], shining and silver, and he knew he must go: unafraid, not hesitating, he paused only at the garden's edge where, as though he'd forgotten something, he stopped and looked back at the bloomless, descending blue, at the boy he had left behind" (231).

What thus remains largely absent in *Other Voices, Other Rooms* is the physical actualization of same-sex desire between men. Despite this lack of sexual explicitness, however, contemporary readers and critics alike immediately recognized and/or presumed homosexuality and calls for its tolerance as the novel's central preoccupation. A pervasive cultural understanding of gender transitivity to designate same-sex desire no doubt contributed to this recognition, but so too did Randolph's overt demands that all manifestations of love be free of judgment and censorship. "[A]ny love is natural and beautiful that lies within a person's nature," he asserts; "only hypocrites would hold a man responsible for what he loves, emotional illiterates and those of righteous envy, who, in their agitated concern, mistake so frequently the arrow pointing to heaven for the one that leads to hell" (147). Although this plea benefits from neither the cool logic with which Weldon

Penderton defends same-sex desire at the end of Carson McCullers's *Reflections in a Golden Eye* nor the moving simplicity of the balladeer's discourse on the lover and the beloved in *The Ballad of the Sad Café*, Randolph's assertion is nevertheless clear regarding men's love of other men. Society must change so that "the world's ridicule" is no longer so fierce that gays and lesbians "cannot speak or show our tenderness" (147–48).

Reviewers of Capote's novel not only recognized these gay themes but in fact spoke of this "tenderness" far more directly than Capote did himself, noting almost without exception the centrality of homosexuality to the text. Such observations were rarely, however, positive.[10] The novel received almost as much criticism for its themes as for its form, and the dismay at the latter was substantial. Charles J. Rolo, for instance, characterized the book as "a poetic Grand Guignol with a Southern accent," one that is "intense, brilliant, and—as a novel—a half failure: too formless and too choked with gaudy blossoms" such as Randolph, "an exotic homosexual who spends most of his time sipping sherry, pasting bluejay feathers onto cardboard birds, and staring out of windows, dolled up in a Louis XVI ball dress and a silver wig." After establishing the book's central focus as the adolescent hero's "recognition and acceptance of his homosexuality," the *New Yorker* noted that *Other Voices, Other Rooms* "can hardly be called revolutionary" and that Capote is not "the trail-blazing writer that his publishers claim he already is." The most caustic criticism, however, came from *Time*. A review entitled "Spare the Laurels" deemed Capote's book "immature," with a theme "calculated to make the flesh crawl." The "languid and effeminate Cousin Randolph" is singled out as one of Skully's Landing's more "sinister fascinations" for Joel and condemned for seducing the boy. The scathing review ends with an overt condemnation of homosexuality: "But for all his novel's gifted invention and imagery, the distasteful trappings of its homosexual theme overhang it like Spanish moss."[11]

Even when reviewers did not overtly identify the novel's representations of homosexuality, its presence was usually still implied. John Farrelly, for instance, mentioned that Joel is prone to "sadism and other perverse variations," while W. E. Harriss nodded to the "gossamer mood of horror, perversity and poetic somnambulism" associated most closely with the "asthmatic, effeminate, sherry-drinking cousin, Randolph." Jesse E. Cross comparably noted with awkward but significant repetition that Joel enters into a "queer household" in which the inhabitants are "all queer." "Much lush writing," Cross concludes, "frequently trailing off into illusory fancies of sick brains, losing its way, yet withal picturesque. Not recommended for libraries."[12] And so continued the litany of adjectives that indirectly bespoke the presence of homosexuality: perverse, effeminate, queer, sick.

By far the most substantial—and potentially problematic—of the reviews was that of Diana Trilling in the *Nation*. She too overtly identified the novel's gay theme that culminates when "the young Joel turns to the homosexual love offered him by Randolph." This focus did not, however, temper her praise for Capote. "I can well understand what the shouting has been about," Trilling asserted; "not since the early work of Eudora Welty has there been an instance of such striking literary virtuosity. . . . In one so young this much writing skill represents a kind of genius." Nevertheless, Trilling was disturbed by what she understood to be Capote's "artistic-moral purpose." "What his book is saying," she felt, "is that a boy becomes a homosexual when the circumstances of his life deny him the other, more normal gratifications of his need for affection." The implications of this depiction are, according to Trilling, that, "having been given an explanation of the *cause* of Joel's homosexuality, we have been given all the ground we need for a proper attitude *toward* it and toward Joel as a member of society. For what other meaning can we possibly draw from this portrait . . . than that we must always think of him in this light—that even when Joel will be thirty or forty, we shall still have to judge him only as the passive victim of his early circumstances?" This supposedly inevitable conclusion is, Trilling warns, "a very dangerous social attitude." "Is no member of society, then, to be held accountable for himself, not even a Hitler?" she asks.[13]

Regardless of the validity of Trilling's presumptions that Capote's novel promotes "dangerous" determinism, the fact remains that her review contributed significantly to the ongoing discourses that centralized *Other Voices, Other Rooms*'s homoerotic elements and their intricate relationship to gender transitivity. And yet, reviews such as hers were only the few opinions that saw public print. Within the private realm, acknowledgment of these gay themes was even more candid, if frequently less homophobic, than the majority of these reviews. Indeed, Clarke relates that when Capote pressured his one-time mentor George Davis, fiction editor of *Mademoiselle*, into an evaluation of the novel, a hesitant Davis finally asserted, "I suppose someone had to write the fairy *Huckleberry Finn*."[14]

* * *

In contrast to Capote, William Goyen does not signal gender transitivity as a consistent, culturally readable marker for homosexuality. In *The House of Breath,* his approximation of "the fairy *Huckleberry Finn,*" Goyen posits same-sex desire and the physical interactions fueled by this desire to be as pronounced in aggressively masculine men as they are in effeminate ones. He conspicuously parallels the narrator's two uncles—the foppish and therefore aptly named Folner "Follie" Ganchion and his older, masculine brother, Christy—as both desiring other men and engaging in same-sex activity despite their exaggerated differences in gender. However, in Boy Ganchion's privileging of Christy's model of same-sex desire over Folner's, Goyen seemingly deems the masculine man preferable to the feminine one. He thus differs from Capote and his foreclosure of gay desire in the gender intransitive man and instead seems to replicate Halperin's suggestion that during at least the second half of the twentieth century the "highest expression" of male homosexuality is the "straight-acting and -appearing gay male." And yet, in that Christy, despite his same-sex acts, has little understanding of gay identity, he is perhaps more correctly considered akin to Foucault's pre-modern sodomite.

Goyen does nevertheless acknowledge his understanding of male homosexuality as presented in Capote's Randolph, offering in Folner a gay man who is gender transitive to the similar extreme of cross-dressing. It begins as a child, Folner recalls, when his mother "dressed me like a girl when I was little and called me 'Follie.'" Yet with adult freedom to dress himself, he continues to cross-dress, despite Charity's strict demands for gender conformity. Granny Ganchion recalls her son's initial steps toward this adult cross-dressing: "You know Folner's done strange things like goin away with a show and everyone says there was something wrong with him—the time he came home in patent leather shoes and even had a permanent wave in his blonde hair proved it." Such behavior intensifies once he abandons rural arenas for urban ones. When he commits suicide in San Antonio and his body is returned to Charity for burial, it is accompanied by trunks stamped "GAYETY SHOWS AND COMPANY" and packed with the paraphernalia associated with continued cross-dressing: "false faces, with tragic-gay bent down eyes, women's wigs, tubes of make-up grease, and spangles spilled over the clothes like dried fishscales." Granny remembers "box after box of costumes with spangles and rhinestones and boafeathers" and, like the townspeople of

Charity, wonders, "Can this be all that's left of Folner Ganchion to come back from San Antone: spangles and rhinestones and boafeathers?"[15]

But even before this ultimate revelation of Folner's violations of masculinity, the novel establishes his gender transitivity. He is among Charity's misfit youths devoted to the Methodist church's Epworth League: "The fine speeches made by my boys and girls and the readin out of the Bible verses. The hymns we sang, all of em settin before me, young and bright, Clara Lou Emson, Joe David Barnes, Folner Ganchion, Conchita Bodeen, and all of them, singin loud and joyful" (78). The boys of the Epworth League are consistently effeminate, choosing to sing and read the Bible rather than hunt and play ball. As the group dissolves with time, Hattie Clegg recalls that the only ones who remain are "a few old reliables like Sarah Elizabeth Galt who had a hare-lip, pore thing, and that kind of a sissy Raphael Stevenson, but both good Christians" (79). Boy Ganchion has comparable memories of his uncle, recalling his effeminacy even in his casket: "Folner was sad and cheap and wasted, a doll left in the rain, a face smeared and melted a little, soft and wasted and ruined" (119).

As Granny's musings reveal, this effeminacy disturbs Charity, prompting it to deem that "there was something wrong with him." Yet it seems less these violations of gender norms than the exaggerated, flaunted performances of them that ultimately alienate Folner from family and community. He acknowledges that, even in his adolescence, the acts of an ostensibly dutiful son are done simply to secure an arena for performance and attention: "Behold my talents: Started out in the Church with good Hattie Clegg, led Young People's programs, gave the main speech, sang a solo, then a duet with some girl, then said the final Benediction—it was all my show. . . . [A]t Grace Methodist Church I was always directing plays, sang in the choir, sang solos, did impersonations on programs in Fellowship Hall, played the piano by ear, anything that was make-believe" (139). When the church can afford only limited types and amounts of theatricality, he seeks arenas than can and will accommodate more elaborate and even transgressive performances, such as his cross-dressing. With hindsight, Boy can assess Folner's evolving roles: "Brave and noble, Folner? Clean and fine? Boys Scouts and the Epworth League and all that, Folner? Pshaw! You didn't want to flicker around East Texas, you wanted to *blaze* in the world, to sparkle, to shine, to glisten in the great evil world. You wanted tinsel and tinfoil and spangle and Roman candle glamor, to be gaudy and bright as a plaster ruby and a dollar diamond" (122). This desire for spectacle makes Boy's apostrophized meta-phor for his uncle seem all the more appropriate: "You were no sparrow in that coffin, Folner; you were a plumed and preened gorgeous bird, hatched in a borrowed nest, cuckolded, meant for some paradise garden" (126). As for exotic birds of paradise, spectacular performance is everything for Folner.

In keeping with the novel's effeminization of Folner, such spectacles link him with certain women rather than other men. These women are, however, neither his dependable, docile sisters nor his retiring nieces but rather his flamboyant niece Sue Emma "Swimma" Starnes and his mother, Hannah Ganchion. Both women not only hyperfeminize and therefore make spec-tacles of their female bodies but also, driven by what the community deems excessive erotic desires, use these bodies for transgressive sexual gratifica-tions. The gossiping voice of the Ganchions' anthropomorphized well overtly compares Folner to Sue Emma: "Then she went on the stage (just like Folner Ganchion, everbody could all see it)—that little country girl Swimma Starnes that everbody knew in Charity Texis." Although he must clothe himself to feminize his body, Sue Emma disrobes to do so most fully: "prancin round half-nekkid in some personality show" (64–65). Neverthe-less, both make spectacles of these feminine bodies.

Folner and Sue Emma further resemble one another by using these spec-tacular bodies to the same end as the promiscuous Granny Ganchion: to arouse male desire. To the community's disgust, Granny, like Faulkner's Addie Bundren, does not remain monogamous within her marriage. Al-though prompted in part by her husband's own infidelities with African American women, she capitalizes upon her good looks and sexual adventur-ousness to conceive Christy by a man she meets at a carnival: "But in some year, when it twas I don't know now, the Carnival come, and I spun a wheel and he knocked niggerbabies down to win these beads—he wanted to brush the sawdust that we had laid in off my skirt but I said let it be you'll *never* brush that sawdust off. Then Christy come. When Christy was made in me his maker made him in sorrow and tears in a wet tent and on sawdust" (151). Glancing at Granny at Folner's funeral, Boy delineates the town's keen ob-servations of her infidelity: "When desire failed you, you had nothing left but the betrayal of desire . . . and a pair of ruby beads given you once by a dark alien youth who found you at a carnival and loved you and stayed to love you longer and again. You would steal away at night and run to him at the City Hotel and all the town knew" (129). A generation later, Folner and

Sue Emma incite comparable gossip with their apparent engendering of male desire. Granny recalls "what happened around Charity and the commotion he [Folner] caused among the young boys, and everyone sayin he acted just like a girl" (147–48). The town, spoken for by the well, notes much the same of Sue Emma: "Naturally she attracted men like flies—that's what she *wanted*. Like her old grandma, had to have whiskers round her, had to have a pair of pants round her noon and night" (65).

With both Sue Emma and Granny, these spectacles of femininity used to such ends elicit only communal condemnation, suggesting the misogyny that circulates through Charity. The town cannot and does not tolerate conspicuous performances of femininity that reveal the power generated by such productions. Women who "misuse" social scriptings through an emphasis on and employment of the feminine body to control men incite such anxiety that Charity must censure them. With such circulations of misogyny, Folner is thus doubly transgressive and therefore damnable in Charity's eyes. With his cross-dressing, he not only performs the "wrong" gender for his biological sex but also enacts a sexualized variation of that gender that is socially condemnable even if performed by persons of the "correct" sex.

Goyen's narrative further links Folner to Granny and Sue Emma in that, to the understanding of this censorious community, all three ultimately suffer punishments for their transgressive behaviors. Granny suffers from a "vile goiter, round and swollen and strutted with purple veins big as a chicken's intestines" (127), the manifestation of her sins. Sue Emma comparably bears hydrocephalic babies that refuse to die: "First one was a boy with a head big as a watermelon and shaped like one. That little freak lived and lived, head kept gettin bigger and bigger, and they would come and measure it and measure it, but it wouldn't die, really got strong and healthy as an ox, and jes lay there in its bed, huge and strong and an idiot, thrashin like a whale and slobberin all over the bedclothes." Deeming the child to be what Sue Emma deserves, Charity smugly concludes that the "wicked have their hell right here on earth" (65–66). The town determines much the same when Folner is driven to suicide, his appropriate end in Charity's opinion. Boy senses this public disapproval at Folner's funeral, noting that they "are burying like a foul thing in the dirt this twisted freak, like Sue Emma's two little monsters, little slobbering freaks with bloated watermelon heads" (127).

It is not, however, merely nameless townspeople who reject the effeminate Folner. With the exception of his mother and Boy, Folner's family despises him. Boy recalls to Folner that at the funeral "Aunty sat hating you, even dead. Even laid in a coffin she despised you like a snake," and Christy "sat out in front of the church in the car, would not come in, sullen and wretched" (123). The minister even uses the occasion to air his repugnance of Folner. "The sermon was a long and sad one," Boy remembers, one that emphasizes Folner's sinfulness: "It told about all the family, about your young life in Charity and your work in the Church. (Once you had stood, at ten, before the whole congregation and recited the books of Bible first forwards, then backwards. You had been a bright boy. You had sinned. The Lord save your soul.)" (126). The acts of Folner's adult life negate the catalogue of youthful achievements, irrevocably damning him in Charity's eyes: "What does he say, Brother Ramsey, in his talking, in his sermon? He is condemning Follie to hellfire" (128).

What remains consistent is that these condemnations of Folner focus on his violations of gender rather than manifestations of his sexual desire for men. And yet Goyen includes ample allusions to Folner's homosexuality that might be used to fuel such condemnations. True, Goyen does not present Folner as engaging in overt sexual interactions with other men or desiring a specific partner, as Capote does with Randolph's ill-fated infatuation with Pepe Alvarez. But throughout the novel, hints of Folner's sexual interactions emerge from the obfuscatory lyricism. As mentioned, his mother suggests that, even before he leaves Charity, Folner has affairs with other boys. His own narrative of escaping with the carnival centralizes the sexualized mentor he finds there, "a trapeze man with thighs in black tights" (141).

But perhaps the most significant of these allusions hint at incestuous sexual interactions between Folner and Boy, as James Levin suggests. Again, although Goyen does not graphically represent sexual acts between the two or even symbolize them as he does with the manifestations of Boy's and Christy's desire for one another, Goyen nevertheless insinuates that Folner's relationship with Boy contains a sexual element and even that Folner initiates Boy into same-sex interactions. As Robert Phillips notes, Goyen experiments with Christ figures throughout his fiction, and *The House of Breath* is no exception, with Christy being the most obvious of these figures.[16] But the narrative also associates Folner with Christ, subtly conflating Folner's possible introduction of Boy into same-sex activity with the Resurrection. "But Boy, we had a time of it, didn't we?" Folner asks Boy. "You little frightened thing, always frightened. On one Easter Sunday I taught you a secret. We rolled away some stone, remember?" The narrative immediately shifts to Boy's anxious response: "You made me feel so full of sin that I never mentioned your name to anybody; and when once and a while they would say your name I would tremble and think they knew" (143). This shame, like Boy's desire for Folner, persists even to his death, and Boy is oddly aroused at the funeral: "for a moment at the Charity Graveyard there was a reunion of blood and a membership of kin over your grave (the odor of lilies and carnations gave me a sensuous, exotic elation that I was ashamed of)" (130–31).

Despite the ambiguity of such passages regarding erotic investments, the bond between Folner and Boy is nevertheless clearly deeper than that between most others in the family. This bond arises in part because of Folner's mentorship of Boy. Both before and after his death, Folner repeatedly seeks to guide and assure his nephew. For instance, Folner attempts to rescue Boy from Charity's destructive confinement, cautioning, "Nothing is made right around here" but is instead "crooked and warped and twisted" (122–23). And when Folner leaves with the circus, he mourns the loss of only Boy: "As we rolled away in our gay wagons, the last thing I saw of the house where you lay sleeping was the wheel turning over it, and the only one in that whole house that I cried for was you, Boy O Boy" (141). Folner is just as meaningful to Boy, and at the funeral he pays a final tribute by dropping "a little purple spangle into your cheap coffin as I passed by. It was a little purple spangle stolen from a gypsy costume in one of your trunks in the loft. You loved it! It was put in the earth with you" (124). And yet Folner's pull continues long after this moment. Years later Boy still pines for "Follie, our Follie" and, as he explains to his uncle, is "called back to the loft where your relics lie stored; and I am here among them rummaging for some answer" (132). Even mere sounds remind Boy of his grief: "oh the sound of the rain on the castorbean leaves, how forever after Folner's funeral that sound reminded me of the funeral" (8).

Robert Phillips has persuasively argued that this bond arises from Boy's resemblance to Folner, one of which the older man is acutely aware. Much like Randolph, who sees himself in the proto-gay Joel Knox, Folner finds a youthful mirroring of himself in Boy. The nephew also senses these similarities, as Goyen suggests by making these reflections concrete. When Boy mentally inventories the Ganchions' loft, he imagines Folner speaking to him: "'I give you this glass,' your voice whispers, 'in which to see a vision of yourself, for this is why you've come. My breath is on the glass and you must wipe away my breath to see your own image.' In the mirror I cannot see myself but only an image of dust. I brush it off—and then see my portrait there. For a moment I look like Folner!" (136–37). Boy's reflection of Folner's image and, by extension, his identity is so pronounced that he does indeed seem to function as "an alter-ego for the narrator," as Phillips suggests.[17] Thus, as in Capote's representations, the adolescent struggling with negotiations of sexual identity finds the effeminate gay man the most accessible model.

Although there may be security for the adolescent in realizing the existence of this model, it is nevertheless an unsettling one. As with Randolph's, Folner's model suggests a direct and inescapable correlation between same-sex desire and gender transitivity. This is further complicated by ambiguities of contingency. Which precedes and therefore dictates the other: the transgressive desire or the transgressive performance of gender? If one desires other men, must one therefore be effeminate? Or, if one is effeminate, must one therefore desire men? Goyen leaves these questions unanswered but emphasizes that the requisite performances of gender in this model secure the gay man's alienation from his society. Given this alienation, that which Boy witnesses directly in Charity's responses to Folner, Boy's is an uneasy acceptance of the model of homosexuality that Folner offers. To him Boy confesses, "It is hard to be in the world and bone of your bone" (132). At no time does he realize this more strongly than as he sits listening to Brother Ramsey's homophobic sermon at Folner's funeral. Boy reflects that his homosexuality, which supposedly must replicate Folner's, is an immense burden: "The Lord hath hung this millstone upon my neck, and I know what for and I have never told. It is a lavalier of wickedness. It is the enormous rotten core of Adam's Apple" (128).

Folner is not, however, the only model of a man who engages in sexual acts with other men that Goyen presents to Boy. Unlike Capote, Goyen significantly complicates the circulations of erotic desire and their relationships to Boy's identity with the inclusion of his other uncle, the masculine Christy. Being "black-headed and swarthy among the other towheads" (129) of the family, he is the physical opposite of Folner in popular concepts of gender: "Christy was big and had dark wrong blood and a glistening beard, the bones in his russet Indian cheeks were thick and arched high and they curved round the deep eye-cavities where two great silver eyes shaped like bird's eggs were set in deep—half-closed eyes furred round by grilled lashes that laced together and locked over his eyes" (157–58). Unlike the diminutive Folner, Christy is enormous, so much so that, when the Ganchions hold his funeral, "they had the services in the old house, not in the church, and the casket was so big (he was a big man) they had to putt it through the winda under the chinaberry tree" (70).

Although Goyen's imagery repeatedly animalizes Christy, no flitting exotic birds characterize him as they do Folner. Goyen instead conveys Christy via great hulking beasts or those given to violence—oxen, dogs, falcons, horses—and typically associated with masculine realms. Boy, for instance, recalls Christy as a "man with a long houndface and a glistening silver eye" (157), and Christy himself notes how the family perceives of him as a beast of burden: "because I was big and big-handed they used me like a plowox" (183). Even when treating Christy's devotion to his mother, Goyen couches the relationship in terms of hunting, animalizing both mother and son: "He was a hunting man; and hunted; and his mother Granny Ganchion was a shaggy old falcon that had caught him like a surrendered bird and held him close to her, home; as though he had been hunted in his own hunting, the hunter hunted; and captured: by trap or talon; or treed; or set or pointed at and stalked in his own secret woods and brought home, driven towards stall and what forage, at nightfall, to her, the hunter's huntress" (158). Although casting Christy in terms of prey, this animalization does not call his masculinity into question. He may be a "surrendered bird," but he is still a "hunter," an active seeker and seizer rather than a detached, effeminate performer like his brother.

Christy's links to animals are more than imagistic, however. The narrative repeatedly poses his fascination with and incessant discussion of animals' genitals and their violent sexual acts. A titillated Boy remembers that Christy "would say whispered things about animals: udders, the swinging sex of horses, the maneuvers of cocks, bulls' ballocks and fresh sheep—he was in some secret conspiracy with all animals" (161). Christy even admits to the voyeuristic, erection-forming pleasure he takes in watching animals mate: "(Lyin in the fields all afternoon one afternoon, watchin for the stallion to take the mare. . . . I waited and waited and just about dark Good Lord it happened. How the mare screamed and how the stallion leapt with's hooves in the air like a great flyin horse of statues . . . As I laid in the fields, somewhere in me was fillin with blood, and suddenly somewhere I was full and throbbin with blood.)" (177). The focus here is conspicuously on males and their genitals, including Christy's own engorged penis. A somewhat less-than-subtle Goyen goes so far as to establish Christy's hypermasculinity as to make him a personified phallus. "He had a circumcision-like scar," Boy recalls, "pink and folded, on his brown neck over which he would gently rub his fingers and tell me how it was a knifecut because of love" (159).

The literally phallocentric Christy is himself as violent as rutting stallions or hunting falcons, exceeding stereotypical masculinity's demands for activity. In a scene that anticipates his first encounter with Boy in the woods, Christy leads the foray that kills the Ganchions' cow. The sensitive Berryben recalls to his mother the trauma of Roma's bloody end: "the men (Christy was the leader) with the axe over the poor ugly cow Roma caught in the ice. ('Mama,' I said, 'she is crying so loud, now, like the dog the time he was sick under the house. Mama!' I cried, 'they have hit her hard on the head with the axe, hard! hard! hard! Mama—she is quiet, now; Mama—she is not crying anymore. Mama . . . Roma the cow is dead'" (114). Cast in binarisms, Christy's masculine activity and ability must eradicate Roma's feminine inactivity and inability symbolized by the trapped cow's paralysis.[18] Although Christy arguably kills Roma for her own good, his axe-blows only add to Berryben's associations of violence with his uncle. The sound and images of Roma's death haunt Berryben, as do "Christy's songs and stories and his scars, the blood of his killed creatures" (115).

Even given this terrifying violence, Christy's withdrawn personality, and the rarity of his interactions with Boy, a significant bond forms between the two, especially from Boy's perspective. He invests far more heavily in the experiences he shares with Christy than in those he shares with Folner and tends to find meaning in even the most casual and laconic of Christy's comments. Boy recalls the thrill he feels at "one of the few words he ever said to me," when Christy holds the family's seashell "out to me once and said, 'Listen!'" (15). Yet there are moments, such as when examining Christy's map of the world, when these interactions are much more substantial and therefore perhaps more understandably invested with value for Boy. "Christy often sat at night," Boy remembers, "(and I sometimes with him) and looked and looked at the map, almost as if he were talking to the world and adoring the world and taking each part of it into himself as he looked" (18). As Folner does with his example of leaving with the circus, Christy offers Boy an escape from Charity, albeit only a metaphoric one: "Sometimes he showed me that by looking a long time at the map and then closing your eyes, you could open them again and look out into Bailey's Pasture and see there, radiant and throbbing, the lighted shape of the world" (18–19). More important for Boy than this escape, however, are the shared experiences that bond him to Christy: "Here, tacked on this wall in the kitchen of the house you held, Charity, was the world's body showing all the life in it; and all the life was in Christy and me—and our skulls became lighted globes of the world, that the map had stamped there, which each of us held in his hands, turning it round to find the worlds that each of us had given to the other" (20). In this case, comfort for Boy lies in the means rather than the end.

To his surprise and elation, this contact with his uncle and the resulting importance of the bond increases when Christy facilitates—perhaps unwittingly and perhaps not—Boy's first orgasm and thus circuitously introduces him to masturbation. The anthropomorphized river reminds Boy of his awakening to autoeroticism and Christy's role in that experience: "Once, when you were swimming, naked, it happened for the first time to you in me. Christy stood on the bank and told you and Berryben to jump in and touch my bottom and see who could come up to the top first" (29–30). Goyen's lyricism is again obfuscatory, yet the diction and actions imply that Boy gets an erection and ultimately climaxes. The River continues: "and you were struggling to come up first, rising rising rising, faster, faster, when some marvelous thing that can happen to all of us happened to you, wound up and burst and hurt you, hurt you and you came up, changed, last to the top trembling and exhausted and sat down on my banks in a spell" (30). Although the orgasm bewilders Boy, Christy fully understands what has occurred and even encourages Boy to attempt another climax.[19]

Once his initial confusion subsides, Boy needs little encouragement to explore autoeroticism further. He repeatedly returns to the River to masturbate, so much so that in its memories the River casts Boy in terms of its lover:

> By me, in these woods, you once made up for what you never had, . . . and lay against my sandstone and ached and cramped and burned and I know what happened there. Just you hard against my rock; and in your trousers, all over you, hot and running like glue—you washed you in my waters . . . O we were lovers, I had you rising and falling in me and you left something in me and it was mixed with my rich sediment and my spume, O we were lovers; and I cast your sperm

mixed in my spume and sediment onto the land, the country of your beginnings, and we made it rich. (30)

Despite the heterosexual paradigm that these images of fertilization suggest, the descriptions nevertheless hint at same-sex desire fueling Boy's ongoing masturbation. He returns to the woods because it is not only private but also the site in which male homosociality as orchestrated by Christy allows for the boy's initial sexual gratification through orgasm. And yet these vague associations between Christy and the pleasures of autoeroticism are all that Boy can make at this point. As the River tells him when reflecting on the fateful swimming trip, "This was the way you learned what could happen to you, but not why; like a clock that could wind up and chime in you down there" (30).

Although Boy remains oblivious to this potential same-sex desire for some time, the novel's progression clarifies that Christy *is* the likely fuel of Boy's autoeroticism. The narrative is nonchronological, but the progression of his recollections of his uncle nevertheless replicates Christy's increasing sexualization during Boy's youth. By the second half of the novel, yet before the final pages in which Boy acknowledges his erotic desire for Christy, practically every description of him is sexually charged. Boy casts even Christy's playing of his French harp in erotic terms. He recalls his uncle's "trembling hands" and, immediately after noting Christy's fascination with male animals' genitals, emphasizes the "blowing and sucking sounds like birdcalls and moaning voices of animals" (161) that come from Christy's control of the instrument. In particular, Boy eroticizes Christy's mouth—"his pale wet lips curled like some delicious membrane"—and imagines it to give voice to all that Christy has not said to Boy. Perhaps most important, he also describes the profound effect this performance has on him: "and before I knew him I lay in my bed hearing these sounds like a mystic music played from the moon that rocked like an azure boat in our sky, framed by my window" (161–62).

Just as Boy's same-sex desires crystallize as Goyen's narrative progresses, so too do Christy's own desires for men become more identifiable. They are initially ambiguous in large part because Goyen adroitly manipulates the instability inherent in male homosociality or, in an even more complicating move, has Christy do so. As in the scene of Boy's first orgasm, Christy seemingly stands as the masculine man who thrives on and even orchestrates fraternal interactions. At least on his part, however, these interactions do not necessarily work to discipline and/or exclude sexual activity, as they most frequently do. Rather, he may gratify same-sex desires by exploiting the physical contact and even displays of sexuality that male homosociality "legitimately" allows between men. Consider, for instance, the "fishing trip with some uncles and other men" that Boy remembers from his childhood:

> I had lain listening all night to a conversation against the stitching call of katy-dids about women and certain Charity women; and then one man had said (it was Christy, my uncle) while he thought I was asleep, that he wondered if I had any hairs down there yet and drank his homebrew and said let's wake him up to see, and chuckled. I had lain trembling and waiting for them to come, knowing they would find what they came to see, quite a few, and lovely golden down, and they had been my secret; but they never came, only made me feel a guilt for secrets. (23)

Although this passage documents Boy's not fully conscious desire to have other men subject his pubescent body to their gazes, it also establishes the ambiguity of Christy's desire to subject Boy to this scrutiny. Simple curiosity may prompt Christy's urge to examine Boy's genitals, to see if his body has become mature enough for his full participation in the homosocial and ostensibly heterosexual realm of the hunt and its talk of women. On the other hand, Christy may be manipulating homosociality's allowances for these supposedly asexual interactions to gratify his desire to view Boy's adolescent body.

Christy's vexed relationship with his brother, Folner, suggests that this gaze may indeed be prompted by homoerotic desire and that Christy sets up Boy as a sort of surrogate for Folner. As discussed, Christy rejects Folner, refusing even to attend his funeral, since, like the rest of Charity, Christy despises Folner's violations of gender. "He hated Folner," Boy recalls of Christy, "said he had to squat to pee and didn't have enough sense to pour it out of a boot" (160). Goyen complicates this hatred, however, by preceding it with Christy's intense love of Folner as a child. This devotion is so fierce that Christy violates his otherwise consistent performances of masculinity with displays of affection that he—and presumably the rest of Charity—perceive to be feminine. At least in Christy's eyes, however, familial hardship necessitates his mothering of Folner: "I was Follie's mother all those years, makes me part woman and I know it and I'll never get over it. How I rocked him and how I slept warm with him at nights, rolled up against my stomach and how I never left him day or night, bless his little soul, settin on the gallry with him on my knee while I watched the others comin and goin across the pasture to town and back from town, to Chatauquas and May Fetes" (160). Christy is clearly anxious at having performed in this manner; however, the gratification that arises from this transgression of gender outweighs this anxiety, and he remembers his parenting of Folner with amazing tenderness.

The loving relation between the two brothers falters when the transgression of gender is no longer momentary and terminal with Christy and does not ensure a gratification that compensates for the social disapproval engendered by the supposedly deviant performance. When Folner too begins to enact roles socially scripted as feminine, Christy's gender anxiety reaches such levels that he reassumes only strict masculine roles and rejects Folner almost altogether because he will not perform comparably. "What was it got hold of him?" Christy asks of Folner: "Took to swingin in the gallry swing all day, by hisself, turned away from me, somethin wild got in his eyes, and then Mama took him back. Began to wear Mama's kimona and highheeled shoes and play show, dancin out from behind a sheet for a curtain; and then I turned away from him" (160–61). In this case, a temporary sacrifice of masculinity leads not to a reinscription of stable masculinity but rather to even more exaggerated violations of gender norms. In his tending to Folner, Christy may be less than conventionally masculine, but he is far from crossdressing. Moreover, as Christy's reflections suggest, Folner's rejection of his brother is equally anxiety-inducing in that the social approval that Christy sacrifices to mother Folner is not compensated by his reciprocal devotion. Quite the contrary to exhibiting such affection, Folner flatly rejects his brother. Boy thus seems correct in his assessment of his uncles, that Christy "had raised him like a mother until Folner turned away from him and hated him, and then Christy said he was a sissy and a maphrodite" (161).

As Boy further recalls, the relationship between the two brothers does not end here. Despite their mutual rejections, "they joined again in the woods—where I joined them too; and now we all join in the world" (161). As usual, Goyen's prose is vague; nevertheless, the narrative suggests that the nonsexual physical contact expressive of the brothers' original mutual devotion metamorphoses into sexual physical contact that is perhaps so gratifying that it outweighs the reciprocal disgust. Their antithetical performances of gender and their willingness to engage in same-sex acts allow the brothers to become what seems compatible—albeit clandestine—sexual partners. That is, through an enactment of recurrent cultural elisions of gender and sexual preferences—ones in which activity (and sexual activity such as penetration in particular) marks masculinity and passivity (and sexual passivity such as being penetrated orally and/or anally in particular) marks femininity—the brothers find themselves able to enact a sexual relationship that ostensibly replicates the gendered roles of normative heterosexuality.

Although Christy's sojourn into the Merchant Marine does not necessarily confirm that his relationship with Folner is sexual, it nevertheless establishes that the relationship is at the very least as strongly informed by love as by the publicly displayed hatred. Not unlike Boy at the novel's open, or Goyen himself during World War II, Christy finds himself acutely lonely in his alienation from childhood friends and family.[20] Homesick and separated from his comrades from home, Christy falls into reveries that conjure up only Folner:

> In the ship I was lonesome and afraid, but I did my work. At night I'd lay in my bunk and think of everthing. And then I saw a face, fair in its youngman's bearded beauty, and so much like Follie that I almost cried out "Follie!" I watched this face while I worked and it swam before me in my nights in my bunk. I wanted to putt my hand on this hand and hold it still under mine, made still by his made still. Oh he was bright and I was dark and I gave him all my darkness on that ship; but we joined, for all good things in the world, and to find somethin together . . . . (36)

These erotic apparitions of his brother so affect Christy that even the town notices the changes in him upon his return. "You know how Christy Ganchion left with the Skiles boy for the Merchant Marines," the gossiping Ganchion well asserts. "Somethin happened to Christy, somewhere, that nobody'll ever know. Christy's quiet as a tomb . . . Anyway when he come back they had a time with him for awhile" (67).

Goyen's narrative never clarifies exactly what goes on between the two brothers in the woods or if it is these interactions that haunt Christy. It seems clear, nevertheless, that something significant occurs between the two there, even if only in Boy's imagination. He repeatedly speculates on the scenario, asking himself of Follie, "Was *he* what Christy hunted for in the woods, going with his birdbag and his gun and returning with bird's blood on him and a chatelaine of slain birds girdled round his hips" (121). If Folner has indeed been Christy's sexual prey in the woods, then the intentions of his subsequent invitations for Boy to go there with him become increasingly suspect of being sexually motivated. These invitations may be Christy merely seeking to establish more firmly Boy's position within homosocial realms typified by hunting, as celebrated in *Go Down, Moses*. Or, as in the cases of the hunting trip and the day of swimming with Berryben, Christy may be manipulating these homosocial interactions to allow an arena for expressions of his desire for other men. That is, Christy may use the supposedly nonsexual fraternal bonding of the hunt to have sex with his nephew, as he has possibly done with his brother.

At this point, before the two ultimately fateful trips to the woods with Christy, Boy remains simultaneously confused, frightened, and intrigued by his elder uncle and his mysterious ways. Boy recalls that Christy "would go off hunting (in Folner's same woods)," consistently promising, "One day when you're old enough I'll take you huntin with me, we'll go huntin, Boy." When Christy returns from his forays, Boy, like Berryben, senses the brutality that Christy has unleashed. He would "then come back to us as though he had been in some sorrow in the woods, with birds' blood on him and bouquet of small, wilted doves hanging from his waist over his thigh, or a wreath of shot creatures: small birds with rainbowed necks, a squirrel with a broken mouth of agony." These artifacts of Christy's violence do not, however, repulse Boy as they do Berryben. Rather, although hesitant, Boy thrills when Christy "would come to me and speak, for he had found words, 'Listen Boy, listen; come out to the woodshed with me quick and let me show you somethin, come with me, quick; by Gum I've got somethin . . . '" (159).

Twice Boy succumbs to his curiosity and goes into the woods with Christy, investing each time with significant—albeit not always fully understood—meaning. In the first instance, even the ostensible reason for the trek into the woods—to hunt a mother opossum and her offspring—works to create an exclusively male sphere. As with the destruction of the cow Roma, the hunt for the opossum and her young is to culminate with the eradication of the female and the results of procreation. That this sphere is to be exclusively male does not, however, foreclose circulations of eroticism. Rather, Goyen's diction almost immediately begins to establish the sexual charge to the homosociality and, somewhat later, offers a coherent symbol of homosexual interactions. "I trembled to go, and slipped away and met him," Boy remembers. "I saw him waiting for me (like a lover), I saw him sitting on a stump watching me as I came, closer and closer, feeling evil, feeling guilty. We rejoiced (without words) at our meeting secretly" (163–64). The uncle and nephew thus embark like lovers and soon begin the work of excavating the creatures from a stump. Just as Goyen's earlier conflations of Christy's violence and sexual desire help for his ferocious chopping to assume sexual overtones, the symbolism needs little deciphering. As Christy hacks at the stump, he unintentionally strikes Boy and thus comes painfully close to a brutal penetration of the boy: "Because I came too close to him once he came down on my thigh with his axe—so gently that he only cut a purple line under the skin and no blood came." Even though this penetration is ultimately checked, thus suggesting Christy's ambivalence about engaging in such sexual acts, his actions nevertheless traumatize him: "Christy wept and begged me not to tell anyone and tied his bandanna tightly round the wound and hugged me and trembled; and I have never told" (164). At least for the moment, despite his crystallizing desire for Boy, Christy cannot consummate the relationship sexually.

In contrast to Christy, whose frantic demands for silence about the incident betrays its illicitness, Boy reacts not with terror or hysteria but rather with an elation comparable to that of his first orgasm. "I almost fainted and fell to the ground," he recalls, "but did not cry." Indeed, he thrills to bear the proof of his uncle's physical violation and, like Christ to doubting disciples, does not hesitate to display his marked body: "I have carried on my thigh the secret scar he left me (O see the wound on this thigh left by the hunter's hand!) and have never told." Yet, as with his first orgasm, Boy remains confused about the meaning of this mark and the significance of Christy having given it. Boy senses only enough to know that Christy is vitally central and that the episode is not finished. "After that, there was a long time of waiting in which I knew there was a preparation for something," Boy reflects. "Within this waiting (was Christy waiting too?) we looked at the map together or I watched him make the ship in the bottle or heard the french-harp in the woodshed" (164).

Unlike the long-anticipated beast in John Marcher's jungle, that in Boy's woods springs with a force rivaling the blows of Christy's axe to Roma, bringing with it what is as close to clarity as one can expect in a Goyen novel. Boy confesses his epiphany as abruptly as he has it: "And then one summer night I learned his truth (and mine)" (164–65). Squatting outside his uncle's window, Boy sees Christy asleep, naked and sexually aroused, and is transfixed by the beauty of his uncle's virile body, "hairy with a dark down, and nippled, and shafted in an ominous place." Instantly and, for the first time, fully aware of his desire for another man, Boy immediately articulates his embrace of this desire ("I whispered to myself 'Yes!'—as though I was affirming forever something I had always guessed was true") and envisions a scenario in which the desire is not only mutual but acted upon. He recreates the laconic Christy's earlier beckonings and adds to them an explicitly sexual charge: "From where I watched him from below it seemed he might at some moment dive down to me and embrace me and there speak and say, 'Listen Boy, listen, let me tell you something . . .'" Although confined to heterosexual paradigms, Boy expands the scenario so that it is literally Edenic, with him, the mirrored image of the effeminate Folner, assuming the role of Eve and Christy functioning as Adam: "There, in the garden, I, like Eve, found him leaf-shadowed (and, like Eve, leaf would forever after make me stop to remember). There he lay, among vines now, so beautiful in his naked sleep, and so stilled (I thought)—a hot liquid summer night filling the world with the odor of greengrowing and moonlight—green-golden under the light he had fallen asleep with still on, little cupids of gnats wafting round him" (165). In language reminiscent of the River's articulation of his masturbations, Boy sets his goals motivated by an acceptance of this desire: *"O when I am ready, really ready, and filled with blood, I will go, . . . hung with my beauty blooming close upon my flesh and this vision burned upon my brain, in the spring, through all the land, sowing it with my substance . . . And we will fill the world with our sighs of yes! and make it sensual like rain, like sun, like scents on wind, being blossoms and pollen"* (167).

Boy's opportunity to act on these desires arises when Christy again invites him into the woods, for the novel's—if not necessarily Boy's—climax: "And then, finally, it was the time Christy had whispered about" (168). Yet, when the scenario develops, Boy is not nearly so eager as when he is the voyeur, safely distanced from his object of desire. That this very person may gratify these desires thrills him, and he recalls, "For a time he was leading me like a piper to the river; and for a time I was following in a kind of glory, and eager, and surrendered, and wanting to follow—just as he was, in his own dumb sorcery and splendor, leading me, victor, proud, like a captive." At the same time, however, "the uncaptured, unhypnotized part of me was afraid, wanting to run home (where was home to turn to, towards where?); for I knew he was leading me to a terrible dialogue in the deepest woods. All his hunting, all his shooting and gathering up of shot birds was a preparation . . . in which he would tell me some terrible secret" (171). Only slowly does Boy realize the actual source of this anxiety. He, already the youthful image of Folner, is about to become a surrogate for the person whom the family, Charity, and, perhaps most important, Christy reviles. Although mute at the time, Boy later imagines he could now name the anticipated interactions with Christy: "'Yet that's what Folner did and you despised him,' I would answer him if we could have a conversation now" (172).

Irony thus permeates this culminating scenario. On the one hand, Boy fears that sexual interactions with Christy will dictate for him an identity like Folner's: passive and effeminate and therefore subject to familial and communal ridicule and rejection. On the other hand, Christy, functioning out of a radically different logic, initiates these actions to prevent Boy from becoming like the detested Folner. If Christy's indulgent mothering of Folner, that contingent on Christy's sacrifice of masculinity, supposedly causes—or at least is a significant factor in—Folner's problematic effeminacy, then Christy's antithetical treatment of Boy may possibly ensure Boy's acceptable masculinity. Since violence and sex have been such effective means of eradicating the feminine, as symbolized in the cow and the opossum, it provides Christy the most likely method to squelch whatever burgeoning displays of femininity Boy may make. Thus, for Christy, Boy's introduction into sex between men within an exclusively masculine realm may prevent him from replicating Folner's transgressive performances of gender, perversely allowing Christy to fulfill his role as a Christlike savior. Because Christy understands gayness to be primarily contingent on transgressive performances of gender rather than same-sex activity, Boy's literal rather than symbolic penetration will, as Christy reflects, "keep him from the fruits like Follie, my own brother." In short, according to this logic, Christy can fuck the threat of gayness out of "this cleanpeckered boy" (174).

This logic is not, however, coherent even for Christy, and it is his own ambivalence, that already marked on Boy's body with the scar of the axe-blow, that ultimately prevents the sexual consummation of the relationship. Despite his thrill at maleness engaged in violent sexual acts, Christy falls back upon the puritan notion that all sex, regardless of the object choice, is corrupting. Just as he honors the virginity of Otey Bell, his by-then drowned wife, he feels he must not violate his nephew: "Boy, Boy you are so good, what made you so good? I am spoiled and he is clean; O I am vile, a shitten lamb. I will corrupt him, do not let me corrupt him when we get to the thicket. I didn't spoil Otey, I let her wait; I can let him wait—but what will get him, what will claim him eventually and spoil him?" (184).

Christy cannot negate this desire for Boy, however, by an act of will. Physical urges counter well-meant resolutions, and the possibilities for pleasure offered in Boy's body tantalize Christy as incessantly as his own naked body has done Boy earlier. As the two walk deeper and deeper into the woods, Christy fantasizes about both of their bodies, focusing specifically on their genitals: "O myself, how splendid myself, good as a stallion, and pretty, and circumcised (is he?), for who, who got me?" Just as Boy's fantasies bring the two bodies together, so too do Christy's: "Does he do it? How will I ask him? (If your Uncle Jack was on a mule and couldn't get off would you help your Uncle Jack off?)" (184). For all of Christy's anxieties about corruption supposedly being inherent in sexual interactions, he acknowledges the pull of the sadomasochistic pleasures they offer: "For I knew, even then, that we all have got somethin in us that will give pain, that will make somebody go *uhuh uhuh uhuh* and wag's tongue and roll's eyes and breathe as though he is gaspin or suffocatin with the croup, or say *whew! whew!* as though he is burnt; and almost die. To give this pain, and to get it, we will do almost anything" (176). To consummate the relationship with Boy thus seems doubly attractive. The sexual union will not only arrest his further evolution toward Folner's transgressive performances of gender but also provide Christy the release of orgasm.

When both men reach the woods, these conflicting circulations of desire and anxiety almost overwhelm each of them. They desperately crave sexual interaction yet fear its consequence. For Christy, although the interaction will not necessarily call Boy's masculinity into question, it will forever spoil his presumed virginity, while for Boy the act may validate a gay identity that offers ridicule, alienation, and ultimately suicide. Not surprisingly, then, the climax of *The House of Breath* is without actual climax. When Christy pauses in his preparations for the symbolic penetration, Boy flees: "His look asked for something that I could not give because I had not yet learned how to give it. I backed away, backed away and he sat still on the stump. He pointed his gun at me to shoot me like a bird; and I backed away. And then he lowered his gun and watched me and let me get away; and then I ran" (185).[21]

Although this flight relieves Christy of the anxiety prompted by Boy's approaching defilement, his escape does not resolve his uncertainty about his desires and the identity he holds to be contingent upon these desires. Christy does not shoot Boy and therefore, in Goyen's symbolic order, sexually penetrate him; nevertheless, Christy unwittingly sets into play a ritual that functions comparably for Boy. A yoke of birds shot by Christy beats against the fleeing Boy's body, and when he eventually pauses, he imbues the wounds the birds have inflicted with enormous significance: "I saw that I was dappled by the blood of birds and that the beaks had beaten against my bare arms as I had run and brought my own blood there, mixed with the blood of birds. I ran on again with his yoke of birds swinging against me, Christy's message to me. I ran blessed with his yoke of loves, of words, his long sentence of birds, bloody and broken and speechless, sentences of his language shot out of his air and off his trees' boughs that were his words' vocabulary" (186). For Boy, the wounds mark Christy's desire, and he knows that he "really *loved* Christy, longed for him, calling to him." Indeed, this love is so intense that Boy feels he should have succumbed to the intuited sexual advances. "I betrayed Christy!" Boy thinks. "I failed him in the woods, he who gave me all these gifts of birds, who spoke for the first time to me and waited for me to answer!" (187).

To the frustration of Boy and readers, Goyen ends this facet of the relationship between the uncle and nephew here. When Christy eventually returns from the woods, there is no mention of the events that take place there. "No one even seemed to know that I had ever been away," Boy remembers, "and Christy never mentioned it. We never went hunting again" (189). The novel ends a scant five pages later, with Boy's outcome uncertain. Goyen never clarifies whether or not Boy assumes the transgressive gender performances of Folner. All that is clear is that, in his reflections on his two uncles, it is not Folner's model and expression of desire that Boy most strongly recalls. Rather, it is Christy's, and in vivid contrast to the conclusion of *Other Voices, Other Rooms, The House of Breath* ends with Boy's hymn to this masculine uncle: "O Christy, our great lover! Reach down your bird-bloodied hand to me, you who decorated me with your garland of news, crowned me with your birdbays of love, blessed me with the flowers and the songs of our woods, hung me with the trappings of our woods to send me, wrought like a frieze with all this beauty, all this knowledge" (191).

With this concluding image, Goyen again establishes how his understanding of the gendering of male homosexuality diverges from Capote's collapsing of male same-sex desire and gender transitivity. In *Other Voices,*

Other Rooms, gay identity is contingent upon an inversion of gender in which performances of femininity take precedence over those of masculinity. On the other hand, in Christy Ganchion, Goyen allows for the existence of a masculine man who, like an effeminate one, can physically act upon sexual desire for other men. In fact, much as Halperin describes, Goyen posits this figure as the cultural ideal of male homosexuality. And yet *The House of Breath* crucially offers two coexisting and competing models of the nexus of gender and desire and foregrounds the conflicting understandings that Boy and Christy hold about the relationship of same-sex physicality and identity. Scripted as such, Goyen's novel thwarts the reification of homosexuality that Sedgwick identifies in both Foucault's and Halperin's delineations of sexuality's history; instead, *The House of Breath* anticipates her demands to interrogate gaps between understandings of same-sex relations. Goyen thus not only queers Twain's famous tale of adolescent boyhood but also forcefully destabilizes "the" homosexuality of "the" American South at midcentury, calling into question the paradigms that Capote offers as immutable in his own "fairy *Huckleberry Finn.*"

3

Richard Wright and Compulsory
Black Male Heterosexuality

IN HER NOW-CLASSIC "Compulsory Heterosexuality and Lesbian Existence," Adrienne Rich offers a sustained interrogation of "heterocentricity" and catalogues various methods by which "male power" enforces heterosexuality among women.[1] Why, Rich implicitly asks, would a woman, if presented with the option of an attainable and culturally sanctioned same-sex relationship, place herself within the currents of oppressive heterosexuality? What Rich's essay does not consider in its original articulation, however, is how heterocentricity is culturally contingent, how patriarchy is not monolithic. In particular, the essay does not significantly examine how heterocentricity is potentially racialized. How do African American communities, for instance, differ from European American ones in the enforcement of compulsory heterosexuality for women, if indeed they do? This sort of question is precisely that taken up by black feminists such as Mary Helen Washington. She builds upon Rich's ideas, particularizes these methods as exerted on African American women, and identifies within their histories a "deep alienation from and anxiety about heterosexual relationships" that make it highly likely that "these women considered taking women as lovers" far more frequently than one might suppose merely by looking at their public writing.[2]

Using these models of inquiry, I suggest that comparable—although by no means identical—conditions have structured certain African American men's explorations, understandings, and expressions of their sexualities in mid-twentieth-century southern milieus. The literature that many of these men produced exhibits a pronounced anxiety about heterosexuality, and, although one expects to find this anxiety in the works of overtly gay men, it persists in the fiction of the ostensibly heterosexual Richard Wright. In two characters in particular—Big Boy Morrison in "Big Boy Leaves Home" (1936) and Fishbelly Tucker in *The Long Dream* (1958)—Wright offers black men whose sexualities evolve (though not without significant pauses and returns) along the lines scripted by Sigmund Freud: infantile polymorphous perversity gives way to bisexuality and ultimately, assuming the "correct" maturation of the individual, to stable heterosexuality. However, unlike the ahistorical psychoanalytic theories in which Wright was so heavily invested, his narratives centralize historically and culturally contingent issues, such as the societal devaluing of African American women, an insistence on European American women as forbidden sexual objects, and the threat and presence of lynching and castration for sexually transgressive African American men in the American South in the 1920s and 1930s. (Because expatriation apparently distanced Wright from the ever-changing racial climate of the American South in the post–World War II era, *The Long Dream,* although set in the 1940s and 1950s, features events more typical of Wright's experiences in the 1920s and 1930s, such as discussed in *Black Boy.*) Just as those methods of male power that Rich and Washington identify as having prompted them to speculate about the general appeal of lesbianism or other exclusively women-focused relationships, these issues of race as identified and put into narrative by Wright seem to have prompted him to speculate about the attractiveness of same-sex relations between adult African American men and to allow fictional sites for idealized, often erotically charged homosociality.

Although Wright's primary sexual identification was heterosexual, issues of same-sex desire and gender transitivity recurred within his life and engendered significant anxiety. Perhaps the most noted scenario was Wright's relationship with the gay James Baldwin. Much critical ink has been spilled about this relationship, but a persisting scholarly strain maintains that Baldwin's homosexuality fostered much of Wright's distaste of the younger writer who ultimately overshadowed him in the 1950 and 1960s. Wright often discussed Baldwin with an emphasis on his lack of masculinity, writing, for instance, that "there existed between Chester Himes and me on the one hand, and Baldwin on the other, a certain tension stemming from our view of race relations. To us, the work of Baldwin seemed to carry a certain burden of apology for being a Negro and we always felt that between his sensitive sentences there were the echoes of a kind of unmanly weeping. Now Chester Himes and I are of a different stamp."[3]

Wright's own physical appearance and performance of gender augmented this anxiety. In an era when gender transitivity was often taken to designate homosexuality, as *Other Voices, Other Rooms* suggests and participates in, Wright's slight frame and fastidious behavior prompted speculations about his object choice. For instance, in her biography of Wright, an admittedly biased Margaret Walker recalls her close interactions with him in Chicago in the 1930s and subtly questions his virility, implying that his relationships with women were little more than platonic. "Richard Wright," she asserts, "was no ladies' man at all," and he "definitely had problems" with women. "He was intensely shy and naive where women were concerned." Walker further recalls that his appearance, like his behavior, was hardly masculine. He "gave the appearance of an almost effete, slightly effeminate personality. He had a pipsqueak voice, small and delicate hands and feet, smooth face with very light beard, and rather fastidious ways or mannerisms." In short, Wright "did not exude a strong maleness or masculinity."[4]

Yet perhaps the most significant incident of Wright's life concerning stereotypes of effeminate men and the conflation of gender transitivity with male homosexuality concerned Wright's younger brother, Leon. Walker cites Inmon Wade to recount how the handsome Leon Wright was abducted in an instance of what Wright later bitterly termed "punk hunting": "Dick's brother was smart too, but he had a misfortune. He was taken by foul play and beaten half to death in the 1930s. . . . They took him for the ride no one knows where or who they were." Walker does not specify if the men abducted the effeminate Leon to be the passive partner in a homosexual interaction or even rape, as the term usually designated, or if the incident was a homophobic beating. She implies the former, however, when she explains, "Young boys were no safer on the streets and in the vice holes of Chicago than young girls. There were examples of male prostitution and brothels, including one reported incident in which a fourteen-year-old boy, whose father was dead, was threatened with a gun. Kidnapping young boys on the streets and initiating them in homosexuality was common practice on the city streets."[5]

That these victimizations could prompt ambivalence in Wright toward homosexuals seems clear. One can understand anger directed toward gays who, propagating "faggot" stereotypes, reified cultural presumptions that effeminacy designated male homosexuality. This reification put "innocent" heterosexual men who happened not to be masculine at risk of homophobic violence. On the other hand, having experienced prejudice because of his blackness as well as having vicariously shared his brother's beating, Wright could sympathize with the injustice and humiliations suffered during homophobic brutalities. Walker herself seems unsure of Wright's final stance toward homosexuals. According to her, he positioned himself within and attempted to adopt the liberal views of "the bohemian world of artists and intellectuals" who maintained a "'live and let live' attitude" toward the numerous gays and lesbians within its circles. In the early 1940s, for example, Wright and his family lived in George Davis's three-story brownstone at 7 Middagh in Brooklyn Heights, a household that featured a "queer aggregate of artists" including Carson McCullers, W. H. Auden, Paul and Jane Bowles, and Gypsy Rose Lee.[6] It was in this environment, where sexual currents were hardly the mainstream, that Wright chose to place himself and his family.

Just as Wright surrounded himself with gays, lesbians, and bisexuals in Brooklyn and elsewhere during his life, his library suggests that he kept their writings and writings about their sexualities handy. In his catalogue of Wright's books, Michel Fabre lists the works of many of the most noted gay, lesbian, and bisexual writers of the day: James Baldwin, Truman Capote, Carson McCullers, Lillian Smith, Gertrude Stein, Parker Tyler, Carl Van Vechten. But Wright's shelves also contained numerous works of nonfiction about "deviant" sexuality. In addition to general surveys, such as Alfred Kinsey's *Sexual Behavior in the Human Male,* Theodor Reik's *Psychology of Sex Relations,* and Kenneth Walker's *The Physiology of Sex and Its Social Implications,* Wright also possessed several studies specifically of homosexuality: Freud's *Leonardo da Vinci, a Psycho-sexual Study of an Infantile Reminiscence,* Richard von Krafft-Ebing's *Psychopathia Sexualis,* John Addington Symonds's *A Problem in Greek Ethics: Being an Inquiry into the Phenomenon of Sexual Inversion,* and D. J. West's *Homosexuality.*[7]

In an earlier study, Fabre suggests that this fascination with homosexuality bordered on obsession for Wright and on more than one occasion turned him into an unapologetic voyeur. Addison Gayle concurs, offering a detailed account of Wright's intrigue with same-sex relations between women: "Once, when Himes was forced to move to another room, he discovered that two lesbians lived in the room directly beneath his new one. On visiting Himes, Wright had noticed the two girls, and at the first opportunity rushed to engage them in conversation. . . . The girls became embarrassed, retreated to their room, only to find Wright following as far as the threshold, peering 'about inside their room as though it were a cage at the zoo.' Finally, one of the girls slammed the door in his face." Himes observes with laconic understatement that Wright "had a sharp curiosity . . . about the sexual behavior of odd couples, lesbians, and prostitutes [and] was greatly stimulated by these encounters." Walker reiterates many of these observations, noting that "[g]roup sex, daisy chains, trains, *ménage-à-trois* and odd couples all interested Wright, not because he was so kinky himself, but because he was always so sexually curious—because he had a compelling curiosity to know everything."[8]

Yet, just as these biographers detail Wright's fascination with sexual otherness, they almost invariably counter with his homophobic overtones. Walker notes that, although "Wright discussed homosexuality in males almost obsessively," he always "spoke of it with derision, bitterness, and genuine concern." She recalls Wright's similar views on lesbianism: "One day he spoke to me in great distress after he had seen me talking to two Jewish women on the project: 'Don't let them put their hands on you and give you candy. Don't you know those women are homos?'" In her biography of Wright, Constance Webb comparably asserts that he maintained "a horror, religious in intensity," for sexual acts between women and "felt soiled and angry . . . at having [once accidentally] embraced a lesbian." Finally, in her biography, Hazel Rowley cites Wright's own journals: "The sight of men holding hands in the streets or two men dancing together closely gave him 'a sense of uneasiness . . . deeper than I could control.' He did not think it was homosexuality. Nevertheless, he wrote, 'my Puritan background makes me disturbed when I see anything like this so blatantly exhibited in public.'"[9]

Wright's biography thus suggests that he had an intense ambivalence about homosexuality. He seems to have been neither unquestionably and exclusively homophilic nor homophobic. On the one hand, a fascination with same-sex desire persisted throughout his life; on the other, an equally persistent repulsion supposedly made him feel "soiled and angry" merely by interacting with gays and lesbians. And, although one hesitates to argue for a causal relationship, it is precisely this ambivalence toward male sexuality and homosexuality that Wright's fiction displays.

Although *The Long Dream* was published at the end of Wright's career and therefore some twenty years after *Uncle Tom's Children* (1940) and its reprinting of "Big Boy Leaves Home," the novel seems the obvious place to begin an exploration of Wright's handling of male homosexuality, since he here offers in Aggie West a rare overtly gay character and suggests an awareness of both an alternative to compulsory heterosexuality and the vehemence with which this alternative was disciplined in homophobic African American communities at midcentury. A seemingly stereotypical gender-transitive gay man, complete with a gender-inspecific name, Aggie walks "mincingly," sports "a wide, sweet smile," and speaks in a "too feminine voice." When he attempts to interject himself and his effeminacy into the homosocial realm of boyhood baseball, the foursome of players bombards him with derogatory names: *sissy, pansy, fruit, fairy, homo,* and *queer nigger.* Aggie's indifference to the name-calling prompts the boys to change their attack to a physical one. With typical Wrightian violence, they brutally terrorize the boy and drive him away: "Lifting the bat, Sam lashed Aggie across the chest. Tony, Zeke, and Fishbelly kicked, slapped, and punched Aggie, who walked groggily, turning, stumbling toward a field, not protesting the raining blows. They followed Aggie to the edge of a stretch of young, waist-high corn where they paused and silently watched the retreating Aggie, staring at his sunlit, blood-drenched shirt gleaming."[10]

This violence suggests that Wright perceives in certain African American communities much the same homophobia that Barbara Smith does. "This attitude," she offers, "is much too prevalent among people of color. Individuals who are militantly opposed to racism in all its forms still find lesbianism and male homosexuality something to snicker about or, worse, to despise. Homophobic people of color are oppressive not just to white people, but to members of their own groups—at least ten per cent of their own groups." The reasons for this sentiment are contested and, of course, multiple. Many of the same cultural factors that informed the white homophobia of the Agrarians—investments in the family and Christianity—influenced that circulating in southern black communities at midcentury, but black homosexuality was also dismissed as an infection of a white culture that featured a range of deviant sexualities. For many African Americans, Smith proposes, homosexuality was "a white problem or even a 'white disease,'" just as for many Africans, Rich offers, homosexuality was "a leftover from colonialism and decadent Western civilization."[11]

Particularly during the rise of Black Power in the years immediately following *The Long Dream,* key black leaders in the United States employed similar rhetorical moves, exaggerating these homophobic sentiments in broader protests of white culture. LeRoi Jones, for instance, offers that "most American white men are trained to be fags. For this reason it is no wonder their faces are weak and blank, left with the hurt that reality makes—anytime. That red flush, those silk blue faggot eyes. . . . the most extreme form of alienation acknowledged within white society is homosexuality." These men simply are, he declares, "effeminate and perverted." Eldridge Cleaver offers much the same, asserting in *Soul on Ice,* after a scathing assessment of James Baldwin and a defense of Wright: "I, for one, do not think homosexuality is the latest advance over heterosexuality on the scale of human evolution. Homosexuality is a sickness, just as are baby-rape or wanting to become the head of General Motors."[12] For Cleaver and Jones, as for the early Capote of *Other Voices, Other Rooms,* gayness is inescapably structured by effeminacy, and both are the unique characteristics of European Americans. If a black man is gay, according to this understanding, he has become metaphorically white and is therefore guilty of being a traitor to his race.

Had Wright ended the scene with Aggie's departure, the episode might be read as being as homophobic as the sentiments of Jones and Cleaver: gender transitivity and/or homosexuality must be punished, silenced, and removed from black male spheres. Wright continues the scene, however, to allow Fishbelly and his cohorts didactic insight into their actions. Tony mumbles, "Hell, mebbe we oughtn't've done that," and Zeke uneasily jests, "We treat 'im like the white folks treat us." When Fish attempts to justify the group's actions, arguing, "But he ought to stay 'way from us," Wright again has his characters compare African Americans and homosexuals: "Mebbe it's like being black . . . That's just what the white folks say about us" (37). Although Fish will not admit it publicly, he concedes the validity of the comparison: African Americans and homosexuals resemble each other in that dominant society oppresses each group for its otherness, whether racial or sexual. Such a conflation is, of course, vastly oversimplified, since, as Sedgwick offers, "it was the long, painful realization, *not* that all oppressions are congruent, but that they are *differently* structured and so must intersect in complex embodiments," but Wright nevertheless here offers a homophilic nod to just such a congruency.[13]

Wright reinforces this stance by having the boys seriously contemplate Aggie's performance of gender and attempt to understand his gender asymmetry. Following a brief pause in the conversation after the boys have attacked Aggie, Fishbelly soberly questions, "Why you reckon he acts like a girl?" With comparable seriousness, Tony replies, "They say he can't help it," and Zeke maintains, "He could if he really *tried*" (37). Yet the boys have not given Aggie the chance to prove his gender conformity and thus produce a readable masculinity for himself. He is not the hesitant sissy coerced into a performance of athletics; rather, he readily interjects himself into the homosocial arena and, complete with glove, asserts his desire to participate. When Fishbelly refuses, Aggie asks: "'Why don't you want to play with me?' Aggie enunciated correctly. 'Play the piano, you fairy,' Tony said. 'That's all you fit for!' 'I love to play the piano and I also love to play ball,' Aggie explained. 'Homo, leave us alone!' Fishbelly's eyes were like brown granite" (35). Aggie's desires are thus not wholly gender transitive by dominant conventions. Although he enjoys playing the piano, he also enjoys playing baseball, so much so that he will risk abuse to engage in the activity. Yet Fishbelly and his friends ironically will not allow Aggie the chance to interact within the "appropriate" gender arena that their later conversation demands of him.

Wright also reveals a potentially homophilic stance by not having the soundly beaten boy vanish from the narrative. Aggie instead twice reappears in the novel, continuing the rare overt homosexual presence in Wright's fiction. Given the conflation of gender transitivity and homosexuality, Aggie's sexual preferences become, if anything, all the more blatant when, as an adult, he is the organist at the Mount Olivet Baptist Church. His childhood effeminacy intensifies into "too-cultivated and swishing behavior," and when Fish asks Aggie if he has found a job to support his family, "Aggie had rolled his eyes, put his hands on his hips and exclaimed: 'Heavens, no!'" Moreover, like Capote's Randolph, Aggie confines himself to the feminine domestic sphere, prompting his mother to boast naively: "And he's a *good* boy; he sews, cooks, washes, irons, and takes care of the house. . . . He's polite, tidy, and bright as a button." Despite this intensification of gender asymmetry and Fish's residual homophobia—"Whenever he was in Aggie's presence he wanted either to hit him or laugh at him"—Fish does act upon a developing sensitivity. He overcomes his distaste for Aggie and, at the request of Mrs. West, promises to help him find employment. Indeed, Fish commits himself so strongly to this task that he risks facing the disgusted outrage of his father. When Fish asks if Aggie can work at the funeral home, Tyree explodes, "Hell naw, Fish! Nothing like that can't *never* happen! What would folks think if we had a 'fruit' working around them stiffs! . . . Naw, Fish; no Aggie or nothing like 'im can ever come in this 'shop'" (205).

Again, however, Wright deflates the homophobic overtones of such an outburst. The hale organist conspicuously reappears to perform the awe-inspiring music for the mass funeral of Clintonville's forty-three dead: the heterosexual frequenters of the Grove, as well as Tyree himself. Throughout the scene, the narrative focalizes through Fish and persists in noting Aggie's continued gender transitivity, as displayed again in his "too-careful manner" of walking. However, when he begins to play, his abilities eradicate preoccupations with his performance of gender: "Suddenly Aggie wet his lips with his tongue, bent forward, touched the organ keys, and there rolled forth a deep-voweled hymn of melancholy sound in which the audience and choir joined" (342). His music so moves the grief-stricken crowd that several sobbing women must be escorted from the service, and even the hard-hearted Fishbelly is touched. Thus, with Aggie's final appearance, Wright suggests through Fishbelly that, although homophobia may persist, there is a place within an African American community for effeminate gay men.

Wright does not, however, confine his exploration of sexual relationships between men to this sole overtly gay character. He also traces in Fishbelly an ambivalent evolution toward adult heterosexuality in a narrative that both begins with and later pauses significantly on moments of intense homoeroticism. The novel opens by establishing Fish's not-yet-crystallized sexual preferences, ones that vary contingent upon context. Filled with as much dread as curiosity about the fish his father will bring home, young Rex Tucker falls asleep, soothed by a dream in which he derives gratification from active participation in the homosocial realm of baseball. The scenario soon narrows to an intimate interaction between Rex and an adored older neighbor, Chris Sims: *"Chris had a baseball in his hand and said: 'Rex, you want to play ball?' and he said: 'Yeah, Chris!' and Chris said: 'Okay. Try and hit this one!' and Chris threw the ball and he swung his bat:* CLACK!, *the ball rose into the air and Chris said: 'You only five years old, but you hit like a big-league player!'"* (4). The erotic implications of Rex's dream are inescapable: at the invitation of an older, more experienced partner, Rex eagerly enters into homoerotic sexual acts that manifest themselves as the athletic play of baseball, a sport redolent with terms, such as *pitcher* and *catcher*, that gay slang continues to appropriate to designate inserting and receiving partners during anal sex. In these interactions, Rex more than fulfills that partner's expectations with mature expertise and gains immense satisfaction from this ability.

As the dream continues, however, the pleasure-giving and -receiving homoeroticized Chris metamorphoses into an enormous fish with a gaping, toothed mouth. The horrified powerless Rex cannot fend it off, and his last image in the dream is of *"the fish's mouth opening to swallow him"* (4). When his mother, Emma, awakens Rex at Tyree's return with the fish, the boy's anxieties are no less pronounced. The fanged mouths, symbolic of the fabled castrating vagina, terrify him, and Rex hesitates to touch the creatures, wailing, "They bite!" Moreover, the smell of fish, stock popular designation of female sexual arousal, disgusts Rex: "Then he sniffed distrustfully. 'They *smell!*' 'Sure.' His father chuckled. 'All fish smell.' 'But they smell like . . .' His voice trailed off. His limpid brown eyes circled and rested wonderingly upon his mother, for that odd smell associated itself somehow with her body." Rex clearly finds nothing pleasurable in the fish and demands, "Kill 'em, Mama" (6).

Rex's fear disappears when he realizes the control he has over the symbolic woman by inflating the fish's bladder. Precise terminology eludes the boy, and he maintains that he inflates the fish's belly. With a pleasure and excitement matching that of his dreamed interactions with Chris, Rex screams, "'I blowed up the fish's belly! . . . I'm going to make a *big* belly this time,' he vowed, taking the bladder and blowing eagerly into it." Belaboring these symbolic impregnations, Wright has Rex himself associate the inflated bladders with pregnancy: "But in his mind there was floating a dim image of Mrs. Brown who had a baby and her belly had been big, big like these balloons." Giddy with power, forgetful of his previous disgust with the fish, and unconscious of the pleasure of his recent homoerotic dream, Rex resolves simply, "I like making fish bellies" (6–7).

As proud of his abilities as the resulting playthings, Rex later displays both to his friends. Instead of being met with delighted smiles, however,

Rex finds only "laughing, derisive faces" that indict his misnaming of the bladders. That is, the boy encounters only humiliation for displaying his symbolic mastery of perhaps the definitive male heterosexual act, the impregnation of a woman. The episode therefore not only results in the permanent renaming of Rex, who becomes "simply *Fishbelly*" (7), but also confuses the boy about his heterosexual capabilities and a desire to exert them. Although the power he perceives himself to have in these inflations gratifies him, his homosocial sphere does not wholly approve of the actions, and Fish himself retains some of his lurking fear of the engulfing mouths and his distaste for the stench of fish.

This opening chapter functions even more broadly to establish Wright's investment in Freudian narratives of sexuality, those already hinted at with Rex's Oedipal name. Wright meticulously presents a young boy who, in the refinement of object choices following infantile polymorphous perversity, has arrived at situationally contingent bisexuality. The latent content of his dream reveals his homoerotic desires as well as his displeasure at heteroeroticism, yet his actions with the fish bladders establish his potential desire for women and/or the pleasure he may eventually receive in wielding power over them and their bodies. But with his careful construction of a particular familial scenario in these opening scenes, Wright suggests that, at least at this point in Fish's life, his desires are more strongly for men. The novel opens with the configuration that Freud posits as conducive to the formation of male homosexual identity: an overprotective, empowered mother and an absent father. Freud asserts in *Leonardo da Vinci and a Memory of His Childhood:* "In all our male homosexual cases the subjects had had a very intense erotic attachment to a female person, as a rule their mother, during the first period of childhood, which is afterwards forgotten; this attachment was evoked or encouraged by too much tenderness on the part of the mother herself; and further reinforced by the small part played by the father during their childhood." Freud concedes, however, that these mothers are also "frequently masculine women, women with energetic traits of character, who were able to push the father out of his proper place." The boy's homosexual identity arises when he

> represses his love for his mother: he puts himself in her place, identifies himself
> with her, and takes his own person as the model in whose likeness he chooses
> the new objects of his love. In this way he has become a homosexual. What he
> has in fact done is to slip back to auto-eroticism: for the boys whom he now loves

as he grows up are after all only substitutive figures and revivals of himself in childhood—boys whom he loves in the way in which his mother loved *him* when he was a child. He finds the objects of his love along the path of *narcissism.* [14]

When this repression of the love for the mother is complete, pronounced misogyny simultaneously arises with the crystallization of homosexuality. Freud explains that, with the boy's discovery that his mother lacks a penis, "this longing [for the phallic mother] often turns into its opposite and gives place to a feeling of disgust which in the years of puberty can become the cause of psychical impotence, misogyny and permanent homosexuality." Freud succinctly concludes his discussion of Leonardo and male homosexuality: "We should have to translate it thus: 'It was through this erotic relation with my mother that I became a homosexual.'" [15]

Within *The Long Dream* Wright replicates precisely this Freudian scenario. Tyree is physically absent when the novel opens, leaving an empowered Emma to discipline the young Rex and put him to bed. Even upon Tyree's return, she wields the most dramatic power over the threatening fish. Rex is adept at the trick of inflating the bladders, but she actually dresses the fish with matter-of-fact deftness. Fish fully recognizes this power, demanding that she rather than Tyree kill them. Her efficiency does not disappoint: "He watched her take up a knife, scrape scales, whack fins, then slit a fish down its side. . . . His mother's fingers groped inside the fish's white belly and drew forth a small batch of entrails" (6). Thus, like Leonardo's mother in Freud's understandings, Emma is "masculine" because of her "energetic traits of character." Therefore, so long as Tyree remains displaced within the Oedipal triangle, she is apt to help maintain into adulthood Fish's nascent homosexuality suggested by his dreams and his misogynistic fear of women.

Yet Wright immediately begins to devalue Emma's power within her son's life and to establish the growing influence of his father. While Rex watches with fascination at his mother's display of dressing the fish, Tyree notes with a hurt tone, "Rex, you don't seem to like my fishes." The boy's attention, however, promptly turns to Tyree: "His father unfolded a bit of sticky fish entrail and put it to his lips and puffed into it and, lo and behold!, a translucent, grayish ball swelled slowly, glistening in the morning's sun. 'Aw . . . Can I make one, Papa?' he asked breathlessly. 'Sure.' His father handed him a fish entrail" (6). In effect, when Tyree symbolically reveals his masculine power of impregnation and thus his gratifying abilities to control women's bodies, he begins to counter Emma's fostering of Rex's homosexuality and to promote in his son a heterosexuality based on Tyree's own. This process is complicated, however, by the ridicule that Rex later encounters. What ultimately results is a countercheck of sorts to his crystallizing desire for women. His friends specifically jeer at Fish's misnaming of the bladder and thus, in the scene's symbolic system, at his ignorance of female bodies and his role in heterosexual control of these bodies. Tony, Zeke, and Sam instead force upon Rex a name that reduces him to the very part of female bodies he does not understand: the uterus. Thus, within the Freudian script for male homosexuality that Wright appropriates, Rex has symbolically become a woman and is therefore free to pursue and love the "substitutive figures and revivals of him in childhood."

Although perhaps more subtly, the scene of Fish's nicknaming also functions to establish the paradigm for how Wright appropriates Freudian theories of sexuality in the service of a racialized construction of self. The chapter begins with a presentation of the family effectively outside history and culture. The setting is geographically and historically unspecified, and, except for the dialect, Wright does not indicate the family's race or races. In contrast, the chapter ends and the next begins with Fishbelly outside the self-contained familial unit and instead within a firmly established cultural and historical moment: an African American household in a racially mixed town in the Deep South just after World War II. The rest of the novel focuses incessantly on this setting and the roles it plays in the formation of Fish's sexual identity. Thus, although Wright's understandings and subsequent representations of sexuality may at first seem doctrinal espousals and replications of Freud's ahistorical theories, Wright ultimately offers these images only within the context of given historical and cultural moments that he seemingly understands to support Freud's theories.

At least three components of this sociohistorical moment emerge within *The Long Dream* as crucial to the currents of sexuality that inform Fish's identity: a general devaluing of African American women within both black and white communities, an insistence on European American women as forbidden sexual objects, and whites' use of lynching and castration to punish black men's real or supposed violations of the taboo against sexual interactions with white women. The first of these, the devaluing of African American women, has been repeatedly documented in southern literary production and particularly punctuated in texts by Zora Neale Hurston, Alice Walker, and similar black southern women. One recalls the famous discussion in *Their Eyes Were Watching God* when Nanny relays her under-standing of southern social realities at the turn of the twentieth century: "Honey, de white man is de ruler of everything as fur as Ah been able tuh find out. . . . So de white man throw down de load and tell de nigger man tuh pick it up. He pick it up because he have to, but he don't tote it. He hand it to his womenfolks. De nigger woman is de mule uh de world so fur as Ah can see." Walker echoes these sentiments throughout her writings but no-where more directly than in Albert's assessment of the long-suffering Celie in *The Color Purple:* "You black, you pore, you ugly, you a woman. Goddam, he say, you nothing at all." As Hurston and Walker imply, black southerners were rigidly differentiated—and self-differentiating—along the lines of sex but only *after* they had been racially discriminated from white southerners. Thus, although ostensibly of the same sex, white and black women would rarely have been perceived as an undifferentiated unity. Hazel Carby flatly offers that "[b]lack women were relegated to a place outside the ideological construction of 'womanhood.' That term included only white women." With this understanding in place, black women would have been only fur-ther devalued, not even allowed the second-class status granted white women within southern patriarchy.[16]

At times blatantly sexist and yet at others seemingly intent on exposing sexism, Wright's fiction often offers attitudes much the same as Albert's, that black women are "nothing at all." *The Long Dream* continues this devaluing within the narrative and the opinions of male characters. Consider, for in-stance, Sarah West and Emma Tucker. As suggested, in her brief appear-ance Aggie's mother naively overlooks her son's sexuality and the communal homophobia he faces: "He needs a job and nobody'll hire him. Why? I don't know." Wright underscores the ignorance suggested by her misunderstand-ings of her son's situation by having Aggie virtually flame. He is so ostenta-tiously gay that Fish cannot comprehend Mrs. West's blindness: "Fishbelly could not believe that Mrs. West did not know what was 'wrong' with Ag-gie, for that 'wrong' was so obvious in Aggie's too-cultivated and swishing behavior" (204–5).

Emma Tucker is likewise both naive about the social realities around her and, for most of the novel, insignificant within the narrative. Her initial im-portance in the first scene dissolves, and she effectively disappears, emerg-ing only briefly much later as the resurrected stereotype of the fanatic evan-gelical Christian that Wright offers in Bigger Thomas's mother in *Native*

Son and Wright's own grandmother in *Black Boy*. Like Bigger's mother and Sarah West, who "took a kind of mute pride in [her crippled son] Bunny's state of idiocy, for that was a kind of proof that God had, for reasons unknown, noticed her" (204), Emma reveals herself unable to deal directly with the intricacies of the racial conflict that destroys her family. When, in the wake of Chris Sims's lynching, Tyree attempts to explain the social taboo against miscegenation to Fishbelly, Emma protests that he is too young to hear such things. She refuses to acknowledge the harsh facts that Tyree attempts to have her—as well as Fishbelly—realize: "In white folks' eyes he's a *man!*" (64) and therefore susceptible to as horrific an end as Chris's should he violate or be accused of violating white codes of black sexuality. Unable to cope with these unpleasant realities, Emma turns to Christianity and the passive dependency Wright holds it to offer as the solution to racial injustice. In the aftermath of the fire at the Grove, Emma blubbers, "Son, if you got any problems, take 'em to Gawd," just as Tyree predicts she will. Even in a moment of rare compassion for his wife, Tyree emphasizes her ineffectualness: "'And Fish, go kind of easy on your mama . . . She don't understand these things'" (298).

This lack of comprehension resurfaces at the mass funeral. As Fish stares at his father's corpse, the result of white racism, he weeps, and his mother assumes it is because of the minister's fiery sermon: "'You feel Gawd, don't you, son?' she asked in a whisper." Disgusted, Fish wants to scream, "Naw, it ain't Gawd I feel; it's the white man!" (351). Because he, like his father, does not or cannot force Emma to face this reality, she only grows more devout in her religious beliefs. Therefore, when she later visits Fish in jail, she whispers, echoing Bigger Thomas's mother, "Pray, son . . . Gawd'll deliver you" (395).

If, among Wright's female characters, Sarah and Emma represent feckless religious fanatics, Gladys, Vera, Maud, and Gloria represent the other persisting type: the hypersexual whore or kept woman who either passively accepts her fate as a sexual object or cunningly uses her sexuality to manipulate men. And yet African American men devalue these women as cruelly and inexorably as they do their naively religious wives and mothers. Tyree is perhaps the most outspoken. When he begins to train Fish as a rent collector, Tyree offers an impromptu lecture on "nigger bitches," categorically damning them as coldhearted and dishonest: "Fish, if they can't pay five dollars *this* Sat'day, how in all hell can they pay ten dollars *next* Sat'day? Be hard on these nigger bitches. They so crooked they could hide behind corkscrews and you couldn't see 'em; they so bad they don't even throw a shadow in the sun; they so evil they could steal the sweetness out of a ginger snap without breaking the crust" (210). Tyree lectures Fish with similar misogyny about his sexual interactions with prostitutes. When he tells his father that, after his first afternoon with the whore Vera, he is planning to visit her again on Saturday, Tyree counters, "Son, you starting all *wrong*. Try the others. They all the same. Take it easy; you got all your life to fool with that stuff. . . . For Gawd's sake, don't go gitting crazy about the first girl you took" (164). For Tyree, African American women such as Maud, Gladys, and Vera are inter-changeable objects—"stuff"—for men to "take" at their will. Their only purpose, Tyree tells Fish, is "to serve you, give you pleasure" (157).

As his lecture to Fish demonstrates, black men such as Tyree seemingly value these women only for their bodies and the sexual pleasure they can provide men. Yet these same men consistently conceptualize these bodies as offensive. Early in the novel, when Fish finds a used condom and proudly uses it to adorn his baseball bat, Chris demands that Fish remove it. He presses Chris for an explanation of the object, and the older boy explodes: "'You monkeys don't understand nothing!' Chris became furious. '*That* rub-ber's been in a woman's "bad" thing.' Four pairs of eyes began to clear. In rough terms they understood that men were different from women, and, if that rubber tubing had been in a woman's 'bad' thing, then it was nasty *in-deed*" (26). Although Wright establishes the boys' gynophobia as perhaps arising from fear of the unknown here, this gynophobia and accompanying misogyny do not disappear. As Fish and his friends become active sexual participants with women, the boys still characterize women and their geni-tals as "bad" and as mere pieces of meat. Tyree is no better. When he in-structs Fish about collecting rent from the whorehouses, he cautions, "Watch Maud. She's sly. She'll try to tempt you with meat, sicking gals on you. Don't touch a deal like that. Meat and money don't mix. . . . Business is business and meat's meat" (198).

In Wright's understanding of southern race relations, this devaluing of black women occurred simultaneously with an overinvestment of worth in idealized white ones. As Earle Bryant and others point out, these women were so highly esteemed within popular myth that they were to be kept pure from sexual violation and particularly from African American men.[17] Ac-cording to Wright, however, the taboo functioned with ironic efficiency. Late in the novel, as Fish sits in jail for supposedly molesting a white woman, the narration focalizes through him and succinctly offers Wright's understanding of the taboo, a passage that bears quoting at length:

> White men made such a brutal point of warning black men that they would be killed if they merely touched their women that the white men kept alive a sense of their women in the black men's hearts. As long as he could remember he had mulled over the balefully seductive mystery of white women, whose reality threatened his life . . . In the presence of a white woman there were impulses that he could not allow to come into action; he was supposed to be merely a face, a voice, a sexless animal. And the white man's sheer prohibitions served to anchor the sense of his women in the consciousnesses of black men in a bizarre and distorted manner that could rarely ever be eradicated—a manner that placed the white female beyond the pitch of reality. (387–88)

According to Wright, the taboo shores up the cultural myth so effectively that the forbidden object of desire assumes such value that obtaining it becomes African American men's omnipresent concern, even if only subconsciously. As Fish confesses to himself after his first visit to Maud's whorehouse, despite his physical gratification with the black prostitutes, "he knew deep in his heart that there would be no peace in his blood until he had defiantly violated the line that the white world had dared him to cross under the threat of death" (165).

The scene at the carnival early in the novel establishes the dynamics of this taboo and the resulting circulations of desire. Fishbelly and his friends respond "with suppressed excitement" to a white barker's hawking of a "daring, forbidden" white woman, but their hopes fall when the boys notice the sign proclaiming "NO COLORED." Tantalizing sexual gratification seems within their reach, offered by white men themselves for a small price, and yet, just as the idealized white women whom the boys encounter every day can never be legitimately obtained as sexual objects, so too can the boys not peek at the carnival's Eve. When Sam attempts to explain to his friends, "White man don't want you looking at their naked women," Fishbelly bitterly points out the contradictions in the scenario: "Why they call this Colored Folks' Day?" (40).

As this scene continues, it also suggests that the taboo tempted more persons than African American men into sexual transgression. Just as European American women were forbidden to black men, so too were these men unavailable as socially legitimate objects of desire for white women. Yet, at least within Wright's representations, the lure of the forbidden is just as strong on these women, and it is they who more willingly transgress the taboo. As Fish and his friends later meander through the trailers of the performers, the white woman of the sex show accosts them: "'Come closer. Don't be afraid. I'll take you in for five dollars apiece,' she said, unbuttoning her blouse and baring her big white breasts in the half-light." Although the boys momentarily stand transfixed at the opportunity, they eventually bolt, not stopping until "they were far beyond the trailers" and the "lynch-bait" (46). Although inaccurate according to the research done by historians such as Neil McMillen, Wright even goes so far as to suggest that women were always the initiators of miscegenistic liaisons with black men. Every sexual interaction between white women and black men in the novel is at the instigation of women, who are thus depicted as flirting with black men's very lives.

Thus denied European American women as legitimate sexual partners, yet constantly impressed upon that lighter-skinned women have intrinsically greater value than darker-skinned ones, African American men within the novel turn with disruptive effects to near surrogates: mulatto women. At Maud Williams's brothel Fish and Zeke choose lighter-skinned girls, leaving the spurned black Maybelle furious: "'Go to hell, you white-looking bitch! . . . They want *white* meat! But you sluts ain't *white!* You *niggers* like me! But you the nearest thing they can git that *looks* white! . . . Ever since I been at this table, you goddam black sonsofbitching niggers ain't got eyes for nothing but *yellow* and *white* meat!'" (177–78). Refusing to be appeased, Maybelle continues with a logic sound even in her drunken anger: "What she's got smells just like mine! It feels the same. Even if you eat it, it tastes the same. You think it's better'n mine just 'cause it looks *white*, but it ain't white. . . . You goddam *white-struck* black fools just hungry for the meat the white man's done made in nigger town!" (179). The brutal reality is that Maybelle's points are no less than accurate. Only because Gladys's and Beth's skin is lighter than Maybelle's do the boys choose them. Yet, because they have internalized the cultural value of white femininity, they feel their selections allow them more meaningful sexual conquests.

Tyree ostensibly attempts to instill in Fish much the same sentiments that Maybelle rehearses. In the aftermath of Chris's lynching, to prevent a similar fate for Fish, Tyree explains to his son that a woman's value is *not* contingent upon her color: "Son, there ain't nothing a white woman's got that a black woman ain't got" (64). To prove his point, he orchestrates Fish's indoctrination to the pleasures of Maud's. Both before Fish enters the brothel and after he leaves it, Tyree punctuates his points: "A woman's just a woman. . . . When you had one, you done had 'em all. And don't git no screwy ideas about their color. I had 'em white as snow and black as tar and they all the same" (158).

Tyree's own sexual behavior, however, suggests otherwise. He confesses to Fish that he *has* had sex with white women: "I was fool enough once to risk my life to see what it was like." Although Tyree says the experience teaches him that "them white women ain't *nothing*" (164), he is just as "white-struck" as Fish and Zeke. The color of his sexual partner's skin *does* matter to Tyree, and he chooses for his mistress the "young mulatto woman" Gloria. She dazzles Fish—and presumably Tyree—with "her yellow skin" and "her smiling brown eyes." Her manners as well as her appearance captivate the boy, who fills "with wonder because she did not speak in that whiny way so characteristic of the black people he knew. She held her head high, enunciated her words clearly, her attitude brimming with confidence. . . . [S]he had the air of a white woman" (171–72). Despite his bravado to the contrary, Tyree values Gloria's enactment and appearance of whiteness and has chosen her as his mistress for precisely these attributes.

As a result of Tyree's impromptu lectures about women's color and his hypocrisy with Gloria, his instruction of Fish is less than successful. As Katherine Fishburn has argued, immediately after Tyree's first lecture, Fish secludes himself in the bathroom and gazes fixedly at a picture of a near-naked white woman. Thus, "Tyree's warning . . . has only increased Fish's fascinated preoccupation with the type. So far, the lesson is backfiring on Tyree."[18] His plans for his son are further complicated once Fish learns of Gloria and her color. When he returns to Maud's after meeting Gloria, the darker Vera will no longer do as his partner; Fish opts instead to the light-skinned Gladys. She is "as white as the whites" (184), "so white that he felt he ought to be afraid of her" (176). As Bryant suggests, Fish is following his father's model and chooses Gladys as his girlfriend because, although "she was not as pretty as Gloria, . . . she reminded him of her" (177). Fish eventually grows to love Gladys because of her color, and despite his periodic jealousy that she can "pass," there is the thrill of fucking a woman who can do so. He even choreographs his sexual encounters with her so that she can pass for him: "'You want me to put the big light on, honey?' she asked. 'Naw,' he breathed. She rose and went into the far corner of the room; there, in the shadows, she looked *completely* white. And it had been for a woman who had the color of Gladys that Chris had been killed" (185). Fish thus orchestrates his sexual interactions so that he can be almost as transgressive as Chris and experience an approximation of a pleasure supposedly worth dying for. And yet, even if Fish has not fully learned the lessons that Tyree and Maybelle have attempted to teach, he has effectively denied himself Chris's indulgence of miscegenistic heterosexuality. Fish will not and does not cross that line—and for good reasons.

Within the novel, the results of black men's transgressions into miscegenistic interactions or accusations of doing so are, quite simply, horrific. Whites orchestrate lynchings replete with violence, humiliation, and dismemberment to punish black transgressors and terrorize potential violators, and one of the most memorable scenes describes the corpse of the lynched Chris Sims: "Dr. Bruce's fingers probed delicately into the mass of puffed flesh that had once been Chris's cheeks; there was no expression on those misshapen features now; not only had the whites taken Chris's life, but they had robbed him of the semblance of the human. The mouth, lined with stumps of broken teeth, yawned gapingly, an irregular, black cavity bordered by shredded tissue that had once been lips. The swollen eyes permitted slits of irises to show through distended lids" (76). The scene only grows more horrific when the men remove Chris's clothes. His neck has been broken twice, his nose abraded to nothing, and his cheek split open by the butt of a gun. But Wright withholds until last what is, in the eyes of the men gathered around the corpse, the most significant violation of Chris's body: "'The *genitalia* are gone,' the doctor intoned. Fishbelly saw a dark, coagulated blot in a gaping hole between the thighs and, with defensive reflex, he lowered his hands nervously to his groin. 'I'd say that the genitals were pulled out by a pair of pliers or some like instrument,' the doctor inferred. 'Killing him wasn't enough. They had to *mutilate* 'im. You'd think that disgust would've made them leave *that* part of the boy alone'" (78). Wright implies, however, that the offending whites *are* immune to such disgust at their own behavior. Because Chris's violation of southern racial dictates has been sexual, the mob of three thousand deputized men feel themselves bound not only to kill him but first to deny him sexuality altogether and by whatever bloody means necessary.

Although historian Neil McMillen's research marks Wright's depiction of "black-hungry" white women as perhaps a distortion of actualities, his representations of Chris's lynching is, on the other hand, historically accurate. McMillen maintains that between 1890 and the Great Depression, Mississippi was the "most race-haunted of all American states," and, of all the "interracial proscriptions" within Mississippi's system of Jim Crow, "none was more fiercely held by whites . . . than the taboo on interracial sex." While white men's sexual interactions with black women were tacitly tolerated, "it was the presumption of both white public and white law that intercourse between white women and black men could result only from rape." As a result, when such violations were presumed to have occurred, white men typically reacted with violence. Although vigilantism and mob violence were by no means directed at only African Americans in the South during the years of McMillen's study, lynchings were omnipresent in the lives of most black Mississippians. McMillen asserts that between 1889 and 1945, "Mississippi accounted for 476, or nearly 13 percent, of the nation's 3,786 recorded lynchings. If the date is pushed back to include the 1880s, the bloody decade immediately preceding disfranchisement, the toll in Mississippi exceeded 600."[19] Of these victims, only twenty-four were white; by far the vast majority who suffered were African Americans.

Perhaps even more shocking than the statistics are the techniques of torture that accompanied the recorded lynchings. Both McMillen and Trudier Harris, in her study of literary representations of lynching, cite as one of the most horrific abuses the burning of Luther Holbert and his wife, as reported in the *Vicksburg Evening Post:*

> When the two Negroes were captured, they were tied to trees and while the funeral pyres were being prepared they were forced to suffer the most fiendish tortures. The blacks were forced to hold out their hands while one finger at a time were cut off. Holbert was severely beaten, his skull fractured, and one of his eyes, knocked out with a stick, hung by a shred from the socket. . . . The most excruciating form of punishment consisted of the use of a large corkscrew in the hands of some of the mob. This instrument was bored into the flesh of the man and women, in the arms, legs and body, and then pulled out, the spirals tearing out big pieces of raw, quivering flesh every time it was withdrawn.[20]

Although the fate of the Holberts was perhaps more violent than that of many lynched African Americans, both Harris and McMillen suggest that it was, on the whole, typical. Thus, in his descriptions of Chris Sims's corpse, Wright is historically grounded.

Wright strays from strict historical accuracy, however, when he strongly implies that these lynchings arose only as punishment for black men's miscegenistic sexual liaisons. Although other African Americans suffer violence at the hands of whites within the novel, only the offending Chris Sims meets with such terrifying physical abuse. Moreover, when Cantley wishes to discipline Fish through violence, the corrupt police chief can justify his abuses only through Fish's orchestrated violation of a white woman. McMillen maintains to the contrary that, "[m]ounting white fears of the black 'beast-rapist' notwithstanding, sexual congress in any form was a relatively minor 'cause' of mob violence in Mississippi or any southern state." Rather, "[m]urder, not rape, was the allegation most often leveled against Mississippi's mob victims." The Holberts, for instance, were lynched for supposedly murdering a planter. McMillen continues, explaining that white mob violence against black Mississippians arose from any number of scenarios: "But the record abounds in lynchings for lesser affronts: 'insubordination,' 'talking disrespectfully,' striking a white man, slapping a white boy, writing an 'insulting letter,' a personal debt of fifty cents, an unpaid funeral bill of ten dollars, a $5.50 payroll dispute, organizing sharecroppers, being 'too prosperous,' 'suspected lawlessness,' horse killing, conjuring, and, of course, mistaken identity."[21] Wright disregards all these in *The Long Dream.* He instead has all white vigilante action toward blacks instigated by real or supposed sexual transgression, thus suggesting that, at least for Wright, it was African American men's sexualities that white southerners most feared and disciplined.

Wright's account of Chris's lynched body also differs from McMillen's findings in that Wright emphasizes the eroticism of the lynched black male body for white women. Just as he suggests that miscegenistic liaisons between white women and black men arose from the former's instigations, Wright implies through Dr. Bruce that the lynchings were held, in part, to satisfy white women's curiosity about African American men's bodies and sexualities. As the doctor analyzes Chris's corpse, he asserts that to "get a chance to *mutilate* 'im was part of why [the whites] killed 'im. And you can bet a lot of white women were watching eagerly when they did it. Perhaps they knew that that was the only opportunity they'd ever get to see a Negro's genitals" (78). Dr. Bruce concludes, "You have to be terribly attracted toward a person, almost in love with 'im, to mangle 'im in this manner. They hate us, Tyree, but they love us too; in a perverted sort of way, they love us" (79).[22]

Regardless of what erotic fantasies the lynchings such as those of the fictional Chris Sims or the real Luther Holbert may have fulfilled for white participants and onlookers, male or female, for Wright these acts of violence clearly achieved their main goal: to strike fear in and therefore exercise white control over African Americans. As noted, one of Tyree's first responses to Chris's lynching is, as Bryant phrases it, to channel "his son's sexual drives . . . in the right direction—that is, away from white women and toward black ones."[23] Despite his preferences for light-skinned women, Tyree holds that whites' social dictates about sexuality must be followed, and, since the parameters are painfully clear, any African American man who breaks them deserves his punishment. Tyree callously assesses Chris's downfall to Fish: "'Chris was just twenty-four. But he should've known better than to touch a white woman. . . . That boy was tempted by that white gal and he had no more sense'n to bite, like a damn fool!' His rage was so furious that he was speechless" (71). Tyree has so internalized the white dictates of control that he can hardly function. When he regains control, his response is precisely that hoped for by white southerners: he makes an imperative to his son that he must not interact sexually with white women under any circumstances.

With Tyree's livid response at this moment, it becomes evident to Fish that, while southern racism has literally castrated Chris Sims, it has, in Wright's terms, also metaphorically emasculated Tyree and any other African American man who responds as he does to such displays of white power. To survive in the racist South, Tyree repeatedly sacrifices masculine authority and assertiveness and instead plays the weeping and shuffling Uncle Tom to Cantley and other whites. Although Tyree, echoing the grandfather of Ralph Ellison's *Invisible Man,* explains to Fish that "the only way to git along with white folks is to grin in their goddamn faces and make 'em feel good and then do what the hell you want behind their goddamn backs," Tyree's "code of living" (148) repels Fish and forces him to the sickening realization that "no white man would ever need to threaten Tyree with castration; Tyree was already castrated" (151). Even more troubling, Fish realizes that, although he escapes the physical castration threatened by the white policeman, white society inexorably works to emasculate him just as it does his father. After Tyree's death, because of Fish's own fear of white violence, he finds himself playing the exact repugnant role with Cantley as Tyree does earlier: "Yes, in spite of himself, he was 'acting' as Tyree had 'acted,' and he hated it, and he hated the man who was making him do it" (362).

Through depictions of this use of lynching and castration to discipline and punish African American men's sexual desires, as well as his contrasting representations of devalued African American women and overvalued European American women, Wright re-creates an historically grounded South that is an environment that, rather than promoting gratifying heterosexuality for African American men, fosters only one that is anxiety fraught. Black women are represented as little more than animals who, although useful objects for the release of sexual tension or the breeding of children, are not fit partners for meaningful, long-term relationships. White women, in contrast, have enough cultural value ascribed to them to fulfill these roles, yet any black man's sexual interactions with these women bring threats of lynching, castration, and death that perhaps more than counters the thrill of breaking the taboo. Thus, despite the violence exercised to discipline male homosexuality, the only arena of safe erotic investments for most southern African American men besides autoeroticism would seem to be intraracial homosexuality, and it is precisely within this arena that Wright has Fish repeatedly hesitate in his evolution toward a potentially stable heterosexuality.

It is within these specific sexual currents that ostensibly work against the development of African American male heterosexuality that Wright has Fishbelly mature. After suggesting, in the opening chapter, Fish's bisexuality, with a potential for eventually exclusive homosexual desire, Wright reestablishes the ambivalence of these sexual preferences when the older Fish unknowingly walks in on the heterosexual intimacies of one of his father's extramarital affairs. As with the fish of his nightmares, the boy is at first frightened by the acts; however, as soon as his father assuages the boy's fears, Fishbelly becomes fascinated with what he has seen. Yet Fish's memories of this scene focus not on his father's female partner but rather on Tyree, and the sexual symbols that fill Fish's subsequent dreams are conspicuously phallic trains, "hurtling, sleek, black monsters whose stack pipes belched gobs of serpentine smoke, whose seething fireboxes coughed out clouds of pink sparks, whose pushing pistons sprayed jets of hissing steam—panting trains that roared yammeringly over far-flung, gleaming rails only to come to limp and convulsive halts." Although Fish appears in these dreams, he does not associate the trains with extensions of himself that might be used to penetrate women. Rather, he strokes and caresses the locomotive's extended levers: *"he grasped hold of the steel bar and hoisted himself up into the cab gee whiz . . . he timidly caught hold of a jutting bar and pulled it and the locomotive began to throb and move slowly at first and then with increasing speed"* (22–23). Wright leaves unclear whether the symbolized masturbation is auto- or alloerotic. In either case, however, Fish handles male rather than female sexual organs, suggesting that the boy's desires are by no means yet exclusively heterosexual.

Although Fish may continue to entertain these homoerotic fantasies, potentially about Chris, the lynching makes clear that the bellhop does not reciprocate, since he instead prefers women and specifically white ones. These heterosexual choices are, of course, disastrous to Chris, as attested to by his mangled, emasculated corpse. These horrific images so disturb Fish that whatever steps he has taken toward a development of a heterosexual identity seem to be momentarily halted, if not reversed. His disgust with female sexuality and sexual organs, those things that have caused Chris's death, now dominates his dreams as strongly as ever: *"Mama sat upon . . . a strange little thing he stooped yes it was a fish belly wet stinking crumbled with fuzzy hair."* Even the impregnation of the fish's belly, that which so delights Fish as a preschooler, becomes horrific. The phallic *"locomotive's stack pipe touched the fish belly* HUMPFF HUMPFF *and the fish belly began swelling pumped up by the stack pipe and getting like a balloon like Mrs. Brown's stomach before she had her baby and glowing yellow* HUMPFF HUMPFF *and the clock said* DON'T DON'T *and then the fish belly was so large he had to step back and make room for it to swell."* Thus, in the dream, as in the reality of the novel, heterosexual intimacy leads to a catastrophic end for Fish's homoeroticized male. The womb subsumes Chris, suffocating him, only to eject his *"naked bloody body"* amid a torrent of blood that kills Fish as well: *"it was too late it was engulfing his head and when he opened his mouth to scream he was drowning in blood"* (82–83). With this symbolism Wright suggests that, although the heterosexual acts horrify Fish and provide him no vicarious pleasure, they do prevail in his dream, thoroughly eradicating the homoerotic bond between Chris and Fish. Terrifying though it may be, Fish is mastering a repression of same-sex desire and accepting heterosexual ones.

Homoerotic images are correspondingly not nearly so distinct or frequent after Fish's nightmare as in the first dozen chapters; however, Wright still includes elements that remind readers of Fish's residual same-sex desire. A litany of praise, for instance, marks the exquisite adolescent male bodies in the crucial episode of the mud fight: "Eight black bodies flashed in the sun. . . . Glistening black bodies leaped behind tree trunks." Wright continues, describing how, almost as if in the labor of a sexual act, the boys scoop the mud into balls "silently, breathing heavily, now and then cocking their heads" (111). The diction and imagery recall the baseballs of Fish's dreams of Chris. Wright counters these images, however, by simultaneously establishing the boys' uneasiness with homoerotic and even intensely homosocial bonds. In the dramatization of the relationship between blacks and whites, Tony momentarily plays a white woman, simpering to his friend, "Sam, darling . . . What a big, strong man! You done killed my husband . . . Winner take all . . . Kiss me . . . All I have is yours!" yet Sam stands *"confused, blinking"* as the production abruptly stops (110). His fears are multiple: physical intimacy with an imagined white woman is terrifying, yet so too is actual same-sex interaction.

As suggested in this episode, whatever traces of homoerotic desire that linger within Fishbelly or his comrades are rapidly being replaced by heterosexual urges. Certainly the boys' anticipation of the losses of their virginities, their bragging about future sexual exploits, and their obsessive discussion of women seem to indicate so. Wright's narrator confirms that for Fish and his cohorts, "the pending gift of woman was something delightful, a gratuitous pleasure that nature had somehow showered down upon the male section of life alone, and he waited for that gift as one would wait for a new and different kind of Christmas with Santa Clauses going up instead of coming down chimneys" (85). Therefore, when Tyree arranges his son's visit to Maud's whorehouse, Fish displays his mastery of the skills necessary for pleasure with women and his triumph over his previous fears of them so well that Tyree can hardly believe his son's prowess.

Fish's heterosexuality would thus seem stable. The lengthy second part of the novel certainly suggests so, since here Wright consistently portrays Fish as desiring women, sometimes voraciously so. In the final pages, however, he conspicuously checks this hunger. Having been set up by the corrupt Cantley for not surrendering the canceled checks that will incriminate him in the Clintonville vice ring, Fish has been imprisoned for molesting a white women but is finally released from jail. When Cantley ushers Fish out of his cell to freedom, the former police chief asserts, "Come on, Fish. Get in my car. Now, where do you want to go? To Maud's for something hot? A bar? Or to your mama's." To Fish's terse reply, "To my flat, sir," Cantley continues his offer of women: "You don't want to wrassle a gal tonight?" (402). Fish, however, turns down the suggestion, just as he does with Maud's subsequent offer to "celebrate. Everything's on *me* tonight" (403). These rejections, however, are not surprising, given the way in which Cantley has trapped Fish—by playing on his heterosexual desire and, in particular, his yearning for a miscegenistic encounter.

Fish's desire for women resurfaces only once he is aboard the airplane bound for France. There the white woman sitting ahead of him fascinates him: "For more than two hours he had avoided looking in front of him, had always kept his eyes to left or right. Finally he stared directly at the object that rested under the dreadful taboo; the young women ahead of him had a head of luxurious, dark brown hair, the wispy curls of which nestled clingingly at the nape of her white, well-modeled neck." Yet his internalization of disciplined desire for whiteness leaves him anxious: "His heart pounded as he stared at close range upon the alluring but awful image and, while looking at it, its aspect of sentient, human life evaporated and was replaced by a dubious, disturbing reality that resided more in the balked impulses of his heart than in the woman's existence" (405). Try as he may, even within an environment that ostensibly will not punish him for interracial heterosexual desire, Fish cannot savor the potential sexual gratification that the woman holds.

Fish's anxiety about his fascination with the woman is soon interrupted, however, by his fellow passenger, a young white man. Although the interaction between him and Fish is brief, the narrative nevertheless reveals undercurrents of homoeroticism. The man conspicuously parallels the previously eroticized woman, with Fish surveying the entirety of the man's body as carefully as he does the woman's: "Out of the corners of his eyes Fishbelly compared the young man's suit with his own and found that his was by far the superior style, cut, and texture of cloth. As though hypnotized, he stared at the back of the man's hairy, white hand that lay but four inches from his own left hand" (407). The verbal exchange between the two men even takes on a certain cruisiness:

> "Hunh?" Fishbelly grunted, coming out of his brooding.
> "Have you a light?" the young man to his left was asking him.
> "Sure," Fishbelly said.
> He held the flame of his lighter to the young man's cigarette.
> "Thanks," the young man said.
> "That's awright," Fishbelly mumbled.

"It's a long flight, hunh?" the young man asked.

"Sure is," Fishbelly agreed.

"Going to Paris?"

"That's right. You?" (405)

This exchange also works to suggest a homoerotic tension between the two men by echoing Shreve and Quentin's famous conversation in *Absalom, Absalom!* Just as Shreve implores that Quentin tell about the South, the friendly white man asks Fish about his home state. Upon learning that it is Mississippi, the man asserts, "Boy, say, that's really the South. . . . Tell me, how is it down there?" (406). Like Quentin but by no means for the same reasons, Fish represses his distaste and even hatred of the South:

Fishbelly grew uncomfortable. What did the man mean?

"It's awright," he said with a slight edge in his voice.

"That's not what I heard," the young man said. "I was told that the whites down there are pretty hard on your people."

. . . .

"That ain't true," he told the young man with quiet heat.

"No?" the young man asked, lifting his eyebrows.

"We live just like anybody else," Fishbelly maintained, feeling a hot flush spread over his body. (406)

When the man reminds Fish about segregation's effects on African Americans, he responds:

"We don't think about that," Fish declared, his teeth on edge.

"God, *I* would if *I* lived there and was *colored*," the young man said.

"Shucks, we forgit that stuff," Fishbelly lied with a forced and nervous laugh.

The young man leaned back and smoked, then smothered his cigarette and slept. Fishbelly brooded. (407)

His response is thus precisely that of the anxious Quentin Compson: outright lies meant to establish a love of a South that has destroyed in the speaker any hopes of a "normal" sexuality: "'I don't hate it,' Quentin said, quickly, at once, immediately; 'I don't hate it,' he said. *I dont hate it* he thought, panting in the cold air, the iron New England dark: *I dont. I dont! I dont hate it! I dont hate it!*"[24] Since Fish and the white man's exchange echoes that produced during the eroticized bonding between Quentin and Shreve, the homoerotic charge between Fish and the white man seems all the more intimated.

Finally, in Fish's city of destination Wright also implies that the heterosexuality that seems to have crystallized may not be as stable as it once was. Whereas during the so-called Great Migration between 1910 and 1920, most black Mississippians, including Wright himself, fled the restrictions of Jim Crow through a trajectory that usually entailed a move first to Memphis and then Chicago or Detroit, with New York as a possible end, Wright has Fish-belly bound from the beginning for Paris. As Zeke's letters establish, this city allows black man and white women the freedom to act upon their sexual desire for each other: "Man, these blond chicks will go to bed with a guy who's black as the ace of spades and laugh and call it Black Market. Man, it's mad. . . . I'm thinking of settling down for a good spell in good old Paris. Man, it's good to live in the grayness where folks don't look mad at you just because you are black" (384). Like Harlem and Greenwich Village in New York, however, Paris also represented an arena of sexual freedom for gays, lesbians, and bisexuals. As a permanent resident of Paris from 1947 until his death in 1960, Wright would have been acutely aware of that city's reputation as a haven for sexual otherness. Moreover, any reader of American fiction who had chanced upon James Baldwin's *Giovanni's Room*, published two years before *The Long Dream*, would have had similar knowledge of that reputation, since in his groundbreaking novel Baldwin depicts Paris as "the garden of Eden" in which David and Giovanni can physically consummate their desire and countless other gays, lesbians, and bisexuals can flourish.[25] Wright even subtly implies as much when Chief Cantley confronts Fish about his suspected flight to Europe: "Those French are dirty" (400). Whether Cantley is referring to interracial sexual interactions or homosexual ones is unclear, but given the context in which Wright wrote the novel, the phrase is certainly readable as both. Thus, in the closing pages of *The Long Dream*, Wright effectively offers yet another site in which Fish can escape from the anxieties of compulsory heterosexuality and explore whatever same-sex desires may arise within him.

Wright wrote *The Long Dream* at the end of his life, a fact that might lead one to conclude that his interrogations of compulsory heterosexuality for African American men was a project that drew his attention only in his final years. However, when one considers the whole of Wright's canon, it becomes clear that an interest in these issues persisted throughout his career. In even his earliest fiction, Wright explores the currents that shaped African American men's sexuality, and nowhere is this exploration more central than in "Big Boy Leaves Home," one of the stories included in the early collection *Uncle Tom's Children*. To link this story with *The Long Dream* is not unusual, and many of the critics who delineate the similarities between *The Long Dream* and *Black Boy* also argue that Wright's fiction comes full circle in the novel, returning to the concerns of the often autobiographical short stories of the 1930s.[26] The novel seems in particular a conscious reworking of "Big Boy Leaves Home," since both texts focus on a young black man's coming of age and decision to leave the South after he witnesses the violent castration and lynching of another black man. In the early story, after he endures the lynching and castration of his friend Bobo, the adolescent Big Boy Morrison escapes to the North, where "colored folks" have "ekual rights."[27] Likewise, plagued with the vivid memories of the lynched, emasculated Chris, Fish ends *The Long Dream* en route to "that cool town" Paris, where "they don't bother colored folks" (268).

Given these numerous ways that "Big Boy" anticipates the themes of *The Long Dream,* it is not odd to find that the two texts also share Wright's preoccupation with submerged homoeroticism that wanes after the initiation into heterosexuality. Like the first part of the later novel, the opening scenes of "Big Boy" focus on precisely such an initiation. Symbolic of female sexuality, the forbidden swimming hole, damp and dark, beckons to be penetrated by the boys, thus anticipating the gape-mouthed fish of Rex's dreams. Yet, like Fish, the boys of the short story are hesitant to undergo this initiation. They appear far more comfortable with the homosociality they share with each other. As in the novel, Wright permeates this homosocial childhood with pronounced homoerotic and even homosexual undercurrents. For instance, the four boys of the short story frequently assume positions associated with male homosexual intimacies. Before the boys swim, they loll on the bank, "flat to the earth, their knees propped up" (18). These, the boys who jest about the unknowns of heterosexual acts with their ribald singing, present themselves not as stereotypically active partners, ready for liaisons with women, but rather as passive partners with raised knees, ready to be penetrated. The boys even note that they are metaphorically in bed together and receive immense pleasure as the sun's rays penetrate them: "'Man, don the groun feel warm?' 'Jus lika bed.' 'Jeeesus, Ah could stay here forever.' 'Me too.' 'Ah kin feel tha ol sun goin all thu me.' 'Feels like mah bones is warm'" (18–19).

If Wright presents the boys as at one moment passive, he also turns that passivity into homoerotic sexual aggression. As the boys vacillate about entering the swimming hole, thereby suggesting an anxiety about heterosexual penetration, they engage in horseplay that, in the images Wright uses to present it, appears extraordinarily homosexual. Big Boy "ran, caught up with them, leaped upon their backs, bearing them to the ground" (20). He "rides" his victims, prompting one boy to ask, "How come yuh awways hoppin on us?" and another to vow to "beat yo ol ass good" (21). Indeed, in a desexualized gang rape of sorts—what Big Boy terms "when a ganga guys jump on yuh" (23)—the other boys join together to conquer him bodily. The language remains focused on their asses, as it has since the opening pages, when the boys play farting games. "Les beat this bastard's ass!" (22), the boys declare, and when the assault falters, Big Boy returns, "Ahm gonna break yo ass nex time" (23).

Throughout this homosocial bonding, the boys remain clothed. However, having "jerked off their clothes and [thrown] them in a pile" (24), the boys unselfconsciously display their naked pubescent bodies in much the same way that Fishbelly and his cohorts do during the mud fight. When the horseplay continues, the homosexual positioning becomes even more dramatic. Apparently meaning to keep his promise of "breaking asses," Big Boy again attacks Bobo. To prepare himself for the advance, "Bobo crouched, spread his legs, and braced himself against Big Boy's body," striking a pose similar to a man about to be penetrated from behind. If this image stays with readers, the following sentence becomes ambiguous: "Locked in each other's arms, they tussled on the edge of the hole" (25). The homoerotic embrace of the two allows the hole to refer both to the pond that the boys hesitate to enter and to Bobo's anus. Indeed, the passive boy's nickname, infantile slang for ass, furthers the suggestion. It is also significant that it is Bobo, the recipient of Big Boy's veiled homosexual interests, who meets with the same fate as Chris Sims, Fish's eroticized hero in *The Long Dream*.

Once entering the pond, the boys' activity retains suggestions of homosexual intimacy. Following Big Boy's precedence, each of the boys "put his mouth just below the surface and blew" (26). Wright offers few details to help readers visualize fully this supposedly harmless bubble-blowing. The pared prose instead allows one to continue the associations established by the boys' intimate actions and preoccupations with male asses and penetrable holes before entering the pond. If so, one can read the surface as male pubic and anal areas, those "blown" or licked in sexual activity. Although such is not an exclusively homosexual act, here the symbolic fellatio or anilingus seems that which men perform on men with gratification and subsequent exhaustion. "Tiring, they came," continues Wright, "and sat under the embankment." Spent and silent, the boys "kept still in the sun, suppressing shivers" (26) during moments of near postejaculatory sensitivity.

Powerful though these eroticized images are, they dissipate by the end of the story, thus anticipating the script that Wright uses with Fish's sexuality two decades later and suggesting that, regardless of the moment in his career, Wright held an amazingly consistent understanding of southern black male sexuality at midcentury. Although his fiction suggests that this South engendered in African American men heterosexual identities so anxiety fraught that they relished homosocial bonds and even intraracial homosexual interactions, persistent African American—as well as European American—homophobia ultimately helped to close down these sites of sexual exploration. Gay black men at midcentury, Wright offers, faced violence almost as intense as miscegenistic straight black men, violence that was, moreover, often directed from within African American communities. He therefore suggests that, even if it was with devalued black women— Hurston's mules of the world—these African American men were compelled ultimately to assume compulsory heterosexual identities.

4

Lillian Smith and the Scripting
of Lesbian Desire

WHEN LILLIAN SMITH'S *Strange Fruit* appeared in 1944, it was by no means the first liberal scrutiny of the twentieth-century American South in fiction. As James Mellard points out, Erskine Caldwell, T. S. Stribling, and Grace Lumpkin, among others, anticipated Smith in literary production that focuses on overtly political issues such as "agrarian reform, industrial change, social deracination, and racial relationships." Nor were these writers the first to interrogate the South's complex race relations from a white liberal perspective. Rather, as Fred Hobson delineates, Smith was the most recent in a line of such liberals who had been "pondering and examining the mind and the soul of Dixie" and arguing for racial justice — or at least what they perceived to be racial justice — since the mid-nineteenth century. Like Quentin Compson, white southern liberals had long felt a compulsion to tell about the South, and by the mid-1940s George Washington Cable, Howard Odum, W. J. Cash, and others had offered many of Smith's arguments, if perhaps without her fervor.[1]

What sets *Strange Fruit* apart from most of these other texts is that Smith's novel initiates a recurring structuring device that allows a literary work to preoccupy itself centrally with calls for racial tolerance yet to establish as a marginalized parallel a plea for an equal tolerance of sexual otherness, especially as structured by same-sex desire. Anticipating Harper Lee's *To Kill a Mockingbird,* Carson McCullers's *Clock Without Hands,* and a number of other lesser-known novels using similar structures, *Strange Fruit* focuses on communal responses to the interracial relationship between an African American woman, Nonnie Anderson, and a European American man, Tracy Deen, detailing how Nonnie's jealous brother kills Tracy, and a white mob lynches an innocent black man for the murder. At crucial and often suspenseful moments in the novel, such as when readers know that Tracy has been killed but the white community does not, Smith shifts her narrative's focus and represents same-sex desire between women and its violent familial censorship through the characters of Laura Deen, Tracy's sister, and her distraught mother, Alma. With each line of plot, Smith clearly intends to chart the existing social conditions that she feels keep in play both the constitutive desires of these sexual practices and the taboos against them and to elicit tolerance and sympathy for those persons who violate these taboos. One of the ultimate goals of *Strange Fruit* is thus to facilitate both racial and sexual tolerance. This chapter seeks to bring the latter of these pleas into sharper focus even while it remains within the context of the former.

Just as race in the South was an enormous burden for Lillian Smith, so too was writing about race in the South, especially late in her career. In the personal correspondences of her last years, she repeatedly reveals a weariness of negotiating race, a feeling for the most part unbelied by her public appearances and work. For instance, during her revisions of *Killers of the Dream* in the late 1940s, she wrote in exasperation, "I hope to God I am through with race when I finish this book. I feel that I have had a thorough breakdown myself and I hope it purges me of certain guilts and so on, forever! I told my secretary—southern, smalltown, sweet and sensitive, and often whitefaced after a day's work on this thing—that my next book was going to be a cook book and she beamed and whispered, 'Oh, yes, please!'"[2] Although neither *The Journey* (1954) nor *Now Is the Time* (1955) was a cookbook or even a book devoid of racial issues, *One Hour,* Smith's next and last novel, was indeed remarkably free of such issues, despite her claims of it being her "big novel" and encompassing all her social preoccupations.

This same period also witnessed Smith's frustration that *Strange Fruit* had been and continued to be exclusively considered a "race novel." A letter discussing how the novel might be adapted into film establishes her irritation at this designation: "Now—this is how I feel about *Strange Fruit* as a movie: It should, under no circumstances, be a 'race' play. It should avoid this stereotype like poison. It wasn't written as a 'race' book; it was interpreted as such. It was from my point of view a book about two families, walled away from each other and themselves, blocked off from life itself by powers, forces they could not grapple with." Such frustrations increased as Smith aged. In 1965, less than a year before her death, she wrote to Wilma Dykeman Stokely, "So, as time goes by and I have another and another attack of cancer (or a new one appears—there have been six up to now) I think 'Am I really going down in history as just the "brave little woman who spent her life helping Negroes.""" 3

Despite these protests and anxieties, Smith now largely seems this "brave little woman." When her work is studied, it is usually *Strange Fruit* or *Killers of the Dream,* her most intense scrutinies of race relations. But even when this is not the case, and one considers Smith's fuller biography and literary production, race emerges as absolutely central to her career. For nearly a decade before the publication of *Strange Fruit,* in the little magazines she jointly edited and published with her partner, Paula Snelling, Smith wrote steadily about issues of segregation and its detrimental effects. Her writing and social activism not only continued but also increased dramatically in the years after *Strange Fruit*'s appearance, as the civil rights movement came to be organized. Her constant speechmaking; her publication of *Killers of the Dream, The Journey,* and *Now Is the Time,* as well as numerous journal and magazine articles dealing with segregation and other issues of southern race; her involvement with the NAACP (National Association for the Advancement of Colored People), SNCC (Student Nonviolent Coordinating Committee), CORE (Congress of Racial Equality), and other civil rights organizations: these all marked Smith's continued preoccupation with race until her death in 1966.

Because Smith did work so ceaselessly and earnestly in this arena, many persons considered her the defining white liberal voice in discourses surrounding race in the midcentury South. By the end of her life, devoted followers even ascribed a near-religious persona to her, often holding her above fallibility. "She was hailed by civil rights workers as something of a priestess," Hobson explains of Smith; "she came to have apostles." Critical work on Smith justifiably continued and frequently persists in much the same vein. In his 1985 foreword to *Strange Fruit,* Hobson himself terms Smith "the most courageous, outspoken, and uncompromising white southern liberal of her generation," adding that "no other white southerner in the first half of the twentieth century was so truly committed to the cause of racial justice as Lillian Smith, and no other was so bold in his criticism of a white South."

Margaret Rose Gladney echoes Hobson in her preface to Smith's letters, asserting that, through "*South Today, Strange Fruit,* and her autobiographical critique of southern culture, *Killers of the Dream* (1949), Smith established herself as the most liberal and outspoken of white southern writers on issues of social, and especially racial, injustice."[4]

Smith may well have been this figure, despite her periodic urges to distance her fiction and other work from exclusively racial issues. In almost every glimpse into her understanding of her literary production, she, like critics typified by Hobson and Gladney, held her interrogations of race to be that which deserved recognition. Yet, as Truman Capote and Carson McCullers with theirs, Smith held her work to have unprecedented cultural and literary value and took repeated offense that this value was not recognized as fully as she felt it ought to have been. She confidently wrote in 1957, "And if I am not the South's best writer I am certainly among the first two or three; and surely my books have made history and will make history." "I know that *Strange Fruit* is an American classic," she asserts elsewhere, "and will in literary and social history be considered so." In the letter negotiating the film rights to the novel, she self-assuredly offers, "In my own opinion, some day I rather think *Strange Fruit* and *Killers of the Dream* plus my other writings will give me the Nobel prize. I am patient; I know my worth; I know my historical value to this country."[5]

When discussing the literary merits and reception of her work, Smith was particularly fond of drawing parallels between herself and Herman Melville, since to her thinking both writers suffered from having their work go unvalued: "This happens again and again to writers; just look at Melville who died virtually unknown after he annoyed the world by writing *Moby Dick.*" "He turned around and dared to write about man's future, about man's depths," she writes of Melville in another letter: "Anyway, the book got not good reviews; and was buried in a heavy silence. Something of this nature happened to *Strange Fruit* . . . Just now, it is being pushed aside, covered with silence, because it struck so deeply into white culture, laying bare so many of our self-destructive values and intellectual habits. But it will come back, find its own—just as *Moby Dick* did." Smith was so adamant about her own preeminent significance to southern culture that she even denigrated other southern liberals' contributions to bolster her own. For instance, although she agreed with much of the argument of Cash's *The Mind of the South* and had invited him to contribute an early chapter for publication in *Pseudopodia* in the 1930s, Smith was nevertheless careful to assert how much more daring her own *Killers of the Dream* was. After noting in a 1965 letter that "*Mind of the South* has sold more than 100,000 copies since I persuaded Knopf to push it again," Smith continues, "But there was no in-depth probing in that book; the man wasn't capable of such, too sick himself, too involved with his own taboos to dare handle it the way I did."[6]

When *Strange Fruit* appeared, it was certainly this handling of race that readers acknowledged as having riveted them, and most contemporary reviewers—especially northern ones—praised the novel for boldly and movingly depicting miscegenation and its violent consequences in a southern community. After noting *Strange Fruit*'s formalistic shortcomings, Francis Downing lauds Smith for making "us know again that the South is stained with racial evil; that it is foul and sick; and that each of us is touched with its foulness and its sickness." "No one," Downing observes of Smith, "is more anguished than she at the obscenity of the race conflict. No one has made it more artistically clear that the South is a system of spoken and unspoken caste, where human life is forfeit to the concept of 'a white man's world.'" Diana Trilling echoes Downing yet also praises Smith for crafting a novel that supposedly speaks beyond its southern contexts: "In her hands the Negro problem turns out to be not only the problem of the whole South but, by implication, of all modern society. To say, for instance, that 'Strange Fruit' anatomizes a small Georgia town at the end of the last war would be to regionalize and to particularize in time a social study which is applicable to any number of other American communities and moments." An equally impressed Edward Weeks compares Smith not with Melville but rather his contemporary comparably invested in issues of race, Harriet Beecher Stowe, calling *Strange Fruit* "a new *Uncle Tom's Cabin*" for the 1940s. "This one comes from the South," he notes, "and this time New England seems afraid of it." Finally, Malcolm Cowley claims *Strange Fruit* to be "the most interesting novel I have read for a long time, even though it deals with what has come to be regarded as the painfully commonplace subject of a lynching." In his opinion, Smith "makes it clear that this lynching was also an episode in a struggle that has continued for three hundred years, ever since the first slaves were landed at Jamestown." He succinctly concludes that, although Smith "seems to lack the specifically literary gifts of William Faulkner, let us say, or Carson McCullers," nevertheless "[h]er book is not a promise but an achievement."[7]

Impressed though they may have been with Smith's treatment of race, reviewers were not, however, uniform in their praise. Several of them who were writing for more conservative magazines and journals found *Strange Fruit* particularly off-putting for its culturally tabooed language as well as its frank sexual scenes. For instance, although deference to social acceptability prompted the perennially graphic Norman Mailer to opt for *fug* rather than *fuck* throughout *The Naked and the Dead* four years later, Smith boldly includes the latter in one of *Strange Fruit*'s most climactic scenes, when the near-imbecilic Henry approaches Nonnie: "'Say,' he said and grinned, 'say, how about fuckin with me?' And as she stared the color had beat through her face and neck. 'You knows,' he grinned, 'fuckin,' and opened his pants."[8] This sexually explicit profanity and other conspicuous elements of the novel—abortion, masturbation, menopause, excrement, venereal disease, graphic violence—offended reviewers like Joseph McSorley, who, after noting that Smith "offers no hint of a solution" to the problem of race in the South, asserts: "Most important of all, presumably for the purpose of appealing to a vulgar multitude, she sins against good taste so grossly as to make her story quite unfit for general circulation. It seems curious enough that 'the daughter of one of the South's oldest families' should recur with such fond frequency to the subject of urine and privies and should employ phrases which decent people regard as unprintable." It is presumably against charges such as McSorley's that Weeks felt compelled to argue that, "despite the shock that is here," he finds "nothing in the novel that is pornographic."[9] Nevertheless, *Strange Fruit* was immediately banned in Boston, and, three months after its February publication, the United States Post Office attempted to prohibit the novel from the mail, a move supposedly foiled only by the efforts of Eleanor Roosevelt.

Noticeably absent in McSorley's and others' litanies of Smith's offenses in *Strange Fruit* is that which has gone relatively unsaid—at least in public forums—by both Smith's champions and her detractors until recently: lesbianism. That McSorley does not identify the novel's representations of the homoerotic relationship between Laura Deen and Jane Hardy suggests the power of the midcentury cultural taboo against same-sex desire between women and thus implies how truly daring Smith was to include lesbian desire in the novel. Although by the mid-1940s American writers from both the South and elsewhere had offered numerous depictions of male homosexuality, those of its female counterpart were still scarce. As I suggested in chapter 1, early critical work on Smith, particularly that done before her death, usually makes scant mention of lesbianism and attempts to dismiss representations of homosexuality in her work as insignificant. Louise Blackwell and Frances Clay's study, for example, heterosexualizes Smith, recording of the late 1910s and early 1920s that she "dated John [*sic*] Hopkins medical students and through all of her various activities made many lasting friends while in Baltimore." The problem is not that Blackwell and Clay mention these interactions, since, as Smith's letters now reveal, she *was* sexually involved with men during her early adulthood. Rather, it is that the critics—although perhaps at Smith's own urging—note only the heterosexual liaisons while labeling Paula Snelling as merely "a close friend of Miss Smith" or "a good friend." [10]

In contrast to their treatment of Smith's own lesbianism, Blackwell and Clay directly address Laura's homoeroticism in *Strange Fruit*. Instead of entertaining this desire as integral or even acceptable to a reading of the novel, however, these critics immediately attempt to explain away this desire, to emphasize that Laura and Jane never form a sexual relationship: "Later Mrs. Deen searches Laura's desk and reads some letters Laura has received from Jane Hardy, an unmarried schoolteacher. Although Laura's affection for Jane indicates tendencies toward homosexuality, Mrs. Deen implies that such a relationship exists when, in fact, there has been no overt behavior on the part of the two women. Her warning to Laura, however, about a possible homosexual relationship, has the effect of disgusting Laura and of destroying her feeling for her friend." Blackwell and Clay thus fall back upon one of the several strategies that Sedgwick charts as having frequently informed literary criticism's negotiations of same-sex desire. "There is no actual proof of homosexuality," she rehearses, "such as sperm taken from the body of another man or a nude photograph with another woman—so the author may be assumed to have been ardently and exclusively heterosexual." Here it is the character rather than the author at issue, but the strategies that Sedgwick identifies nevertheless hold. Laura merely "indicates tendencies toward homosexuality," and certainly "there has been no overt behavior on the part of the two women." Moreover, as Blackwell and Clay read the novel, there is no longer even the potential for a lesbian relationship after Alma's calculated intervention into her daughter's life, and readers can therefore presume Laura to be "ardently and exclusively heterosexual." [11]

Even after Smith's and Snelling's deaths, and in a permissive era in which lesbian representations have proliferated, critics have not substantively treated Smith's lesbian themes or her own lesbianism until of late. In *The History of Southern Literature* her name, like William Goyen's, appears but twice in the volume's entirety. Her only identified work is *Strange Fruit,* noted simply as "perhaps the best known of the many militantly antiracist novels written by whites during the first two decades of the Renascence." As noted, the substantial work of Richard King and the early Fred Hobson on Smith also neglects lesbianism. Even when arguing for her exceptionalism among southern liberals, Hobson does not mention her crucially differentiating sexuality until his recent work typified by *But Now I See.* "Like [Hinton Rowan] Helper and [Edmund] Ruffin and the earlier [Robert Lewis] Dabney," Hobson writes in the earlier *Tell About the South,* Smith "was in some measure isolated from her fellow Southerners, although not for the same reasons they were: her sex, her early experience in China, finally her thirteen-year battle with cancer gave her a unique perspective." With such silences Hobson thus seems to contradict his claim that *Strange Fruit* "treated the most taboo of Southern subjects, miscegenation." For him, as for many others, the sexual mixing of races was at least utterable, while homosexuality—and in particular that between women—remained, until virtually the new millennium, the love that dare not speak its name or even have it spoken of.[12]

Although Anne Loveland's 1986 biography of Smith took steps toward recognizing the importance of same-sex desire between women in Smith's life and work, it was Margaret Rose Gladney's editing of Smith's voluminous letters that definitively established lesbianism as an issue so central to her work that it merits serious scholarly investigation. As Will Brantley notes in his appreciative review of the published letters, they have ensured that discourses circulating around Smith's work must now include those informed by gender and sexuality. "Smith's letters will also prompt new assessments of her complex sexual identity," Brantley writes. "Surely no one will now be able to deny the sexual component of Smith's relationship with Paula Snelling, the woman she called her 'companion.'" Although Smith and Snelling destroyed most of their personal correspondences, a few remain, and Gladney includes several of these letters in *How Am I to Be Heard?* thus documenting not only Smith's persisting interrogations of homosexuality but her own lesbianism. As Gladney argues and Brantley agrees, such letters are crucial: "The absence of those personal letters clearly contributes to, but does not excuse, biographers' and critics' tendency to ignore or minimize the role of gender and sexual orientation in their reading of Smith."[13]

"To create a full portrait of Smith," Gladney continues, "one that ac-knowledges the importance of gender and sexuality, it is merely necessary to bring into central focus her relationship for over forty years with Paula Snelling and the place and work that brought them together—Laurel Falls Camp." This relationship begins to emerge in letters such as that in which, during her stay in New York for the staging of *Strange Fruit*, Smith writes wistfully to her "Paula darling," "But I could do with a little loving for a change. Oh darling, if our full spirits and bodies could effect the marriage that our minds have always had—And that our integrity of spirit had had! . . . I'd love to feel your lips on mine . . . and I can imagine other feelings too." And yet in this handful of letters from the 1940s, one glimpses not only the couple's physicality but also the everyday strains of a long-term relationship. "You know I love you and need you and depend on you in a thousand ways," Smith reassures Snelling before countering, "Relationships change. I think as you have leaned more heavily on me during the past few years, I have protested the weight. It is as simple as that." "Maybe the old wonderful Paula will come back too," Smith hopes in another letter, "the one so rich in ideas and inner vitality. The one who helped me through so many bad spots—so patiently and gently." [14]

The depth and intricacy of Smith and Snelling's relationship resurfaces in another cycle of letters, this time from the early 1960s. Sounding a famil-iar note, Smith expresses her ongoing concern that she has overshadowed and dominated Snelling and affirms her attempts to create a portion of her life apart from Smith. "Honey—I know it is hard as hell. But any new step is," Smith writes: "You realize this, but you hate to acknowledge that my personality does weigh yours down. . . . It will be hard on both of us: we shall miss each other dreadfully; and I shall certainly miss the thousand ways you have lifted details off of me and the work you do around the place. But in the end, it will be better for me and better for you. Each of us will feel more free and let ourselves do what we sometimes need to do as persons and want to do." "I love you better than anybody in the world," Smith ends the letter. "I want you to know that. I respect and honor you as a person. I have real-ized even in my angriest moments, my weakest times when I felt I could not work another hour or take another step, that you wanted to help me in every way you could." Thus, although the arrival at "a full portrait of Smith" is, no doubt, an illusory ideal, Gladney's inclusion of letters such as these does much to establish that, although race was of enormous importance to

Smith's understanding of both her culture and herself, sexuality—and homosexuality in particular—was also crucial.[15]

That Smith held race and sexuality to be inextricably intertwined on the southern social matrix of the first half of the twentieth century is no revelation. In addition to her private letters, both her fiction and nonfiction make this point so incessantly that few critics have not addressed it. As seen, many of these analyses of Smith's understanding of this matrix often prioritized race, even urging that it bases all her other assumptions about southern culture. Gladney, for instance, concludes in her preface to the letters, "Because issues surrounding race so dominated life in the American South from the turn of the century through the civil rights era, it was almost impossible for Smith to address questions of gender, sexuality, or class without first dealing with race."[16] This prioritization is as it should be. As Gladney points out, however, although race is Smith's starting point for her interrogations of southern culture, she by no means considers it her exclusive end. Even *Killers of the Dream* and *Strange Fruit,* with their intense focus on race, spend much time examining Smith's multiple points of conclusion that are often only tangentially related to race and frequently—although, given Smith's letters and biography, not surprisingly—foreground same-sex desire.

Of the two texts, *Killers of the Dream* argues more cogently—if perhaps less interestingly—than *Strange Fruit* how southern race relations foster same-sex desire. The largely autobiographical *Killers* bases its essentializing claims on Smith's memories of growing up in a large upper-class family in northern Florida in the first two decades of the century and repeatedly opts for rhetoric that foregrounds an environment in which southern cultural inscription of sexuality is, if not contingent upon inscriptions of race, at least distinctly parallel to them.[17] Both race and sexuality were largely open secrets in Smith's childhood, ever present but rarely acknowledged. "Neither the Negro nor sex was often discussed at length in our home," she recalls. "I remember that, like *sex,* the word *segregation* was not mentioned in the best circles." And yet, as Smith understands race and sexuality, both were in fact grounded in segregation. Just as nonwhite persons were to be quarantined within the southern social body because of their supposed racial contaminations, so too were sexual zones and the desires and actions they engendered to be quarantined within the physical body because of their equally infectious sinful character. It was these parallel segregations that the young

Smith and most other southerners of her class and generation accepted almost unthinkingly. She recalls "that I was better than a Negro, that all black folks have their place and must be kept in it, that sex has its place and must be kept in it, that a terrifying disaster would befall the South if ever I treated a Negro as my social equal and as terrifying a disaster would befall my family if ever I were to have a baby outside of marriage."[18]

In a strikingly effective rhetorical strategy, Smith continues this parallel throughout *Killers*, thereby not only urging her readers into an acceptance of the parallel but also revealing how firmly she holds it to be an accurate reflection of the southern social conditions of her childhood, those that shaped the dominant generation at midcentury. "By the time we were five years old," Smith recalls in a chapter entitled "The Lessons,"

> we had learned, without hearing the words, that masturbation is wrong and segregation is right, and each had become a dread taboo that must never be broken, for we believed God, whom we feared and tried desperately to love, had made the rules concerning not only Him and our parents, but our bodies and Negroes. Therefore when we as small children crept over the race line and ate and played with Negroes or broke other segregation customs known to us, we felt the same dread fear of consequences, the same overwhelming guilt we felt when we crept over the sex line and played with our body, or thought thoughts about God or our parents that we knew we must not think. (83–84)

Southern social conventions as Smith understands them construct the "race line" and the "sex line" to be not necessarily the same barrier but to function comparably and to be internalized via the same ideologically seamless processes. Thus, although she problematically feels that her ability to delineate this prevailing ideology positions her outside it, Smith persists in using the same terminology to characterize how southern society scripts both race relations and the sexualized body. "Now, parts of your body are segregated areas which you must stay away from and keep others away from," Smith rehearses from her youthful lessons. "These areas you touch only when necessary. In other words, you cannot associate freely with them any more than you can associate freely with colored children" (87).

As *Killers* progresses, Smith clarifies that, although these taboos concerning the "race" and "sex" lines parallel one another and are therefore distinctly separate in children's inculcations, the prohibitions arise from within unique southern social conditions contingent upon the *eradication* of this separability. That is, the ideology of Smith's childhood emerges from a culture based, she feels, on miscegenation, the simultaneous violations of these taboos. Slavery created biracial—if not multiracial—areas in much of the South, and white men, both horrified and fascinated by nonwhite women, begat mulatto children by them: "Temptation and menace twisted together as they see-sawed in the white man's mind. Attraction, fear, repulsion, attraction—so it went. After a few years, lighter faces began to appear in back yards. More and more light faces. And, at the same time that they were finding the back-yard temptation irresistible, these white men were declaring and sometimes beginning to believe that Negroes did not have souls, that they were not quite human, they were different, they were 'no better than animals'" (119–20). Guilt from these miscegenistic transgressions in turn forced white southern men into the ineffectual compensation of idealizing white southern women. "The race-sex-sin spiral had begun," Smith asserts. "The more trails the white man made to back-yard cabins, the higher he raised his white wife on her pedestal when he returned to the big house. The higher the pedestal, the less he enjoyed her whom he had put there, for statues after all are only nice things to look at" (121).

As Sandra Gilbert and Susan Gubar famously rehearsed two decades ago, the creation of the "angel in the house" was by no means an exclusively southern project. In her discussion of the decades' long glorification of white southern women into "Dixie's diadem," Anne Goodwyn Jones argues that this process "has much in common with the ideas of the British Victorian lady and of American true womanhood. All deny to women authentic selfhood; all enjoin that women suffer and be still; all show women sexually pure, pious, deferent to external authority, and content with their place in the home." Yet, self-admittedly building on Smith's arguments and those of historians such as Cash and Anne Firor Scott, Jones immediately clarifies the cultural specificity of this process in the South: "southern womanhood has from the beginning been inextricably linked to racial attitudes. Its very genesis, some say, lay in the minds of guilty slaveholders who sought an image they could revere without sacrificing the gains of racial slavery." Thus, although she is more cautious than Smith in positing a solitary origin of this figurative pedestal, Jones nevertheless agrees that circulations of race are crucial to an understanding of this idealization. "In the knot of race, sex, and class, some find one thread clearer than others," she offers. "But, in general, historians agree that the function of southern womanhood has been to justify the perpetuation of the hegemony of the male sex, the upper and middle classes, and the white race."[19]

As Jones suggests, this idealization of southern white women has as an imperative female sexual purity, usually understood to be virginity before marriage and connubial procreational heterosexuality afterwards. Women tolerated the latter as something of a necessary evil, because only it, this well-rehearsed script goes, can lead to true motherhood, the sanctified and mystical production of new life from one's own body, the process in which a woman's existence supposedly culminates. In fact, Jones clarifies, "in some renditions she [the idealized southern white woman] lacks sexual interest altogether" but withstands sexual advances and interactions simply to appease her more animalistic husband and achieve motherhood. As Jones argues throughout *Tomorrow Is Another Day,* this figure abounds in white southern women's literature, such as in Chopin's Adele Ratignolle, Glasgow's Virginia Pendleton, and Mitchell's Ellen O'Hara and Melanie Wilkes.[20]

Of all the supposed effects that assuming positions on this metaphorical pedestal had on southern white women, it is perhaps this desexualization that Smith holds as most culturally problematic in *Killers.* Because "[s]ex was pushed out through the back door as a shameful thing never to be mentioned" (141) in front of—much less by—southern white women, they eventually internalized this idealization divorced of sexuality and became what Smith depicts in her fiction as little more than frigid mannequins. Alma Deen, one of the least sympathetic characters of *Strange Fruit,* embodies this southern feminine ideal and consequently has the near-requisite intense aversion to sex. "She had been a good wife to Tut, submitting to his embraces quietly, without protest," Alma tells herself, and yet "that part of marriage seemed . . . a little unclean and definitely uncomfortable" (77). Even nonsexual physical contact with her husband appalls her: "Sometimes all she could remember of hers and Tut's nights together was the lifting of his leg off her body. There was something almost *dissipated* about the way Tut slept, letting himself go, so, so uncontrolled, you might say" (74). Her husband's male body so offends Alma that she "occasionally, oh most rarely, . . . slept in Laura's bed, escaping Tut's masculinity. Feeling at times a desperate need, she would slip into Laura's room. And on those nights her sleep would be dreamless and peaceful" (67).

The crucial scene in which Alma discovers the clay torso her daughter has sculpted underscores the elder woman's aversion to sexuality and corporeality. Alma is initially troubled not so much by Laura's potentially homo-erotic motivations to mold female breasts and genitals as by her desire to create and thus expose herself to any physical body. For Alma, the sex of the sculpted body is largely unimportant; it is the nakedness that unnerves and immobilizes her: "And as she stood, unmoving, a bright red spot appeared in each cheek, her clamped jaws squared, shuttling her face into fresh planes, destroying the glaze which gave Alma Deen what her friends ardently called her 'spiritual look.' She held the little figure, stared at each detail as if she saw nakedness for the first time" (67). "If it had any beauty in it!" the narra-tive, focalized through the horrified Alma, exclaims of the clay torso. "But no, only nakedness. Why should Laura want to make naked things? . . . A man, a boy—you could understand men being dirty like that—men seemed made that way. But your own daughter . . . spending her time making naked things . . . What did she do it for! She'd call it art, and her lips would grow tight and thin as she said it" (68). Inculcated to view men as inherently fas-cinated with exposed bodies, Alma can "understand men being dirty like that." She immediately recalls Tracy "playing savages" with Henry as boys, a scene equally permeated with unacknowledged homoeroticism: "Naked, unmindful of the broiling sun, they [Tracy and Henry] were crouched be-fore an upturned washpot, beating upon it. Sweat poured down from their grave faces, down their bodies" (69). Although Alma disciplines Tracy for his transgression, she feels as if she understands his motives for exposing his body. Quite simply, boys do that. But for a fellow woman—much less the daughter Alma has raised to mirror her own feminine sensibilities—to dis-play an equal fascination with naked bodies is almost unimaginable for her, and she recoils when the clay torso forces her to do so.

Alma's emotional frigidity is perhaps even more disconcerting than this fear of corporeality. Her coldness, yoked with her constant need to control her family, decisively alienates her children and spawns their intense resent-ment of her. When confronted with Laura's sculpture, Alma's mental and physical immobilization lasts but minutes, and she quickly remedies the sit-uation. "She had met every exigency of Laura's life," Alma thinks to herself. "This, too, she could take care of": "Then, taking the figure more securely between her plump white hands, she kneaded and pressed and pounded it with slow deliberateness until it was reduced to a shapeless wad; and, walk-ing swiftly through the hall, past Eenie in the kitchen, to the back porch, she dropped it in the garbage can. It lay there among corn shucks, okra stems, tomato skins—no more than the mud pies Laura used to make years ago; just another of the little messes Alma had cleaned up after her young daughter" (72–73). Like Tennessee Williams's domineering Amanda Wingfield, who cares little for her fragile daughter's sensitivity in *The Glass Menagerie*, Alma Deen reveals comparably little care for Laura's feelings. Even if one disregards the clay figure's embodiment of Laura's lesbian desire, as Alma initially seems able to do, and therefore does not consider her act to equate same-sex affections with the familial garbage, one can still take offense at Alma's blatant disregard for the artistic efforts that Laura expends in sculpting the figure. Alma not only puts the torso in the trash but also first demolishes it. And yet this destruction does not surprise Laura when she eventually finds the torso missing from her drawer: "That her mother had destroyed the little clay figure, Laura took for granted. It was one of those things you took for granted" (241).

As the novel progresses and Smith increasingly demonizes Alma, her calculated intrusiveness seems less and less surprising and indeed something to be taken for granted. Throughout her children's existences, she interposes with unnerving precision and emotional detachment to attempt to orchestrate their sentiments and/or behaviors. For years she dismisses Laura's privacy and clandestinely reads her private writings to monitor, among other things, her sexuality. As Alma contemplates the clay figure, she scans Laura's bedroom to note her "bed, her books, her desk. In that desk Laura kept her writings; when little, her diaries; now older, her letters. And it was by means of these that Alma had maintained so intimate, so satisfying a knowledge of her child's thoughts and moods" (67). Tracy too faces Alma's indomitable policing of sexuality. Just as she attempts to retard Laura's fascination with female bodies, destroying both the clay torso and Jane Hardy's letters to Laura, Alma also works to end Tracy's affair with Nonnie, arranging for him to talk with the Reverend Dinwoodie, the visiting revivalist minister championed for reforming youthful sexual transgressors:

> *Tracy* . . . Mother's voice had faltered but her eyes had looked steadily into his, *I've arranged for you to have a talk with Brother Dinwoodie at nine o'clock in the morning.* You kept thinking of it.
> *You've—say that again, will you, Mother?*
> *I think you heard me.*
> *Sure . . . but I want to give you a chance to—take it back.* He'd kept his voice low. *Of all the goddam meddling—* (82–83)

Tracy's mutterings suggest that Alma's fear of corporeality and any sexuality—whether Laura's presumed lesbianism, Tracy's miscegenation, or even Tut's connubial heterosexuality—invariably leads to the frustrating intrusions that irrevocably alienate her family.

Smith seems discontent, however, to let this meddling alone damn Alma and instead parodies her preoccupation with her primped and clothed body, contrasting it to the sensuality of Laura's clay torso and even the brutal eroticism of Nonnie's rape. Smith scripts these bodies as glorious in their nakedness, yet Alma's conventional efforts to beautify herself engender in Tracy a Swiftian horror and disgust. On seeing his mother at her dressing table, he catalogues the offensive actions that compose the "ritual of cleansing and smoothing her body and making it as attractive as she knew how": creaming her neck so that "it glistened in the creases of flesh, catching the light"; yanking wads of graying hair from her brush; "pulling the hairs from that mole near her lip." The last particularly horrifies Tracy, and he notes with some relief, "A pair of tweezers lay near the comb. . . . Glad she wasn't doing that now. It made him uneasy to watch her jerk at herself like that" (190). His uneasiness culminates when her "hand moved toward the tweezers. Good Lord, she's going to do it right now. Women don't have a bit of shyness. 'Don't!' He hadn't meant to say it. Now you feel like a fool. His mother smiled, picked up a small bottle of alcohol, wet a piece of cotton, wiped off the tweezers. She's going to do it, anyway" (191). Thus, contrary to Bakhtinian thought that equates the sexualized body with the grotesque, Smith's imagery suggests that it is the desexualized body that appears horrific and even monstrous, with its cavernous wrinkles and tufts of hair. Even efforts to beautify this body repulse with equal force.

Although the results of this sexual and emotional frigidity in Alma and the white women she represents in Smith's schema are many, perhaps the most prominent is that this sexual purity forces white men into the beds of African American women and thus continues the spiral of miscegenation and pedestalization, even as this schema also reveals Smith's limited ability to complicate white male sexuality with the viability of homosexuality, bestiality (as Faulkner entertains in *The Hamlet*), autoeroticism, and/or other forms of nonnormative heterosexuality. Tracy's affair with Nonnie, which drives the novel's plot, is largely contingent upon the virtue of Dot Pusey, the girl understood to be his eventual fiancée. Like Alma of the earlier generation, Dot apparently holds sex to be tolerable only within the context of marriage, much to Tracy's dismay, frustration, and resentment. With the virginal Dot, his mother, and others like them in mind, he condemns these women with no small amount of misogyny, even as he hurries to the sexual comfort that Nonnie offers:

> All the white women in the world. Yeah . . . they tie their love around you like a little thin wire and pull, keep pulling until they cut you in two. That's what they do. Back there, they're asleep now, stretched out on their beds asleep, ruling the town. White goddesses. Pure as snow—dole out a little of their body to you—just a little—see—it's poison—you can't take but a few drops—don't be greedy—do as I tell you—do as I tell you now—be a good boy—do as I tell you—just a little now—Tracy!—that's not nice—that's not nice— (195)

When one takes Tracy's interior monologue at face value, as Smith seemingly intends, her understanding of white southern men's impulse for miscegenation crystallizes. The very desexualization they supposedly enforce in white women is perceived of as manipulative cock-teasing, a male-debasing strategy for feminine power. As the condescending tone of the monologue suggests, this withholding of male sexual gratification with the bodies of white women not only denies men sexual release with their culturally appropriate partners but also infantilizes these men, casting them in the roles of demanding greedy children in search of instantaneous pleasure. Denied by white women, southern white men can be granted such pleasure only by African American women, those who can either be "legitimately" overpowered through the dual justifications of white supremacy and patriarchal privilege, or who openly value and desire sexual interactions—and the possible social protection they may entail—and therefore welcome whatever advances are made.

With this final step in Smith's social narrative, she seems to reinscribe the hypersexualized racial other who has permeated European Americans' cultural self-definition and literary production. In Nonnie and the remembered black women of Smith's childhood, she romanticizes African American women as inherently comfortable with both their sexualized bodies and casual sexual interactions, providing images reminiscent of Maud and Vera in Wright's *The Long Dream,* if perhaps without the sexist overtones. Yet Smith bases this sexualization not in necessarily racist essentialisms but rather in racial ones allowed by her investments in Freudian psychoanalysis so pervasively in vogue at midcentury. She holds psychosexual identity to form within the familial dynamics of childhood. In *Killers* in particular, because of her presumptions about African Americans' less sexually repressive familial relationships, ones in which sexuality is openly expressed and acknowledged, Smith accords adult African Americans fewer digressions from fully realized heterosexuality than European Americans. That is, for Smith, African Americans' sexuality is generally more liberated than that of whites. Thus, although Nonnie and similar representations may seem to be racial reinscriptions of the nymphomaniacal black wench and perhaps may be regarded as such no matter what the explanation, these figures offer far healthier sexualities in Smith's thinking than those of Alma and Dot.

For all the parody that Smith uses in her descriptions of these desexualized white women and the poor comparisons they suffer with Nonnie, Smith's dual investments in psychoanalysis and theories of cultural determinism also elicit some sympathy for these women. In that they are products of these culturally specific dysfunctional families, these women are victims to some degree. They have little control, Smith grants, for having come—or, rather, not come—to sexual maturity in households dominated by frigid mothers and distant or absent fathers. African American mammies, Smith argues with distressingly romanticized essentialism, offered these young girls and their brothers their only warmth. This love, however, was invariably dismissed as the children absorbed southern racism's devaluing of African Americans. Granted, for Smith, this status of victim does not fully excuse these women's replications of their mothers' coldness and penchant for manipulation, but the victimization does offer the solace of explanation. In her characterization of these women in *Killers*, Smith graciously notes of them, "We cannot forget that their culture had stripped these white mothers of profound biological rights, had ripped off their inherent dignity and made them silly statues and psychic children, stunting their capacity for understanding and enjoyment of husbands and family" (151).

For Smith, the perpetuation of miscegenation and the debasement of these women are not, however, the only results of the sexual frigidity of white southern mothers, and yet it is here that most critics of her work have stopped in their explication of her psychoanalytic schema of southern culture. In both her fiction and nonfiction, Smith argues that these women's desexualizations may lead just as directly to their children's—but especially their daughters'—homosexuality as they do to their sons' tendency toward miscegenation: "We cannot censure—who would dare!—but we know now that these women, forced by their culture and their heartbreak, did a thorough job of closing the path to mature genitality for many of their sons and daughters, and an equally good job of leaving little cleared detours that led downhill to homosexual and infantile green pastures, and on to alcoholism, neuroses, divorce, to race-hate and brutality, and to a tight inflexible mind that could not question itself" (153).

Smith makes precisely this point in *Strange Fruit*. Just as Alma, Dot, and other sexually restrained white girls foster Tracy's desire for miscegenation, so too does Alma's frigidity leave "little cleared detours" for Laura's lesbianism. Smith explains in the 1961 letter to Jerome Bick: "In the white family, there was Tracy's sister, Laura, pushed by the same mother into the by-paths of Lesbianism. This, too, is interesting; and I used it in the book as a deeper shadow of the deviation which the mother forced on both her children. Both cultural deviations, but one (Tracy's) less deeply rooted than the cultural deviation we call 'homosexuality.'" It is worth noting, though, that Smith's focus here and elsewhere on southern homosexuality is almost exclusively on lesbianism, perhaps because of autobiographical factors. Her fiction presents no overtly gay characters, the closest being *One Hour*'s effeminate organist accused of being gay and brutally beaten. Her letters reveal comparably little about male homosexuality except to emphasize its difference from that of women. Smith writes, for example, that "female homosexuality" is "as different as day from night from male homosexuality. There is no such thing as 'the homosexual' anyway." Critics such as Gladney, who have spoken of "Smith's treatment of lesbian and gay male relationships," are therefore perhaps too eager to identify an inclusiveness that her writing does not suggest.[21]

Although Smith does not depict a sexual actualization of Laura's homoerotic relationship with Jane Hardy, as Blackwell and Clay record, Smith nevertheless leaves little doubt about the role Jane plays in Laura's life and how she comes to that role. Girls such as Laura desire a surrogate for their unacceptable mothers, either the frigid white biological women represented by Alma or the idealized African American mammies who, as Smith understands them, already function as surrogates for these white women but whose affections are invariably denied white children when either a new child is born into the family or southern racism demeans African American presences. As Laura lies awake in her bedroom the night her brother is murdered, she recalls how Jane offers what neither Alma nor Mamie, Laura and

Tracy's childhood mammy, no longer provides. "And then one day you had been playing tennis and suddenly had begun to talk," the narrative imagines. "And you knew you could talk to Jane, you could tell her about your sculpture and your verses, about your fears and your feelings. And soon you were feeling with her a security that you had not felt since you were a little girl with your Mother" (246).

Smith bolsters this notion that lesbianism is to some degree contingent upon an asymmetry of ages and/or maturity by not only making Jane significantly older than Laura but also emphasizing the young girl's childishness. Despite her college education in New York, she seems to have internalized and retained the role of little girl imposed upon her by her mother. Laura repeatedly lapses into references to Alma as "Mumsie" and never thinks to question her interference in her daughter's adult life. Instead, when Alma exerts her control, Laura retreats into the comforting—and vaguely erotic— memories of Mamie, her "slow deep breathing" and "her soft breast" (246). This behavior only makes the older Jane seem all the more mature and therefore, in Smith's schema, all the more attractive to Laura.

Smith acknowledges that this particular configuration of a lesbian relationship can be dismissed within homophobic circulations not only because of the wrongness of actualizing same-sex desire but also on the basis that the older woman "abuses" the younger one who is "innocently" seeking a surrogate mother. Certainly this is the rhetorical strategy that Alma uses: "'There're—women, Laura, who aren't safe for young girls to be with. Of course you are young and inexperienced—' Mother was finding this hard going. . . . Now Mother lowered her voice: 'There're women who are— unnatural. They're like vultures—women like that.' Mother's face had grown stony. 'They do—terrible things to young girls.' 'Oh, Mother!' 'I don't believe a woman is the right kind of woman who talks about the naked body as Jane does'" (243). Although Alma's concept of lesbians is strikingly homophobic, casting them as scavenging birds of prey, Smith's figuring of lesbianism in *Strange Fruit* seems to suggest that she too perceives of these relationships in similar—if perhaps not so extreme—terms of age and maturity.

Smith's subsequent depictions of lesbianism do little to counter this circumscribed understanding of same-sex desire between women. The homo-eroticism of *One Hour* is between a fifteen-year-old girl and a camp counselor who is nearly a decade older. Even years afterwards, Grace Channing, the young camper, recalls the depth of her feeling for the Woman: "She was tall and beautiful—and could do everything: swim, ride, shoot, paint. . . . She opened up the world for me, I'll leave it at that. . . . I learned from her about tenderness and passion." And yet, when Grace eventually realizes during a school "lecture on 'normal love' that this amazing creature who had seemed to her to have come out of a myth, who did not quite belong in the ordinary world, was nothing but a homosexual," she fears that her desire for this women indicates a crystallizing lesbian identity. As her eventual husband acutely senses, Grace thus acts out of homophobia to orchestrate a liaison that will confirm her heterosexuality. She begs Mark to have sex with her, but he refuses: "When I make love to you it is not going to be a lab experiment. Let's get that straight. That's what you want? not me—but to be sure of yourself? . . . That you're normal?" The couple ultimately does, however, have sex, and Grace enters into a series of fulfilling heterosexual relationships, recalling her desire for the Woman only when news of her suicide arrives. These images thus remain consistent with the psychoanalytic understanding of lesbianism that Smith establishes in *Strange Fruit* and *Killers*. Although desire for other women is a "natural" and understandable stage within southern contexts, it arises out of childish impulses for a surrogate mother and ought eventually to be superseded by mature heterosexual desire, as is the case with Grace Channing. The choices are grim if such a supersession cannot or does not occur: to embrace an ostensibly infantile lesbian identity, as Smith herself seems anxiously to have done, or, like the Woman of *One Hour,* to commit what film critic Vito Russo has termed the "obligatory suicide" for gays and lesbians.[22]

Even in Smith's more private writing throughout her life, she reveals how strongly she was committed to this problematic concept of lesbianism. Her letters repeatedly focus on bonds formed by older women who take advantage of younger girls' crushes. In particular she recalls her years of administering counselors and campers at Laurel Falls:

> I realized then, without much of a psychological vocabulary that some women are dangerous creatures; and I faced the fact that my responsibility was to protect the girls in their emotional growth from the exploitation of such women. That it was much the same as a similar seduction or exploitation made by men. In fact, I have always treated homosexual affairs just as I do heterosexual affairs.

There can't be a double standard: if we don't let the male life guard cuddle up with a fourteen-year-old kid on a camping trip we don't let a grown woman do it. This came as a shocking surprise to the two or three really confirmed homosexual women in my camp. They were shocked at me and my language[,] not at themselves.

As Gladney points out, it was in this paradigm of lesbianism that Smith understood her own early same-sex relationships. "Smith reflected that her four years at the Baltimore YWCA had made her knowledgeable about 'such attachments' and that she herself had been 'moderately involved,'" Gladney offers, "but she had also been aware of the dangers of older women who 'were unscrupulous in playing with the kids' emotions.'"[23]

One can even argue that, despite being virtually the same age, Smith's relationship with Snelling was structured in similar terms. Instead of fulfilling the role of the dependent girl seeking a more mature woman's sexualized maternal love, however, Smith either was—or understood herself to be—this woman to the emotionally weaker and more dependent Snelling, as the cited letters suggest. In this shift of roles from "girl" to "woman," Smith reveals one of the more dramatic shortcomings of her theory of same-sex desire between women. Although she can explain why the "girl" desires the "woman," Smith never fully accounts for the supposedly more mature woman's desire for the younger one. Even if this desire is the persistent longing for maternal comfort, Smith does not explain how the older woman can transfer the source of her gratification to a less-than-maternal younger figure. Smith's understanding of lesbianism thus seems multiply problematic, being simultaneously essentializing, homophobic, and insufficiently explanatory.

And yet Smith's historical context does much to mediate these ostensible shortcomings. Of southern writers at midcentury, she remains virtually alone in depicting same-sex desire between women. Indeed, as the subsequent two chapters argue, even female writers of the day concerned with same-sex desire studiously avoided overt representations of lesbianism, turning instead to carefully generalized encodings of homosexuality, as with Harper Lee, or to desire between men, as with Carson McCullers. Moreover, as the models of same-sex desire offered by Truman Capote, William Goyen, and Richard Wright document, these understandings are always limited by a number of factors, not least of which are autobiographical preoccupations and impositions. To expect Smith's depictions of lesbianism to transcend these limitations is quite simply unfair. Her representations thus seem vexing starting points for the imaginings of southern lesbianism that have circulated since midcentury. Circumscribed though the female sexualities of *Strange Fruit, One Hour,* and *Killers of the Dream* are, they stand as carefully articulated groundbreaking depictions, radical in their openness and provoking in their limitations.

5

Harper Lee and the Destabilization of Heterosexuality

UNLIKE LILLIAN SMITH'S FICTION, which, after its initial notoriety and even infamy, quickly fell out of popular circulation, Harper Lee's *To Kill a Mockingbird* (1960) met with enthusiastic critical and popular reception upon its publication and has remained one of the nation's most pervasive texts. It was, according to the *Commonweal*'s review, "the find of the year," and Robert W. Henderson raved that Lee had written both a "compassionate, deeply moving novel, and a most persuasive plea for racial justice." Almost without exception, reviewers praised her depiction of small-town southern life. Granville Hicks noted her "insight into Southern mores," and Keith Waterhouse, writing from the other side of the Atlantic, offered that "Miss Lee does well what so many American writers do appallingly: she paints a true and lively picture of life in an American small town. And she gives freshness to a stock situation." This "freshness" arises in part, suggested Frank H. Lyell, because Lee avoids the tropes and imagery of the southern gothic. "Maycomb has its share of eccentrics and evil-doers," he admits, "but Miss Lee has not tried to satisfy the current lust for morbid, grotesque tales of Southern depravity." Perhaps recalling *Other Voices, Other Rooms* and *The House of Breath,* a reviewer for *Time* agreed with Lyell, arguing that Lee's novel includes "all of the tactile brilliance and none of the preciosity generally supposed to be standard swamp-warfare issue for Southern writers." "Novelist Lee's prose has an edge that cuts through cant," this reviewer asserted, concluding, "All in all, Scout Finch is fiction's most appealing child since Carson McCullers' Frankie got left behind at the wedding."[1]

These reviewers' criticisms were few and easily dismissed. Critics seemed intent to disregard the possibility that the narrative might be Scout's adult reflections on her childhood rather than a telling of yesterday's events. Hicks thus identified Lee's central problem as "to tell the story she wants and yet to stay within the consciousness of a child," while the hostile reviewer for the *Atlantic Monthly* deemed the narration "frankly and completely impossible." The only other real concern indicted the novel's didacticism, which most reviewers were content merely to note and then dismiss as minor. The reviewer for *Booklist*, for example, concluded, "Despite a melodramatic climax and traces of sermonizing, the characters and locale are depicted with insight and a rare blend of wit and compassion," and *Time*'s granted that, although "a faint catechistic flavor may have been inevitable," "it is faint indeed." The consensus was, as the *Commonweal*'s reviewer put it, that the "author unknown until this book appeared will not soon be forgotten."[2]

Lee was indeed not forgotten, for the novel won the Pulitzer Prize in 1961 and was soon adapted into a screenplay by Horton Foote. The resulting 1962 film starring Gregory Peck met with critical acclaim and simultaneously made Lee's narrative, albeit significantly altered, accessible to a wider audience. Since this time, the novel has been widely taught in American schools, in no small part, Eric Sundquist argues, because of its "admirable moral earnestness" and "comforting sentimentality." To him, as to early reviewers, the book offers "a merciless string of moral lessons" presented through "a model of conventional plot and character" that is nevertheless "an episodic story of wit and charm."[3] Because of this teachable didacticism, thousands of adolescents have been subjected to Lee's less-than-subtle symbolism and Atticus Finch's palatable liberal dicta to his children for social tolerance.

Despite—or perhaps because of—these popular circulations, *To Kill a Mockingbird* has been for the most part critically neglected, typically being dismissed simply as a popular novel or as children's literature. *The History of Southern Literature*, for instance, devotes but a solitary paragraph to the novel. Martha Cook briefly summarizes the plot and, at odds with Sundquist, tersely concludes, "*To Kill a Mockingbird* is most successful in its unsentimental portrayal of enlightened views on the rights of blacks." More substantial critical discussions of the novel remain few, with an ebbing to almost nothing of late. Only two notable exceptions emerge, essays by Sundquist and Claudia Johnson, the latter of which was expanded into the slim *To Kill a Mockingbird: Threatening Boundaries*. And yet these works share a primary focus of contextualizing the novel's circulations of race within larger historical ones of the novel's setting and period of composition, the mid-1930s and the mid- to late-1950s respectively. Both essays approach the novel through the Scottsboro case, the Supreme Court's ruling in *Brown v. Board of Education*, Rosa Parks's bus ride, and the desegregation of the University of Alabama, and thus keep the lens of analysis primarily that of race.[4]

This evolution of critical approaches from initial fanfare at publication to general dismissal to one informed foremost by race should by now be familiar, since such an evolution parallels the shifting approaches to *Strange Fruit* and Lillian Smith's other writing, and both trajectories of critical reception reflect southern literary studies' increased awareness and interrogations of race. As the previous chapter establishes, however, the scholarship on Smith has of late expanded to incorporate other significant critical lenses and those of gender and sexuality in particular. And, as I hope to have shown, *Strange Fruit* and *Killers of the Dream* prove themselves texts subject to such approaches. This chapter argues that *To Kill a Mockingbird* not surprisingly bears comparable richness under such scrutiny.

Just as Lee's novel shares with *Strange Fruit* a narrative structure that privileges racial tensions, with Tom Robinson's trial for miscegenistic rape and his ultimate death paralleling in importance Tracy Deen and Nonnie Anderson's interracial affair and its tragic results, so too does Lee include as significant an array of sexual otherness as does Smith. But, whereas Smith overtly addresses homoerotic desire in Laura Deen, Lee explores sexual difference more obliquely through transgressions of gender, the absence and parody of heterosexual relations, and the symbolic representation of closetedness. What nevertheless emerges in *To Kill a Mockingbird* is a destabilization of heterosexuality and normative gender that seems far more radical, because of its cultural pervasiveness, than the momentary presences of overt same-sex desire in Smith's novel. That is, whereas Smith depicts struggles of isolated lesbians within southern society understood to be as homophobic as it is racist, Lee presents this society to be, without it ever being fully conscious of the fact, already distinctively queer.

Like so much southern literary production during and after World War II, *To Kill a Mockingbird* centrally preoccupies itself with gender transitivity. These violations of normative gender manifest themselves in characters as diverse as Dill Harris, Scout Finch, Miss Maudie Atkinson, and even, to a lesser degree, Atticus Finch, as well as in a number of minor figures. Lee draws attention to such transgressive performances through their alterity to normative ones, such as those of Aunt Alexandra, and by overt communal demands for gender conformity. Lee does not, however, use these transgressions as consistent cultural shorthand for homosexual or proto-homosexual identities, as Capote and Goyen do. Unlike the effeminate Joel Knox and Boy Ganchion, whose narratives culminate in struggles to negotiate and, albeit uneasily, to accept same-sex desire, Lee's gender-transitive characters do not face such moments of crisis. Their narratives end without comparable culminations and thus suggest that she is as interested in gender transitivity when it is not indicative of same-sex desire as when it is, and she seems concerned at broadest with how rarely normative gender is *ever* performed.

Of *To Kill a Mockingbird*'s central trio of young protagonists, only Jem Finch is conventionally gendered, behaving as a southern white boy his age ostensibly ought. In contrast, Scout and Dill struggle with such behaviors and seem more comfortable in gender-transitive roles. Consider first Dill. Lee not only scripts him as effeminate but also underscores his sissiness through the contrast to Jem and his crystallizing masculinity. Although the elder boy is underweight for Maycomb's football team, he nevertheless dwarfs Dill, and even Scout stands almost a head taller. Dill is in fact so small that, when the Finches first encounter him sitting in his aunt's collard patch, "he wasn't much higher than the collards." Scout and Jem are amazed when, after guessing Dill to be four-and-a-half years old based on his size, he informs them he is almost seven. "I'm little but I'm old," Dill demands when Jem offers, "You look right puny for goin' on seven."[5]

Comparisons of Dill and Jem become overt when they offer up their individual sizes and names for inspection, and, given the cultural valorizations of masculinity, Dill fares poorly when placed alongside Jem:

> Jem brushed his hair back to get a better look. "Why don't you come over, Charles Baker Harris?" he said. "Lord, what a name."
>
> "'s not any funnier'n yours. Aunt Rachel says your name's Jeremy Atticus Finch."
>
> Jem scowled. "I'm big enough to fit mine," he said. "Your name's longer'n you are. Bet it's a foot longer."
>
> "Folks call me Dill," said Dill, struggling under the fence. (11)

At least in his own opinion, Jem physically measures up to his full name, whereas Dill, metaphorically a foot deficient, does not and is instead forced into an appropriately truncated nickname.

If Dill's prepubescent body is less than masculine in size, his dress and actions do little to counter this effeminacy. Like Capote's delicate Joel Knox, Dill dresses in clothes perceived to be sissy, wearing "blue linen shorts that buttoned to his shirt" rather than Maycomb County boys' customary overalls. Although perhaps not necessarily feminine, his actions and desires are nevertheless likewise unconventional. He is, Scout says, "a pocket Merlin, whose head teemed with eccentric plans, strange longings, and quaint fancies" (12). Foremost among these fancies is to establish contact with Maycomb's reclusive Boo Radley. After hearing Scout and Jem rehearse communal gossip of Boo, the "Radley Place fascinated Dill" and "drew him as the moon draws water" (12–13). For all the intensity of these longings, however, he is conspicuously cowardly and will go no closer to the Radleys' than the light pole at the corner, and the resulting scenario allows Lee yet another arena to establish Dill's lack of daring in contrast to Jem's bravery. Not surprisingly, it is he rather than Dill who first enters the Radleys' yard and touches the house.

It is common knowledge that, in this characterization of Dill, Lee drew heavily upon Truman Capote's effeminate childhood identity, as he readily acknowledged. In a series of interviews with Lawrence Grobel, Capote reflects on this childhood in Monroeville, Alabama, and recalls his friendship with Nelle Harper Lee and her family: "Mr. and Mrs. Lee, Harper Lee's mother and father, . . . lived very near. Harper Lee was my best friend. Did you ever read her book, *To Kill a Mockingbird?* I'm a character in that book, which takes place in the same small town in Alabama where we lived." He clearly implies Dill, whose childhood replicates Capote's so closely as sketched by biographer Gerald Clarke:

> As the years passed, the differences between him and other boys became even more pronounced: he remained small and pretty as a china doll, and his mannerisms, little things like the way he walked or held himself, started to look odd, unlike those of the other boys. Even his voice began to sound strange, peculiarly babylike and artificial, as if he had unconsciously decided that that part of him, the only part he could stop from maturing, would remain fixed in boyhood forever, reminding him of happier and less confusing times. His face and body belatedly matured, but his way of speaking never did.[6]

With Dill, Lee draws upon not only these generic effeminate mannerisms but also Capote's ubiquitous short pants, his precociousness, his string of surrogate- and stepfathers, and even his distinctive white hair that "stuck to his head like duckfluff" and formed "a cowlick in the center of his forehead" (12).

Although the lascivious photo of Capote on the dust jacket of *Other Voices, Other Rooms* still haunted readers in the 1960s, when *To Kill a Mockingbird* appeared at the beginning of the decade, this image of Capote was but a few short years away from being replaced by comparably vivid others, ones that readers of Lee's novel might, if they knew Dill's biographical basis in Capote, bring with them to the text and thus to their understanding of Dill. In 1966 Capote not only published to wild acclaim *In Cold Blood* but, to celebrate the novel's completion, also hosted the Black and White Ball at Manhattan's Plaza Hotel. The publicity of each event was phenomenal, but that of the ball in particular inundated Americans with images of Capote's over-the-top campy effeminacy. As the photo spreads in *Life* and other magazines attested, the evening was, in Capote confidante Slim Keith's terms, "the biggest and best goddamned party that anybody had ever heard of" despite being "given by a funny-looking, strange little man."[7]

Having thus captured the public eye, Capote refused to leave it. In his remaining years, as his creativity and productivity waned, he shamelessly compensated by crafting an eccentric public personality for himself, which he flaunted, such as during his recurring appearances on Johnny Carson's *The Tonight Show*. As with those persons who saw the photographs of the Black and White Ball, Carson's viewers internalized images of Capote as an unabashed aging gossipy queen or, as Kenneth Reed has characterized Capote, a "madcap social butterfly and late evening television chatterbox."[8] Thus, for Lee's readers aware of Dill's basis in Capote, these images of him circulating throughout the 1960s and 1970s extratextually reinforced Dill's effeminacy.

And yet it is not Dill's gender violations but rather Scout's that command the most stringent communal surveillance and discipline. Her extended family and community—virtually one and the same—incessantly work to force her out of her tomboyish ways and into those appropriate for a young southern girl of the 1930s. As Claudia Johnson notes, however, Maycomb faces no small task. Scout abandons her feminine, given Christian name of "Jean Louise" for an adventurous and boyish nickname, invariably chooses overalls over dresses, and demands an air rifle for Christmas rather than a doll so that she can, among other things, terrorize her cousin.[9] Only rarely does she abandon such behavior to aspire to perform feminine roles, and these aspirations usually meet with scant success. Scout recalls, for instance, her "burning ambition to grow up and twirl in the Maycomb County High School band" but notes that she develops this talent only "to where I could throw up a stick and almost catch it coming down" (105).

Just as Lee uses Jem as a foil to Dill to establish his effeminacy, so too does she present Aunt Alexandra, Atticus's sister, to force Scout's tomboy-ishness into sharp relief. Alexandra is the period's model of white southern femininity and casts a figure reminiscent of Alma Deen, Smith's fictionalization of the stereotypic frigid southern mother of a decade earlier. Like Alma, Alexandra subjects her body to fashion's requisite contortions so that it may be read as feminine. "She was not fat, but solid," Scout remembers of her aunt, "and she chose protective garments that drew up her bosom to giddy heights, pinched in her waist, flared out her rear, and managed to suggest that Aunt Alexandra's was once an hour-glass figure. From any angle, it was formidable" (130). Her manners and actions are comparably ladylike, and Maycomb responds to them with considerably more appreciation than Scout does: "To all parties present and participating in the life of the county, Aunt Alexandra was one of the last of her kind: she had river-boat, boarding-school manners; let any moral come along and she would uphold it; she was born in the objective case; she was an incurable gossip. . . . She was never bored, and given the slightest chance she would exercise her royal prerogative: she would arrange, advise, caution, and warn" (131). "Had I ever harbored the mystical notions about mountains that seem to obsess lawyers and judges," Scout offers when recalling her aunt, "Aunt Alexandra would have been analogous to Mount Everest: throughout my early life, she was cold and there" (82). Yet, because of the very aspects of this personality that Scout finds so distasteful, the town welcomes Alexandra, allowing her to fit "into the world of Maycomb like a hand into a glove" (134).

Just as Aunt Alexandra ascribes to and performs proper southern white femininity, so too does she demand the same of others—and the transgressive Scout in particular. As Johnson observes, "Aunt Alexandra brings with her a system of codification and segregation of the human family according to class, race, and in Scout's case, sex."[10] Alexandra is correspondingly adamant about enforcing normative mappings of gender onto biological sex. Lee is hardly subtle in her condemnations of such strictures, manipulating readers' sympathies through both Scout's first-person narration and its rehearsals of Alexandra's seemingly endless carping about Scout's appearance and behavior. A description of Finch's Landing, where Alexandra and her husband live, allows Scout to clarify:

> Aunt Alexandra was fanatical on the subject of my attire. I could not possibly hope to be a lady if I wore breeches; when I said I could do nothing in a dress, she said I wasn't supposed to be doing things that required pants. Aunt Alexandra's vision of my deportment involved playing with small stoves, tea sets, and wearing the Add-A-Pearl necklace she gave me when I was born; furthermore, I should be a ray of sunshine in my father's lonely life. I suggested I could be a ray of sunshine in pants just as well, but Aunty said that one had to behave like a sunbeam, that I was born good but had grown progressively worse every year. (85–86)

When Alexandra moves in with the Finches for the summer of Tom Robinson's trial, she immediately launches a protracted assault on Scout: "'Put my bag in the front bedroom, Calpurnia,' was the first thing Aunt Alexandra said. 'Jean Louise, stop scratching your head,' was the second thing she said" (129).

The women of Aunt Alexandra's missionary circle are no less relentless in both providing suitable models for Scout and attacking her when she does not internalize them. On the afternoon of Alexandra's tea, Miss Stephanie Crawford pounces immediately upon Scout's entrance into the room. Cattily observing that her presence at Tom's trial has violated traditional separations of spheres, Miss Stephanie demands before the entire missionary circle, "Whatcha going to be when you grow up, Jean Louise? A lawyer?" and responds before Scout can answer, "Why shoot, I thought you wanted to be a lawyer, you've already commenced going to court" (232). When Scout mildly suggests that she wants to be "just a lady," a rebuffed Miss Stephanie shifts from cajoling to outright chastising: "Miss Stephanie eyed me suspiciously, decided that I meant no impertinence, and contented herself with, 'Well, you won't get very far until you start wearing dresses more often'" (233).

Although most readers already sympathize with Scout, Lee reinforces the dismissal of Miss Stephanie and the rest of the missionary circle's criticisms by undercutting the model of their supposedly natural southern femininity. As Scout and the women themselves realize, there is little natural about them at all. Their painstakingly crafted bodies and carefully orchestrated acts and gestures instead attempt to pass as natural or, at worst, artfully artless constructions. "The ladies were cool in fragile pastel prints," Scout remembers; "most of them were heavily powdered but unrouged; the only lipstick in the room was Tangee Natural. Cutex Natural sparkled on their fingernails, but some of the younger ladies wore Rose. They smelled heavenly" (232). As Lee emphasizes with these brand names, Alexandra and her neighbors insist on wearing only "natural" lipstick and fingernail polish and opt for powder but no rouge, since they have communally—although, from a logical standpoint, somewhat arbitrarily—agreed that the bodily alterations of powder do not call attention to and thus expose the artifice of femininity as rouge does. And yet "Tangee Natural" lipstick and "Cutex Natural" fingernail polish are not natural. They are commercially designated, appearance-altering products named to assist women in their efforts to perpetuate the illusion of expressing an inherent femininity. Thus, in that this description makes overt the women's efforts to disguise the feminizations of their bodies, Lee exposes their attempts to conceal the genesis of gender. With the revelation, the implied logical basis of Alexandra's and others' demands for Scout's femininity—that she express the natural gender with which she is born—crumbles, since readers now see the full complicity of these women in their tacit agreements to mystify the immediate cultural origins of femininity.

As this terminology suggests, with Lee's revelation of the missionary circle's conspiracy, she anticipates in fiction precisely what Judith Butler, building upon the work of other theorists and historians of gender and sexuality, has cogently argued concerning the deployment of gender. Like Lee, Butler interrogates—to dismiss as false—gender's presumed expressivity, the enactment of an interior essential gender. In simplified terms, Butler argues that, because gender is performed rather than expressed, "there is no preexisting identity by which an act or attribute might be measured." If such is indeed the case, "there would be no true or false, real or distorted acts of gender, and the postulation of a true gender identity would be revealed as a regulatory fiction." To prevent precisely this revelation, however, gender functions to eradicate signs of its performativity: "Gender is, thus, a construction that regularly conceals its genesis; the tacit collective agreement to perform, produce, and sustain discrete and polar genders as cultural fictions is obscured by the credibility of those productions—and the punishments that attend not agreeing to believe in them; the construction 'compels' our belief in its necessity and naturalness. The historical possibilities materialized

through various corporeal styles are nothing other than those punitively reg-
ulated cultural fictions alternately embodied and deflected under duress."[11]
To Kill a Mockingbird reveals both these concealments, as symbolized in the
accoutrements of "natural" beautification, and, through the disciplinary actions and demands exercised on Scout, the punishments for disbelief in the
naturalness of the performances of polarized genders. Lee's readers thus
have the potential to realize just as forcefully as Butler's that white southern
femininity, like any other sort, is but "a regulatory fiction."

Such observations from Butler concerning gender's performativity are
not, however, the most innovative components of her argument. Both the
fame and critical usefulness of *Gender Trouble* arise primarily out of Butler's
articulations of how the parody of drag has the potential to expose gender
performativity's reification as expressivity: "As much as drag creates a unified
picture of 'woman' (what its critics often oppose), it also reveals the distinctness of those aspects of gendered experience which are falsely natural-
ized as a unity through the regulatory fiction of heterosexual coherence. *In
imitating gender, drag implicitly reveals the imitative structure of gender itself—
as well as its contingency.* . . . In place of the law of heterosexual coherence,
we see sex and gender denaturalized by means of a performance which
avows their distinctness and dramatizes the cultural mechanism of their fab-
ricated unity." Butler does not, however, champion drag's parody as invariably subversive, as some critics have accused. "Parody by itself is not subversive," she offers, "and there must be a way to understand what makes certain
kinds of parodic repetitions effectively disruptive, truly troubling, and which
repetitions become domesticated and recirculated as instruments of cultural
hegemony." Consistently tentative in her claims outside the hypothetical
and conditional, Butler hazards only that a crucial element for the subversion of gender is the exposure of its repetitive structure. Yet this is the site
where all gender transformation, whether ostensibly subversive or not, must
originate: "The possibilities of gender transformation are to be found precisely in the arbitrary relation of such acts, in the possibility of a failure to
repeat, a de-formity, or a parodic repetition that exposes that phantasmatic
effect of abiding identity as a politically tenuous construction." Nevertheless, in that any transformation calls into question "the abiding gendered
self," any of the acts of Butler's catalogue—and not merely parodic repetitions such as drag recognized as such—has subversive potential.[12]

Lee's scene of the missionary circle's tea would seem to bolster Butler's

suggestion that a failure to repeat stylized acts need not necessarily be parodic to expose the performativity of gender. In her description of the ladies'
appearances, Scout notes that "Cutex Natural sparkled in their fingernails,
but some of the younger ladies wore Rose." One could hardy say that, in
having made this choice of fingernail polish, the younger women self-
consciously parody femininity as Butler maintains drag performers to do. Indeed, these women cannot function in the same manner, since Butler understands much of drag queen's subversiveness to arise from their anatomically
male bodies performing femininity. "If the anatomy of the performer is already distinct from the gender of the performer, and both of these are distinct from the gender of the performance," Butler clarifies, "then the performance suggests a dissonance not only between sex and performance,
but sex and gender, and gender and performance." [13] Because the younger
women at Alexandra's tea are, in contrast to drag queens, neither anatomically male nor knowingly parodic, no such valorizable dissonance of gender,
sex, and performance can emerge from them if one retains the criteria of Butler's scenario. Nevertheless, these women's deviations from applying Cutex
Natural to their nails draw attention to the false naturalness of the other
women's bodies, whose nails sparkle as brilliantly as those painted Rose.

In addition to these women with the red fingernail polish, Scout herself
disrupts the illusions of gender's expressivity in this scene. Until this point,
she, like the novel's other gender-transitive characters, has loosely paralleled
the drag queens of Butler's discussion, destabilizing gender through vaguely
parodic performances of the "opposite" gender. Whereas the drag queens often satirically imitate femininity, Scout parodies—although far less self-
consciously—masculinity, and one might argue that this parody operates
with the subversiveness that Butler feels it capable. As is not the case with
the scarlet-nailed ladies, because Scout's anatomy is distinct from the gender
of her performances, they make public the same dissonances of corporeality
as arise from drag performances. In the scene of Alexandra's tea, however,
Lee gives Butler's theories an additional twist and suggests that a comparable
disruption emerges when the drag artist attempts to perform the gender
"correct" for his or, in this case, her anatomy. Scout follows her aunt's dictates
and wears a "pink Sunday dress, shoes, and a petticoat" (231), casting a comic
figure not unlike McCullers's Frankie when dressed for the wedding. Although this attire will supposedly correct Scout's gender trouble in the community's opinion, recollected images of Scout in her customary drag of over-

alls and her internalization of masculine acts and gestures so denaturalize the feminine clothes that communal representatives such as Miss Stephanie and even Miss Maudie can only focus on the absent overalls: "'You're mighty dressed up, Miss Jean Louise,' she said. 'Where are your britches today?'" (232). Scout's appearance in the pink dress thus becomes the equivalent of the drag queen abandoning her sequined gown and pumps to sport a tool belt and work boots or, as *La Cage aux Folles* and *The Birdcage* would have it, John Wayne's jeans, Stetson, and swagger. In these cases, the alterity of performances of normative gender to drag's pervading stylized repetitions establishes the former as, if anything, even more of a drag performance than the latter and thus, in Scout's case, ironically enables her enactment of *normative* gender to destabilize femininity.

Although Lee's readers may savor these destabilizations, they go largely unnoticed or ignored by characters within the novel, and the demands for gender conformity persist, both from the missionary society and elsewhere. Indeed, it is no one from Aunt Alexandra's circle who most dramatically antagonizes Scout. Mrs. Henry Lafayette Dubose, another of the Finches' neighbors, is fierce to the point of being unladylike herself in attempts to coerce Scout into appropriate feminine behavior. Secure in her age and infirmity, Mrs. Dubose has no qualms about public outbursts, as Scout recalls: "Jem and I hated her. If she was on the porch when we passed, we would be raked by her wrathful gaze, subjected to ruthless interrogation regarding our behavior, and given a melancholy prediction on what we would amount to when we grew up, which was always nothing. We had long ago given up the idea of walking past her house on the opposite side of the street; that only made her raise her voice and let the whole neighborhood in on it." In keeping with these brazen outbursts, Mrs. Dubose rejects Alexandra's tactics of wheedling and nagging to alter Scout's behavior and instead opts for cruel shame. The old woman repeatedly resurrects the image of Atticus's dead wife to Jem and Scout, asserting that a "lovelier lady than our mother had never lived" (104) and that her children are a disgrace to her memory. When the shame of not meeting her mother's presumed expectations fails to drive Scout out of her overalls, however, Mrs. Dubose does not hesitate to employ fear: "'And *you*—' she pointed an arthritic finger at me—'what are you doing in those overalls? You should be in a dress and camisole, young lady! You'll grow up waiting on tables if somebody doesn't change your ways—a Finch waiting on tables at the O.K. Café—hah!'" (105–6).

Mrs. Dubose also allows Lee to continue yet another means of damning those persons who would enforce normative gender. Because the novel most centrally calls for an end to southern racism through the manipulation of a sympathetic African American martyr and benign aristocratic paternalism, Lee's narrative invites readers to evaluate the racial attitudes of each of the white characters and judge them racist or not. Although at times she seeks to complicate this binarism, she marks most of the persons who demand Scout's gender conformity—Alexandra, Mrs. Dubose, and the majority of the missionary circle—as both lingering representatives of the antebellum slave-owning South and undeniable racists. While Atticus and Jack Finch abandon the Landing to pursue careers at various times in Montgomery, Nashville, and even Boston, Alexandra chooses to remain on the family's cotton plantation, surrounded by reminders of her ancestor's slave-holding and his own strictures for feminine behavior. Scout recalls both the "old cotton landing, where Finch Negroes had loaded bales and produce, unloaded blocks of ice, flour and sugar, farm equipment, and feminine apparel," and Simon Finch's unique home: "The internal arrangements of the Finch house were indicative of Simon's guilelessness and the absolute trust with which he regarded his offspring . . . [T]he daughters' rooms could be reached only by one staircase, Welcome's room and the guestroom only by another. The Daughters' Staircase was in the ground-floor bedroom of their parents, so Simon always knew the hours of his daughters' nocturnal comings and goings" (84). Via these two observations, Lee suggests how strongly she holds antebellum white southern femininity to have been contingent upon the enslavement of African Americans. It is they who bear the physical burden of unloading the feminine apparel at the landing, that which can be afforded in the first place only because of slave labor's ostensible profits. Likewise, it is this labor that allows Simon Finch to construct a house specifically designed to regulate his daughters' affairs.

Just as Alexandra has retained Simon's sexist notions of gender as represented in the Daughters' Staircase, she has also seemingly retained elements of the racism implicit to this enslavement of African Americans. For instance, she stews when Atticus decides to defend an African American accused of raping a white woman, and Scout trounces her annoying cousin only when he repeats his grandmother's characterization of her brother as a "nigger-lover" (87). Moreover, Alexandra reveals Lee's stance that white southern femininity's contingency on the debasement of African Americans persists in the 1930s. Consider the scene in which Alexandra arrives at the Finches' for the summer. Her command concerning Scout's unladylike behavior follows her initial order for Calpurnia to put away Alexandra's suitcase. As the close proximity of these commands suggests, Alexandra's authority in her dictates to Scout arises primarily out of her own feminine model, and yet this model remains valid only so long as Calpurnia or another black person frees Alexandra from unfeminine physical exertion.

Mrs. Dubose, on the other hand, is a literal artifact of the antebellum South, born just before or during the Civil War. She supposedly keeps "a CSA pistol concealed among her numerous shawls and wraps," and whiffs of earlier slave-holdings permeate her employment of African American servants, for she retains "a Negro girl in constant attendance" yet allows Jessie little of the respect that Atticus has for Calpurnia (103–4). With these links to the stereotypic Old South and its Confederate culmination, it is not surprising that Mrs. Dubose offers opinions similarly conservative to Alexandra's concerning both race and gender. In virtually the same breath that she condemns Scout's overalls, Mrs. Dubose seethes about Atticus "lawing for niggers": "'Yes indeed, what has this world come to when a Finch goes against his raising? I'll tell you!' She put her hand to her mouth. When she drew it away, it trailed a long silver thread of saliva. 'Your father's no better than the niggers and trash he works for!'" (106).

Although Mrs. Dubose's racism is overt and vociferous, Lee even more forcefully condemns that of Alexandra's missionary circle, which is all the more distasteful because of the women's hypocritical investments in so-called Christian uplift. Grace Merriweather, "the most devout lady in Maycomb," sponsors a local program after having offered her profuse support of Christianity's shouldering of the white man's burden: "I said to him, 'Mr. Everett,' I said, 'the ladies of the Maycomb Alabama Methodist Episcopal Church South are behind you one hundred per cent.' That's what I said to him. And you know, right then and there I made a pledge in my heart. I said to myself, when I go home I'm going to give a course on the Mrunas and bring J. Grimes Everett's message to Maycomb and that's just what I'm doing" (233–34). Immediately after this comment, however, she carps about the responses of Maycomb's African Americans to Tom's trial. "[T]he cooks and field hands are just dissatisfied, but they're settling down now—they grumbled all next day after that trial," Mrs. Merriweather explains to Scout. "I tell you there's nothing more distracting than a sulky darky. Their mouths go down to here. Just ruins your day to have one of 'em in the kitchen" (234). Gertrude Farrow, "the second most devout lady in Maycomb," responds with her own complaints, maintaining, "We can educate 'em till we're blue in the face, we can try till we drop to make Christians out of 'em, but there's no lady safe in her bed these nights" (235). With this smug paternalism, fear of black male sexuality, and hypocritical racial enlightenment, Lee underscores that she, unlike Smith, does not consider southern white women less racist than their male counterparts because of an inherent female morality, and tempts readers to dismiss all that these women value and represent, including traditional white southern femininity.

With the exception of the women of the missionary circle, Lee does not, however, allow readers wholly to dismiss these racist characters and instead elicits some sympathy for Mrs. Dubose and Alexandra in particular. Part 1 closes with Atticus's articulation of Mrs. Dubose's heroism in defeating her addiction to morphine: "I wanted you to see what real courage is, instead of getting the idea that courage is a man with a gun in his hand. It's when you know you're licked before you begin but you begin anyway and you see it through no matter what. You rarely win, but sometimes you do. Mrs. Dubose won, all ninety-eight pounds of her." As Atticus suggests to Jem, despite her racism, Mrs. Dubose is "a great lady" and "the bravest person I ever knew" (116). Alexandra garners comparable sympathy in the novel's final pages. Even if she does not necessarily counter her previous racism, she is nevertheless shaken at news of Tom's death and concedes that Atticus has done the right thing, albeit to little avail in the community's eyes: "I mean this town. They're perfectly willing to let him do what they're too afraid to do themselves—it might lose 'em a nickel. They're perfectly willing to let him wreck his health doing what they're afraid to do" (239).

With this confession, Alexandra hints at the complexity of her character. She by no means replicates her brother's saintly attitudes and actions, and, even in the emotional aftermath of hearing of Tom's death, Alexandra tersely says of Atticus, "I can't say I approve of everything he does" (239). Nevertheless, she distinguishes herself from her catty guests who, rather than recognize the significance of Atticus's actions, hold them to be misguided. Yet this ambiguous relation to race has been anticipated by Alexandra's capricious relation to gender. As Scout knows all too well, Alexandra is "fanatical" that her niece appear and behave femininely. However, Alexandra allows and even fosters significant transgressions from normative masculinity in her grandson Francis. Exasperated that her husband's shiftlessness excludes the chivalry necessary to secure her position on the figurative pedestal of white southern femininity as delineated by Smith, Scott, and Jones, Alexandra inculcates in Francis behavior that is strikingly different from his grandfather's and, as a result, hardly masculine. "Grandma's a wonderful cook," Francis boasts to Scout. "She's gonna teach me how." When Scout giggles at this image, Francis counters, "Grandma says all men should learn to cook, that men oughta be careful with their wives and wait on 'em when they don't feel good" (86–87). Alexandra thus reveals her investment in white southern femininity to be so strong that she is willing to sacrifice corresponding southern masculinity so that the former's delicacy not be impinged upon. The result is that Francis Hancock, grandson of one of the novel's most outspoken gender conformists, is a gossiping sissy who slicks back his hair and, as his Christmas wish list reveals, craves the clothes of a fashionable young dandy: "a pair of knee-pants, a red leather booksack, five shirts and an untied bow tie" (85). As his sexually ambivalent name suggests, he does not have a strong masculine identity but instead, at his grandmother's urging, a Wildean penchant for foppery, one often culturally understood to designate effeminacy and, as Capote suggests, homosexuality.

Despite this active promotion of gender transitivity in Francis and hints of racial enlightenment at the novel's conclusion, Alexandra nevertheless remains too exclusively invested in traditional white southern femininity to emerge as a viable alternative to Mrs. Dubose and the women of the missionary society. Lee instead posits Miss Maudie Atkinson, arguably the novel's most sympathetic white adult female character, as the preferable model of southern womanhood for both Scout and readers. Unlike Alexandra, Miss Maudie is not overtly distraught about the transgressive performances of gender and indeed has constructed a public identity contingent upon adroit manipulations of such performances. This is not to suggest, however, that she jettisons social conventions. When she chooses, she can rival her neighbors in her successful enactment of white southern femininity. Just as she appears on her front porch each evening freshly bathed to "reign over the street in magisterial beauty" (47), Miss Maudie can also smoothly integrate herself into that larger world "where on its surface fragrant ladies rocked slowly, fanned gently, and drank cool water" (236). She in fact maintains this role when others falter, as when she coolly orchestrates the remainder of the tea after Alexandra crumbles at news of Tom Robinson's death.

Although not conveyed in the film adaptation, Miss Maudie is, however, "a chameleon lady," and these polished feminine performances are checked by others as transgressive as any of Scout's: working "in her flower beds in an old straw hat and men's coveralls" (46), thrusting out her bridge-work with a click of her tongue as a sign of friendship, nursing charred azaleas at the sacrifice of her hands, and even meditating arson. Indeed, some of the most striking imagery associated with Miss Maudie is blatantly martial, casting her in the role of biblical warrior:

> If she found a blade of nut grass in her yard it was like the Second Battle of the Marne: she swooped down upon it with a tin tub and subjected it to blasts from beneath with a poisonous substance she said was so powerful it'd kill us all if we didn't stand out of the way.
>
> "Why can't you just pull it up?" I asked, after witnessing a prolonged campaign against a blade not three inches high.
>
> "Pull it up, child, pull it up?" She picked up the limp sprout and squeezed her thumb up its tiny stalk. Microscopic grains oozed out. "Why, one sprig of nut grass can ruin a whole yard. Look here. When it comes fall this dries up and the wind blows it all over Maycomb County!" Miss Maudie's face likened such an occurrence unto an Old Testament pestilence. (47)

Minor though this battle may seem, Lee's martial imagery and Miss Maudie's transformation into a prophet of the Old Testament stand in marked contrast to her graceful offerings of dewberry tarts at Alexandra's tea. With her public image thus in constant flux between these two gender norms, the "chameleon" Miss Maudie offers the most appropriate identity for Scout and Jem's "absolute morphodite" (72) snowman to assume. Throughout its construction, the snowman evinces an uneasy coexistence of femininity and masculinity, resembling first Miss Stephanie Crawford and then Mr. Avery. This irresolution is rendered understandable only when Jem sticks Miss Maudie's sun hat on the snowman's head and thrusts her hedge clippers in the crook of its arm. Insofar as the feminine and masculine already commingle in the culturally readable Miss Maudie, the ambiguously sexed and gendered Absolute Morphodite can also be made coherently legible by giving it her personality.

Lee suggests several things with Miss Maudie's "chameleon" self-fashioning, not least of which is that she may function comparably to Scout to disrupt reified southern white femininity. With her constant alternating performances of masculinity and femininity, clad one hour in the work clothes of a manual laborer and the next in Mrs. Dubose's requisite dress and camisole, Miss Maudie undercuts the constancy with which the rest of the missionary circle express their femininity. That is, her public performances, deliberately staged for the entire neighborhood's viewing, make overt the comparable manipulations of gender that the other women wish not to be exposed as so easily mutable. Yet, because these alternations have grown predictable, Miss Maudie's performances do not disrupt with the force that, say, Scout's unexpectedly feminine presence at the tea does. As Butler acknowledges, any stylized repetition of acts—even initially transgressive and/or subversive ones—can be domesticated through their very repetition, since such predictable recurrences promote reification. Miss Maudie's presence nevertheless suggests how token a normatively gendered performance may be and still appease such cultural strictures as Lee understands them. Because Miss Maudie periodically participates in such ostensibly gender-reifying rituals as the missionary tea, even while she understands such participation to be simple performances, her neighbors are content to allow her otherwise inexcusable transgressions of gender. Thus, whereas Butler emphasizes almost exclusively the punishments associated with a rejection of gender's necessity and naturalness, Lee not only identifies such punishments in Scout but also counters in Miss Maudie ways in which such discipline might be negotiated and avoided. One does not have to agree to believe in gender's expressivity, Lee offers, so long as one condescends to *perform* as if one does at strategically appropriate times. Indeed, as the women of the missionary circle prove, such belief is the exception rather than the rule.

Lee further promotes readers' investments in Miss Maudie and her alternatives to southern white femininity by having her harbor little of the overt racism of Alexandra, Mrs. Dubose, and the missionary circle. With the exception of Atticus, Miss Maudie emerges—even if problematically— as the novel's most racially enlightened white character, one of the "handful of people in this town who say that fair play is not marked White Only; the handful of people who say a fair trial is for everybody, not just us; the handful of people with enough humility to think, when they look at a Negro, there but for the Lord's kindness am I" (239).[14] She realizes how pervasively racism permeates Maycomb and therefore both supports and is grateful for Atticus's stirring defense of Tom Robinson: "I was sittin' there on the porch last night, waiting. I waited and waited to see you all come down the sidewalk, and as I waited I thought, Atticus Finch won't win, he can't win, but he's the only man in these parts who can keep a jury out so long in a case like that. And I thought to myself, well, we're making a step—it's just a baby-step, but it's a step" (218–19). And yet, for all her interest in the trial's outcome, Miss Maudie nevertheless refuses to participate in the spectacle. In its aftermath, however, she abandons what may be perceived of until this point as a passive role and deftly squelches the missionary circle's attack on Atticus. Lee has Miss Maudie willing to condescend to participate in the women's charade of femininity but unwilling to tolerate their racism when they attack the sole figure to assume a public—and, in Miss Maudie's opinion, truly Christian—stance for legal equality.

Just as Miss Maudie nurses little racism in comparison with her neighbors, she also holds none of Maycomb's morbid curiosity about the Radleys. When Scout rehearses the lurid tales of Boo to Miss Maudie, she tersely dismisses the gossip as "three-fourths colored folks and one-fourth Stephanie Crawford" (50) and counters by emphasizing tolerance toward Arthur's right to do as he pleases. In a tactic similar to Atticus's suggestion that, to understand a communal outsider or misfit, one must "climb into his skin and walk around in it" (34), Miss Maudie urges Scout to consider Arthur's perspective: "'Arthur Radley just stays in the house, that's all,' said Miss Maudie. 'Wouldn't you stay in the house if you didn't want to come out?'" (48). And yet Miss Maudie sympathizes with Arthur having to function within a family and community intent on controlling and demonizing him. When Scout asks if Arthur is crazy, " Miss Maudie shook her head. 'If he's not he should be by now. The things that happen to people we never really know" (50). Miss Maudie thus proves as exemplary in her tolerance of Arthur Radley's communal otherness as she does with differences of gender and race and emerges to readers precisely as Scout has characterized: "the best lady I know" (49).

Miss Maudie's male counterpart is, of course, Atticus Finch, the novel's almost sainted hero. He not only displays the same ostensibly enlightened attitudes as Miss Maudie but also, via privilege conferred on him by masculine spheres, works publicly for social equality and tolerance. His defense of Tom Robinson is the most significant of these efforts, but Atticus also proves himself equally determined to accord Arthur Radley some degree of communal respect. When he catches Scout, Jem, and Dill "busily playing Chapter XXV, Book II of One Man's Family" (44), their improvised pro-

duction of the Radleys' fabled saga, Atticus immediately halts the performance, just as he later interrupts the children's attempt to leave a note for Boo.
"Son," Atticus says to Jem in perhaps the harshest tones Lee ever allows her
hero, "I'm going to tell you something and tell you one time: stop torment-
ing that man" (53).

Given that Atticus shares these attitudes with Miss Maudie, it is not
surprising that he also is both tolerant of gender nonconformity and, in the
opinion of his family and community, something less than masculine himself. His heroism, like that of Mrs. Dubose, is not contingent upon being "a
man with a gun in his hand." Quite the contrary, Atticus avoids stereotypically male violence to resolve conflict and uses a gun only when forced, as in
the case of the rabid dog. Thus, just as Miss Maudie adroitly deploys her
femininity, so too does Atticus strategically choose when a masculine performance is in order, content in the meantime to forego such behavior. "He
did not do the things our schoolmates' fathers did," Scout recalls; "he never
went hunting, he did not play poker or fish or drink or smoke. He sat in the
livingroom and read" (94). Indeed, Atticus's failure to engage in such activities causes considerable anxiety in his children. "[T]here was nothing Jem
or I could say about him when our classmates said, '*My* father——,'" Scout
confesses. Instead, having internalized the community's rigidly binaristic
understandings of gender, she and Jem feel this failure "reflected upon his
abilities and manliness" (93).

No matter how reassuringly different from the rest of Maycomb in either their ethics or performances of gender, Atticus and Miss Maudie are
nevertheless problematic characters. With the capacity for manifold tolerances located within solitary figures such as these, Lee seems to posit an
identity inherently resistant to any oppression of any cultural difference.
That is, she suggests that all tolerances are congruent, that is if one is tolerant of racial otherness, one will of course be equally tolerant of gendered
otherness and even that difference that can only be speculated about, as in
the case of Boo Radley. In contrast to this understanding, tolerance might
more appropriately be considered similar to oppression as Sedgwick has the-
orized it. As cited earlier, she reminds that "it was the long, painful realization, *not* that all oppressions are congruent, but that they are *differently*
structured and so must intersect in complex embodiments." Just as each oppression is thus "likely to be in a uniquely indicative relation to certain distinctive nodes of cultural organization," so too is each tolerance likely to re-

flect a potentially singular organization.[15] Therefore, despite certain similarities, tolerance of racial otherness is not the same as tolerance of gendered otherness, yet Lee's characters tend to obfuscate these differences and thus leave readers with an oversimplified representation of social mechanisms and interactions.

Regardless of this oversimplification, what emerges from Lee's novel is a portrait of a southern community in which performances of normative gender are surprisingly the exceptions rather than the rule. Not only is the narrator in whom readers so heavily invest a tomboy, but the two most sympathetic adult white characters are figures who defy normative gender roles and instead perform "appropriately" only to strategic ends. Those characters who do subscribe to these roles are hardly sympathetic and racist almost without exception. Moreover, in Lee's handling of them, these same characters unwittingly reveal the constructedness of gender that they seek to conceal and, in the case of Alexandra, even foster overt transgressions. Maycomb is thus, for all its demands for gender conformity, an arena of dizzyingly varied gender performances.

Although perhaps not at first apparent, just as *To Kill a Mockingbird* is a novel permeated with valorized gender transitivity, it is also remarkably deplete of heterosexuality as conventionally represented through traditional marriage. As Claudia Johnson reminds, unmarried people—widows and widowers, spinsters and bachelors—fill the Finches' neighborhood: Atticus, Miss Maudie, Miss Stephanie, Miss Rachel, Miss Caroline, Mrs. Dubose, Mr. Avery, and both of the Radley sons, Nathan and Arthur. One is, in fact, hard-pressed to name a character besides Tom Robinson who both figures centrally in the novel and is within a stable marriage. And yet Tom's marriage seems readable as primarily part of Lee's heavy-handed characterization of him as "a quiet, respectable, humble Negro" (207) who heads a harmonious nuclear family of "clean-living folks" (80) and thus contrasts to the incestuous widowed Bob Ewell. If anything, to shore up how differently Tom and Helen live from the Ewells in their dump, Lee succumbs to stereotypes of African Americans when she sketches crowds of black children playing marbles in the Robinsons' front yard and the little girl standing picturesquely in the cabin's door: "Dill said her hair was a wad of tiny stiff pigtails, each ending in a bright bow. She grinned from ear to ear and walked toward our father, but she was too small to navigate the steps. Dill said Atticus went to her, took off his hat, and offered her his finger. She grabbed it and he eased her down the steps" (242). Indeed, such images are only slightly removed from those of happy plantation darkies that permeate earlier southern literature.

Neither the immediate Finch household nor its larger familial connections offer such a warm portrait of connubial life. Scout explains that Atticus is a widower, his wife having died only a few years into the marriage: "She was a Graham from Montgomery; Atticus met her when he was first elected to the state legislature. He was middle-aged then, she was fifteen years his junior. Jem was the product of their first year of marriage; four years later I was born, and two years later our mother died from a sudden heart attack" (10). That Atticus, already late to marry by Maycomb's standards, allows so many years to elapse without remarrying is something of a travesty in communal opinion. Amid her demands that Scout begin wearing dresses and that Atticus stop defending "niggers," Mrs. Dubose repeatedly offers that "it was quite a pity that our father had not remarried after our mother's death" (104). Despite these communal injunctions, however, Atticus shows no signs of taking another wife and instead seems content to function as the sole parent to his children.

Unlike Atticus, his younger brother, John Hale Finch, never marries and, although somewhat casually, evinces a phobia of reproduction. "I shall never marry," Jack wearily confesses to his brother after mishandling Scout's conflict with Francis. "I might have children" (91). Indeed, Lee offers in Jack a character readable as gay by persons understanding sexuality within a rigid binarism of heterosexuality and homosexuality and thus assuming an absence of the former to designate the presence of the latter. Moreover, Jack's life parallels those of Goyen's gay Folner and Smith's lesbian Laura, and all three characters seem fictional counterparts to queer persons discussed by historians such as George Chauncey, John D'Emilio, and Allan Bérubé. Like so many of these persons at midcentury, Jack is an aspiring professional who leaves familial constraints to study and live in a large urban area and thereby minimize small-town life. After finishing medical studies in Boston, Jack returns not to Maycomb but rather to Nashville and visits his family in Alabama only once a year at Christmas. He remains a bachelor at almost forty and has as his only acknowledged companion a much-doted-upon cat. When, during one of his visits, Jack offers to show snapshots of Rose Aylmer, Scout explains that the cat is "a beautiful yellow female Uncle Jack said was one of the few women he could stand permanently" (83). But even if Lee does not intend Jack to be read as gay, and readers do not understand him as such, he nevertheless stands as yet another character whom Lee chooses to have uninvolved in heterosexual marriage during the course of the novel.

Jack further disrupts communal heteronormativity with his parody of its courtship. Scout recalls the performance he gives with the help of Miss Maudie:

> We saw Uncle Jack every Christmas, and every Christmas he yelled across the street for Miss Maudie to come marry him. Miss Maudie would yell back, "Call a little louder, Jack Finch, and they'll hear you at the post office, I haven't heard you yet!" Jem and I thought this a strange way to ask for a lady's hand in marriage, but then Uncle Jack was rather strange. He said he was trying to get Miss Maudie's goat, that he had been trying unsuccessfully for forty years, that he was the last person in the world Miss Maudie would think about marrying but the first person she thought about teasing, and the best defense to her was spirited offense, all of which we understood clearly. (48)

Regardless of Jack's asserted reasons for instigating these exchanges, they ultimately function to spoof heterosexuality by wrenching its rites of courtship from their usual contexts. Much like Scout during her performance of femininity at Alexandra's tea, Jack and Maudie are ostensibly behaving as their community expects, enacting through appropriately gendered roles the rituals to culminate in heterosexual marriage. Jack plays the role of the aggressive male suitor, while Maudie that of his coy mistress. Yet, just as Scout's customarily transgressive behavior renders her normative performances disruptive, Jack and Maudie's usual silences in expressing heterosexual desire denaturalize their displays of heterosexuality and reveal them to be artificial. Unlike Scout, however, Jack and Maudie are fully conscious of this revelation and artfully stage it in the public arena to create even more of a spectacle.

Such a performance would not be nearly so significant if Lee tempered it with normative enactments of heterosexual desire, ones that reveal such rituals to unfold as they supposedly ought in set cultural scripts. Instead of doing this, however, Lee offers a series of parodies, ones that, although not self-consciously satiric, nevertheless function to establish heterosexuality as existing in the novel primarily in comic deviations from its fictional norm. The first of these parodic heterosexual pairings appears in Miss Caroline's traumatic discovery of Burris Ewell's head lice. When her scream arrests the attention of the entire class of children, the chivalric Little Chuck Little emerges to rescue and console her:

> Little Chuck grinned broadly. "There ain't no need to fear a cootie, ma'am. Ain't you ever seen one? Now don't you be afraid, you just go back to your desk and teach us some more."
>
> Little Chuck Little was another member of the population who didn't know where his next meal was coming from, but he was a born gentleman. He put his hand under her elbow and led Miss Caroline to the front of the room. "Now don't you fret, ma'am," he said. "There ain't no need to fear a cootie. I'll just fetch you some cool water." (30)

Lee strengthens Little Chuck's chivalry when Burris defies Miss Caroline's questions about his hygiene, family, and school attendance. "Little Chuck Little got to his feet," Scout recalls. "'Let him go, ma'am,' he said. 'He's a mean one, a hard-down mean one. He's liable to start somethin', and there's some little folks here.'" Unlike the questionably masculine Atticus, Little Chuck is quite willing to opt for violence, doing so despite his diminutive size: "[W]hen Burris Ewell turned toward him, Little Chuck's right hand went to his pocket. 'Watch your step, Burris,' he said. 'I'd soon's kill you as look at you. Now go home'" (32). The hero ultimately triumphs, and the damsel, although emotionally shaken, as is befitting her more delicate sex, is saved.

Like Jack and Maudie, Little Chuck and Miss Caroline thus enact sex-appropriate roles. Lee undercuts these performances, however, with the situational irony that arises between the ideal of heterosexual chivalry and the reality of the classroom's scenario. The foes from whom Lee's hero must protect the damsel are neither a dragon nor a rival knight bur rather a nomadic head louse and a surly prepubescent first grader. For that matter, the hero is no aristocratically virile Lancelot. Little Chuck Little is only a step above common white trash, far from adult, and, as Lee emphasizes with his name, ridiculously small. As a result, she presents readers not with a reifying performance of heterosexual chivalry but rather with a quasi-sexualized relationship comically deviant in its transgressions of differences in class and age and thus unable to be sexually enacted.

Lee comparably undercuts chivalric courtship in Jem's ritualized visits to Mrs. Dubose. Although these afternoons of reading to her are supposedly penance for the destruction of her camellias, the visits replicate the mythic suitor's persistent wooing of his beloved with stirring pronouncements of affection. Jem composes no sonnets for his partner, but Lee nevertheless keeps him firmly within romantic expression, having him read to Mrs. Dubose from *Ivanhoe,* a novel emblematic of the romanticization of heterosexual courtship. Just as Jem is no Petrarch or Sidney, however, Mrs. Dubose is neither Laura nor Stella: "She was horrible. Her face was the color of a dirty pillowcase, and the corners of her mouth glistened with wet, which inched like a glacier down the deep grooves enclosing her chin. Old-age liver spots dotted her cheeks, and her pale eyes had black pinpoint pupils. Her hands were knobby, and the cuticles were grown up over her fingernails. Her bottom plate was not in, and her upper lip protruded; from time to time she would draw her nether lip to her upper plate and carry her chin with it. This made the wet move faster" (111). Lee thus reverses the asymmetries of the relationship between Little Chuck and Miss Caroline. Although hovering at puberty, Jem is a male suitor of a socially appropriate age to enter into such a ritual, but Mrs. Dubose is, in contrast, a grotesquely old female beloved. The end result, however, is much the same, in that readers encounter yet another image of implied transgressive heterosexuality.

Although with Dill's proposal of marriage and Scout's acceptance, this pair enacts heterosexual rituals further than any of the three couples discussed so far, much the same destabilizing humor emerges from the two. As Scout recalls, Dill "asked me earlier in the summer to marry him, then he promptly forgot about it. He staked me out, marked as his property, said I was the only girl he would ever love, then he neglected me" (46). Like Little Chuck Little, Scout and Dill are too young by societal standards to engage in the heterosexual acts that usually accompany marriage. Their woeful ignorance of these acts' intricacies and results emerges in a discussion of babies' origins, where neither child is too clear on the process. Moreover, in that Scout and Dill are both gender transitive, they present a pairing as superficially disconcerting as Capote's Joel Knox and Idabel Thompkins. In each case, the genders are ostensibly transposed, and the woman rather than the man disciplines wandering affections through violence. When Dill chooses homosocial interactions with Jem rather than pseudoheterosexual ones with Scout, she foregoes feminine tears and coaxing and instead "beat him up twice but it did no good, he only grew closer to Jem" (46).

Lee concludes the novel with a final nonnormative heterosexual pairing, that of Scout and Boo Radley. After he saves Scout and Jem from the malevolent Bob Ewell, the shy Boo is in the awkward situation of himself needing to be seen safely home, and Scout kindly assists him:

> "Will you take me home?"
>
> He almost whispered it, in the voice of a child afraid of the dark.
>
> I put my foot on the top step and stopped. I would lead him through our house, but I would never lead him home.
>
> "Mr. Arthur, bend your arm down here, like that. That's right, sir."
>
> I slipped my hand into the crook of his arm.
>
> He had to stoop a little to accommodate me, but if Miss Stephanie Crawford was watching from her upstairs window, she would see Arthur Radley escorting me down the sidewalk, as any gentleman would do. (281)

As with the other parodic images of heterosexual courtship, this one is marked by socially disruptive elements such as an incongruity of ages, an inverted incongruity in levels of maturity, and, at least with Scout, transgressions of gender norms. This image, however, crucially differs from those that precede it. Whereas the pairings of Little Chuck and Miss Caroline, Jem and Mrs. Dubose, and Dill and Scout are each unself-conscious in its parody of heterosexuality, and the performances of Uncle Jack and Miss Maudie are deliberately satiric so as to expose those characters' distance from heterosexuality, Scout intentionally orchestrates her interactions with Boo to replicate the contours of a heterosexual relationship. She has, in essence, learned the lessons taught by Miss Maudie. Just as she purchases a certain amount of freedom by periodically appeasing the neighborhood through her performances of femininity at the missionary teas, Scout potentially negotiates a comparable freedom for Boo when she crafts the illusion of his normative heterosexuality. That is, although Boo may continue to transgress communal norms by eschewing a public existence, that community is more apt to accord him this transgression because he performs "correctly" during his brief foray into the public arena. Although this image includes disruptive elements, it nevertheless comes closer to fulfilling communal expectations of Boo's appropriate sexual behavior than the rumors of macabre voyeurism circulating in the absence of observed sexual performances.

As these delineated differences suggest, Lee's parodies of heterosexuality are not identically structured, nor do they work to exactly the same ends.

These pairings nevertheless remain parallel in that they fill the text's relative void of normative heterosexuality. Moreover, despite the lack of sexual desire and the often comic or horrific elements in these parodies, they frequently provide far more gratification than the novel's actual marriages. Scout recalls, for instance, her closeness with Dill and the sadness she feels in his absence. "[S]ummer was the swiftness with which Dill would reach up and kiss me when Jem was not looking, the longings we sometimes felt each other feel," Scout remembers. "With him, life was routine; without him, life was unbearable. I stayed miserable for two days" (118). In the novel's final pages she comparably notes the gratification provided by the relationship with Boo Radley and her anxiety about her lack of reciprocation: "We never put back into the tree what we took out of it: we had given him nothing, and it made me sad" (281). Even Jem's horrendous interactions with Mrs. Dubose prove extraordinarily meaningful to him, and part 1 significantly closes with him, having heard Atticus's explanations of Mrs. Dubose's situation, symbolically recanting his hatred. Readers' final image is of Jem meditatively fingering the perfect snow-on-the-mountain camellia she sends him so as to die "beholden to nothing and nobody" (116).

In contrast to the meaningful bonds arising within these relationships scripted as parodies of heterosexual courtships, when Lee does on rare occasion depict marriage, the union seems unenviable. Consider that of Alexandra. One of the novel's least sympathetic characters, she is also married to a virtual nonentity. Scout recalls Uncle Jimmy as "a taciturn man who spent most of his time lying in a hammock by the river wondering if his trot-lines were full" (9) and only reluctantly amends her recollections of Christmases at Finch's Landing to mention him: "I should include Uncle Jimmy, Aunt Alexandra's husband, but as he never spoke a word to me in my life except to say, 'Get off that fence,' once, I never saw any reason to take notice of him" (81). His relationship with Alexandra seems so strained that her protracted visit to the Finches seems a welcomed respite from a less-than-pleasant marriage, a respite not unlike that sketched by Kate Chopin for Clarisse Laballière at the conclusion of "The Storm." Of Alexandra's own childbearing within marriage, Scout explains, "Long ago, in a burst of friendliness, Aunty and Uncle Jimmy produced a son named Henry, who left home as soon as was humanly possible, married, and produced Francis" (81–82). The elder Hancocks' marriage thus seems emotionally and sexually unfulfilling, and, unlike Tom Robinson's children, Henry regards his parents' household as something to escape and then avoid, only a convenient place to deposit his son while he and his wife "pursued their own pleasures" (82).

Although generations of Finches before Atticus and his siblings have married with greater frequency and presumably more gratification, they nevertheless often transgress the boundaries of normative heterosexuality. As Atticus gently reminds his sister, the Finches have something of a penchant for mild incest: "Once, when Aunty assured us that Miss Stephanie Crawford's tendency to mind other people's business was hereditary, Atticus said, 'Sister, when you stop to think about it, our generation's practically the first in the Finch family not to marry its cousins. Would you say the Finches have an Incestuous Streak?'" Alexandra's reply is a cryptic affirmation and denial: "[N]o, that's where we got our small hands and feet" (132). She claims her ancestors' transgressive acts so long as they result in bodies culturally understood as refined, but she implicitly denies that such acts are truly incestuous, presumably because they are not confined within the nuclear family and are therefore socially valid and even welcomed by most nineteenth-century standards. Alexandra's dismissal notwithstanding, Atticus's accusations seem, in hindsight, to designate all the more transgressive acts when readers encounter the novel's only other suggestion of incest, that between Bob Ewell and his daughter Mayella. Although the relationships between sexual participants are markedly different, Lee nevertheless prompts readers to map back onto Alexandra's ancestors the very acts that Atticus publicly condemns.

Just as Lee offers heterosexuality represented through marriage as either absent, unfulfilling, or culturally transgressive in each of these scenarios, so too does she characterize the sexual interactions that come under scrutiny at Tom Robinson's trial in a similar manner. As Atticus proves to no avail, Tom's rape of Mayella Ewell, arguably the novel's central heterosexual act, is a fiction. The sexual interactions that occur between the two are, nevertheless, simultaneously unfulfilling and culturally transgressive insofar as they are miscegenistic. Indeed, this manifestation of heterosexuality is far more transgressive within a southern context than Tracy Deen and Nonnie Anderson's interracial affair in *Strange Fruit*. Rather than have a white man instigate a sexual relationship with a black woman, as Smith does, Lee chooses to have a white woman seduce a black man. As Atticus explains to the jury, Mayella thus violates one of the mid-twentieth-century South's strongest taboos: "She was white, and she tempted a Negro. She did something that in our society is unspeakable: she kissed a black man. Not an old Uncle, but a strong young Negro man" (206). Because of these social strictures, the interaction is hardly fulfilling. Mayella's sexual gratification ceases immediately upon her father's murderous presence, and the hesitant Tom Robinson meets with an end as gruesome as that of Richard Wright's comparably tempted Chris Sims.

Sexuality thus emerges in *To Kill a Mockingbird* in much the same way that gender does: normative expressions are rare, whereas transgressive ones abound, often manifesting in the novel's most sympathetic characters. Although Lee's community sets up enduring heterosexual marriages as the norm, they are almost nonexistent and, with the one exception of Tom and Helen Robinson, never gratifying. Images of transgressive heterosexuality fare somewhat better in Lee's handling but are usually contingent upon the relative presence or absences of sexual desire. In its presence arise, on the one hand, incestuous relationships that either beget elitist whites or accompany the domestic violence of white trash and, on the other hand, interracial relationships that invariably lead to humiliation and death for African Americans. In contrast, the absence of sexual desire in heterosexual relationships often promotes liaisons that are simultaneously disruptive parodies of heterosexuality and mutually gratifying. Moreover, each of the sympathetic white characters engages in neither heterosexual marriage nor transgressive heterosexuality during the novel. And, although this absence of marriage does not necessarily designate a character such as Atticus, Jack, or Miss Maudie to be nonheterosexual or even homosexual, Lee nevertheless offers in Jack a character easily understandable as such to readers who have internalized the absoluteness of a heterosexual/homosexual binarism. Scout and Jem are therefore coming into adulthood not within an utterly conventional "tired old town" (9), as emphasized in Horton Foote's screenplay, but rather within a community whose instabilities of gender and sexuality mark it as, in the broadest sense, queer.

Although southern community as Lee imagines it is thus, as a whole, pervasively queer in its circulations of gender and sexuality, she nevertheless conspicuously creates individuals who emerge as outsiders within this social matrix. Indeed, as the title indicates, the novel's most pervasive and unsubtle symbolism concerns itself with communal negotiations of these outsiders and their alterity to others. The valorized mockingbird becomes the all-too-readable symbol of the innocent Tom Robinson, shot seventeen times by a white guard while attempting to escape imprisonment. In fact, with heavy-handedness justifying Sundquist's critique of the novel, Lee has Braxton Underwood's editorial overtly expose and then explain the symbol: "Mr. Underwood simply figured that it was a sin to kill cripples, be they standing, sitting, or escaping. He likened Tom's death to the senseless slaughter of songbirds by hunters and children, and Maycomb thought he was trying to write an editorial poetical enough to be reprinted in *The Montgomery Advertiser*" (243). Unlike Underwood's editorial, however, Lee's novel more broadly identifies Tom's crucial otherness as his race rather than his physical handicap. Thus, when readers map the defining attributes of the mocking-bird onto Tom, who seems to represent all African Americans in Lee's figu-rations, he emerges as the harmless victim of empowered whites' destructive racial discrimination.

Tom Robinson is not, however, the only figure that the mockingbird symbolizes. With somewhat greater subtlety, Lee uses the bird to represent the equally innocent Boo Radley, who, like the mockingbirds that Atticus saves from Scout's and Jem's rifles, ultimately escapes meaningless slaughter. To expose Boo's heroism and thus bring him to public attention, Scout re-alizes, would "be sort of like shootin' a mockingbird, wouldn't it?" (279). De-spite sharing this symbol with Tom, however, Boo crucially differs in that it is not the color of his skin that dictates his status of cultural outsider. But rather than grounding Boo's communal alienation in an identifiable alterna-tive to race, Lee instead offers only damning speculative rumors about him and his identity, and he remains with few exceptions within the confines of his dilapidated house until the novel's closing chapters. With this figure and his unique relationship to the community, Lee thus shifts her focus away from white southern responses to racial otherness and instead presents a sce-nario that obliquely—if not always coherently—parallels ones crucially in-formed by sexual otherness. That is, because Lee surrounds Boo with so many of the silences and absences that structure the frequent closetedness of same-sex desire, she invites readers to speculate that Boo's reclusiveness is comparable to closeted sexuality and thus explore what bearing this literal representation of closetedness might have on an understanding of the figu-rative. Such a consideration of this parallel in turn invites a reading of the mockingbird to represent persons negotiating same-sex desire as well as social recluses and African Americans.[16]

To assert that Lee's representation invites such a reading is not, however, to argue that Boo is gay. Although the structure of reclusiveness as Lee presents it may strongly resemble that of the closet, they are not the same. Indeed, fissures almost immediately begin to surface if one approaches Boo as directly representative of a closeted gay or lesbian individual. Perhaps foremost, Lee never establishes the transgressive elements of Boo's identity to be anything other than reclusiveness. Although this may at first seem closely akin to closetedness, reclusiveness can be a social deviancy in and of itself rather than a silencing or secreting of deviancy, as closetedness is. The more appropriate comparison of reclusiveness to actual homosexuality, however, reveals how differently these two components of identity are structured and thus how Lee's potential metaphor for a closeted gay individual is somewhat tenuous. Homosexual acts can usually be kept hidden while an individual circulates with relative freedom within a community, whereas a recluse is most forcefully marked by the very desire *to be* hidden, to avoid *any* communal circulations. In short, a homosexual's closet is figurative; a recluse's is literal. By giving Boo a reclusive rather than an identifiably homosexual identity, Lee creates a situation in which he, in effect, cannot come out of the closet, for coming out would erase the transgressive element of his identity.

Although this fissure between Lee's representation of reclusiveness and the actualities of closeted gayness suggests the uniqueness of the gay closet, her depiction's employability as a symbol or parallel to closetedness nevertheless should not be invalidated. In other ways, Boo's reclusiveness does remind readers of closetedness, insofar as it can be essentialized, and the trajectory of his life loosely replicates one of the most pervasive and cherished narratives of coming out. Consider first the parallels between a closeted gay person whose sexuality is not an open secret and Boo as he initially appears—or, more correctly, does not appear—in the novel. Absence is a—if not *the*—crucially defining factor for each. Just as Boo is physically absent within his community, definitive knowledge of a gay person's sexual identity is comparably absent in some or all others' understandings of him or her. As a result, these identities are constituted largely by rumor, conjecture, or otherwise indirect knowledge. A closeted person's hidden sexuality provides his or her community little basis for a more accurate understanding of his or her particular queerness, and he or she is thus usually left to exist within a communal space permeated with, at best, homophilia confirmed through knowledge of others' gay identities or, at worst, homophobia bolstered by derogatory images of homosexuality.

Although sequestered within his house, Boo nevertheless exists within similar currents imposing upon him an identity in his absence. There are those townspeople, such as Atticus and Miss Maudie, who base their opinions of Boo on his youth and, although they have not seen him in years, studiously attempt to squelch gossip. "I remember Arthur Radley when he was a boy," Miss Maudie reflects. "He always spoke nicely to me, no matter what folks said he did. Spoke as nicely as he knew how" (50). On the other hand, the majority of Maycomb thrives on rumors, elaborating on them to create a horrific monster. Jem's thorough internalization of these images, gleaned from "bits and scraps of gossip and neighborhood legend" (44), for instance, allows him to give a full response to Dill's request for a description of Boo: "Boo was about six-and-a-half feet tall, judging from his tracks; he dined on raw squirrels and any cats he could catch, that's why his hands were blood-stained—if you ate an animal raw, you could never wash the blood off. There was a long jagged scar that ran across his face; what teeth he had were yellow and rotten; his eyes popped, and he drooled most of the time" (17). Maycomb's gossip thus demonizes Boo in his absence as savagely as homophobic discourse can.

Jem's description of the imagined Boo also reveals Lee's understanding that popular imagination has a pronounced need to script a transgressive individual as knowable through his or her very body. As a result, Jem conspicuously includes Boo's bloodstained hands as indelible markers of his lack of civility and other deviant behavior. Such presumptions about a transgressive body have also long existed in popular imaginings of homosexuals. The most recurring presumption, of course, is of gender transitivity, but others involve the ostensible effects of same-sex acts on the gay or lesbian body. During World War II, for instance, military physicians reasoned for the detection of gay men during clinical examinations, since sexual activity would have invariably and permanently distended their rectums and made their throats capable of accepting tongue depressors without display of gag reflexes.[17]

These popular images of Boo further parallel homophobic understandings of gays and lesbians in that both script transgressive individuals as disrupting familial unity and ensuring parental fear, anxiety, and embarrassment. Jem, Scout, and Dill revise their "melancholy little drama" of the

Radleys' lives to include precisely this. Scout recalls Mrs. Radley's characterization in particular: "Mrs. Radley had been beautiful until she married Mr. Radley and lost all her money. She also lost most of her teeth, her hair, and her right forefinger (Dill's contribution. Boo bit it off one night when he couldn't find any cats and squirrels to eat.); she sat in the livingroom and cried most of the time, while Boo slowly whittled away all the furniture" (44). In the children's imaginations, Boo's deviancy is so devastating to his family that its members become unfit to function within greater society. Boo's mother can only mourn that which she had lost in her son, even as he continues to destroy the actual house.

Such sentiments parallel those sometimes shown by parents when they learn of their children's gayness. Sedgwick reflects on precisely this when she writes, "I've heard of many people who claim they'd as soon their children were dead as gay. What it took me a long time to believe is that these people are saying no more than the truth."[18] These feelings have historically arisen in no small part because the prevailing and often overlapping ideologies of most twentieth-century social institutions—military, legal, religious, and medical—have labeled homosexuality deviant. A gay or lesbian person was—and sometimes still is—thus often simultaneously treasonous, criminal, sinful, and psychologically disturbed, left without legitimate space in any of these institutions. Not insignificantly, these simultaneous stigmatizations are precisely what Lee rehearses in the communal gossip of Boo. At various moments, he emerges within these narratives as criminal, sinful, mentally ill, or all three. If neighborhood legend is to be believed, Boo's first transgressions are indeed vaguely criminal. As a teenager, he becomes involved with "the wrong crowd," "the nearest thing to a gang ever seen in Maycomb" (14). Mr. Radley's response to his son's transgressions is swift and exacting, and, even if the specifics remain unknown, there is the suggestion that Mr. Radley's punishments are so extreme that Boo is permanently traumatized. After these events, "[t]he doors of the Radley house were closed on weekdays as well as Sundays, and Mr. Radley's boy was not seen again for fifteen years" (15). Despite there being no proof of further illegal behavior, Boo nevertheless becomes within popular imagination "a malevolent phantom" responsible for a range of criminal activities. "Any stealthy small crimes committed in Maycomb were his work," Scout recalls. "Once the town was terrorized by a series of morbid nocturnal events: people's chickens and household pets were found mutilated; although the culprit was Crazy Addie, who eventually drowned himself in Barker's Eddy, people still looked at the Radley Place, unwilling to discard their initial suspicions" (13).

Just as Boo breaks the law but neither to the extent nor with the malevolence that his community wishes, so too does he presumably sin, if only according to the strictures of his father's conservative religion. Miss Maudie explains to Scout that Mr. Radley's religious preferences are not those of Maycomb's stolid Baptists and Methodists but rather the biblical fundamentalism of "a foot-washing Baptist" who believes "anything that's pleasure is a sin" and "take[s] the Bible literally" (49). Indeed, because of these sectarian differences, the Radleys hardly deign to interact with their fellow townspeople. "They did not go to church, Maycomb's principal recreation, but worshiped at home," Scout offers. "Mrs. Radley seldom if ever crossed the street for a mid-morning coffee break with her neighbors, and certainly never joined a missionary circle" (13). Nevertheless, no one presumes the family—and Mr. Radley in particular—to lack either religious conviction or devotion: "Miss Stephanie Crawford said he was so upright he took the word of God as his only law, and we believed her, because Mr. Radley's posture was ramrod straight" (16).

Lee leaves little doubt, however, as to how readers are to accept this figure. Scout's memories reveal that Lee's biblical patriarch displays all the warmth and friendliness of Faulkner's Simon McEachern: "He was a thin leathery man with colorless eyes, so colorless they did not reflect light. His cheekbones were sharp and his mouth was wide, with a thin upper lip and a full lower lip. . . . He never spoke to us. When he passed we would look at the ground and say, 'Good morning, sir,' and he would cough in reply" (16). Moreover, Lee has characters that readers presume to be trustworthy damn Mr. Radley and, by extension, his coercive fundamentalist Christianity. Calpurnia, for example, offers one of her rare comments on "the ways of white people" to curse Mr. Radley's corpse as "the meanest men ever God blew breath into" (16–17). Miss Maudie is somewhat more temperate in her explanations of the Radleys, but she too implicitly critiques the effects of Mr. Radley's religious fanaticism: "'You are too young to understand it,' she said, 'but sometimes the Bible in the hand of one man is worse than a whiskey bottle in the hand of—oh, of your father.'" "There are just some kind of men who—who're so busy worrying about the next world they've never learned to live in this one," Miss Maudie concludes, "and you can look down the street and see the results" (49–50).

As with so much of Boo's story, Miss Maudie leaves unsaid the specifics of these results; however, Miss Stephanie Crawford elaborates on the facts of Boo's narrative to suggest a logical series of causes and effects. Angered by his son's minor infractions of the law, Mr. Radley ensures "that Arthur gave no further trouble" (15), and Boo disappears. The community hypothesizes that Mr. Radley exerts the patriarchal authority invested in him by Scripture to discipline Boo's rebelliousness so excessively that Jem, amplifying communal gossip, judges "that Mr. Radley kept him chained to the bed most of the time" (16). Even Miss Maudie mournfully replies to Scout's inquiry if Boo is crazy, "If he's not he should be by now. The things that happen to people we never really know. What happens in houses behind closed doors, what secrets—" (50). Given the effectiveness and perhaps even excessiveness of this unspecified discipline suggested by Boo's physical absence, a rebellion against this patriarchal authority seems not only understandable but also expected.

Yet, within both familial and communal responses, Boo's reaction to his father's oppression is figured as proof of mental instability. The very placidity and methodicalness with which Boo supposedly interrupts work on his scrapbook to stab his father in the leg with a pair of scissors bespeak his insanity as well as hint at Lee's appropriation of an unresolved Freudian Oedipal conflict. According to Miss Stephanie's polished version of the tale, "As Mr. Radley passed by, Boo drove the scissors into his parent's leg, pulled them out, wiped them on his pants, and resumed his activities" (15). His mother immediately presumes utter insanity in her son and runs "screaming into the street that Arthur was killing them all," and Maycomb as a whole "suggested that a season in Tuscaloosa might be helpful to Boo." Even Mr. Radley concedes that, although "Boo wasn't crazy, he was high-strung at times" (15).

If Lee suggests with this identity, triply damned by crime, sin, and insanity, that Boo's family and community play a significant role in the imposition and, after Mr. Radley's death, self-imposition of the closet, she also depicts the community as equally, if perhaps somewhat paradoxically, preoccupied with making Boo come out of that space. Even as Jem, Scout, and Dill participate in the elaborations on the closet-bolstering rumors, the children are also fascinated with Boo and plot scheme after scheme to lure him into communal interactions and thus supposedly to learn his true identity. "Wonder what he does in there," Dill murmurs before suggesting, "Let's try to make him come out . . . I'd like to see what he looks like" (17). Such a paradoxical response to deviant identity was and, according to Sedgwick, continues to be a staple reaction to homosexuality: "To the fine antennae of public attention the freshness of every drama of (especially involuntary) gay uncovering seems in anything heightened in surprise and delectability, rather than staled, by the increasingly intense atmosphere of public articulations of and about the love that is famous for daring not speak its name."[19] That is, as discourses proliferate around homosexuality, whether homophobic or homophilic, there persists and even increases a fascination with deviant sexuality being made knowable in public arenas.

To Kill a Mockingbird culminates with this knowability of the deviant when Boo literally comes out to rescue Scout and Jem from Bob Ewell, and the final chapters of the novel explore personal and anticipated communal responses to this knowability. Lee's narrative dictates these responses, however, by less than subtly establishing Boo as thoroughly sympathetic despite his cultural otherness. Just as she scripts Tom Robinson as quiet and respectable, she creates in Boo a figure epitomizing self-sacrifice and heroism. Each of his previous interactions with the children has been a gesture of friendliness and consideration: leaving intriguing trinkets in an oak tree as tokens of affection, providing a quilt for the shivering Scout as she watches Miss Maudie's house burn, and mending Jem's ripped pants. Boo's ultimate gifts, however, are Scout and Jem's very lives, as Atticus recognizes. Thus, whereas Tom eventually proves as innocent as Harriet Beecher Stowe's martyr with the same name, Boo, a protector of children as innocent as Little Eva, proves as heroic as the Christian knight to whom his name Arthur alludes.

If Boo's actions are thus antithetical to those attributed to him by gossip, so too is his body at variance with images circulating in popular imagination. Instead of a drooling, bloodstained oaf, Scout encounters a man easily mistakable for an unknown ordinary townsperson. As she surveys Jem's bedroom in the aftermath of the encounter with Bob Ewell, but before she knows Boo's identity, Scout notes the presence of the children's rescuer and finds him immediately readable as benign: "The man who brought Jem in was standing in a corner, learning against the wall. He was some countryman I did not know. He had probably been at the pageant, and was in the vicinity when it happened. He must have heard our screams and come running" (268). He wears the most ordinary of clothes for Maycomb—khaki pants and a denim shirt—and, despite a paleness unsettling in a community of sunburned farmers, verges on being thoroughly generic in Scout's initial notice of him.

Even after Scout learns who this figure is, however, she finds Boo to be anything but the monster of communal gossip. She no longer fears his house and even pauses to savor the view from its porch when she escorts him home. The walk comes close to fulfilling the visions made possible by the maturity she gains during the summer of Tom's trial: "I imagined how it would be: when it happened, he'd just be sitting in the swing when I came along. 'Hidy do, Mr. Arthur,' I would say, as if I had said it every afternoon of my life. 'Evening, Jean Louise,' he would say, as if he had said it every afternoon of my life, 'right pretty spell we're having, isn't it?' 'Yes, sir, right pretty,' I would say, and go on" (245). The novel's final didactic lines underscore this sympathetic character even further. Although Scout drowsily refers to the events of *The Gray Ghost* as Atticus puts her to bed, she might as well be discussing Boo:

> He guided me to the bed and sat me down. He lifted my legs and put me under the cover.
>
> "An' they chased him 'n' never could catch him 'cause they didn't know what he looked like, an' Atticus, when they finally saw him, why he hadn't done any of those things . . . Atticus, he was real nice. . . . "
>
> His hands were under my chin, pulling up the cover, tucking it around me. "Most people are, Scout, when you finally see them." (283–84)

Like the wronged Stoner's Boy whom Scout recalls in *The Gray Ghost,* Boo is an innocent victim of social accusations. When Scout finally meets him and can judge his identity for herself rather than rely on malicious rumors, he strikes her not as a freakish demon but instead as simply "real nice."

In its generic form, this narrative is one often championed as the ideal for the advancement of social tolerance. The cultural outsider is known only in the abstract and accordingly demonized for his or her rumored differences until prolonged or heroic interactions establish reassuring commonalties for the cultural insider and ultimately ensure acceptance. Within gay communities this narrative is particularly familiar, since one of the most consistently promoted courses of action is coming out. Gay persons, the valorized narrative goes, must confront society to demythify homosexuality and thus allow others to understand same-sex desire more accurately, with the ultimate goal being acceptance or at least tolerance of homosexuals. In fact, the narrative usually figures the closet as a site of fear, cowardice, and self-loathing, and persons who remain within this space often stand accused of retarding and even jeopardizing the tolerance fostered by persons who have already come out.

The terms of this acceptance and/or tolerance, however, mark one of the most divisive splits within these communities. At one end of the conventional spectrum are those persons who hold gayness to be radically different from a usually—and inaccurately—homogenized straightness and urge acceptance of this alterity. At the other end of this spectrum are those who emphasize perceived commonalties between heterosexual and homosexual persons, downplaying differences between the two and within each to stress gays and lesbians' "normalcy" when compared to, again, homogenized straight persons. Despite minor differences, this rhetoric implies all persons are first and foremost human and deserve to be treated as such.

Like most persons with culturally minoritized identities, gays and lesbians struggle with these negotiations of difference and sameness, debating the personal and political efficacy of not only these extremes but also the more complex and more common intervening stances. But, as historian John D'Emilio has suggested, such debates did not emerge only when the Stonewall riots electrified gay and lesbian communities in 1969. At precisely the moment when Lee was completing *To Kill a Mockingbird,* a crucial handful of American homosexuals were engaged in one of the most significant rounds of these debates. Nascent homosexual communities such as those considered in George Chauncey's work experienced tremendous growth that frequently solidified a group identity during and immediately after World War II. With this emergent identity, D'Emilio argues, came the struggle for its public acknowledgment. Early advocates for this recognition, such as those persons organizing the Mattachine Society in 1951, tended toward political radicalness, often bringing with them Communist affiliations and usually characterizing their efforts as working toward militant "homosexual emancipation." It is perhaps not surprising, however, that in this era of Joseph McCarthy's Communist paranoia, the probings of the House's Un-American Activities Committee, Dwight Eisenhower's seemingly benign presidency, and the return to prewar cultural and familial normalcy with a vengeance, comparable conservatism also crucially affected emerging gay activism. Indeed, by the mid-1950s the leadership of these organizations dramatically shifted from its radical instigators, such as Harry Hay and Charles Rowland, to persons such as Marilyn Rieger and Kenneth Burns and constituted what D'Emilio terms a retreat into respectability.

The political strategy advocated by Rieger, Burns, and others like them, that which eventually came to characterize much of gay activism until Stonewall, directly countered the strategy of the Mattachine's original and early organizers. Whereas Hay and Rowland considered gays and lesbians a minority with its own unique culture, Rieger and Burns denied such a status. "We know we are the same," Rieger argued at the 1953 Mattachine convention, "no different from anyone else. Our only difference is an unimportant one to the heterosexual society, *unless we make it important*." According to this logic, homosexuals should therefore come out and prove their utter normalcy to gain equality. "[B]y declaring ourselves, by integrating," Rieger continued, "not as homosexuals, but as people, as men and women whose homosexuality is irrelevant to our ideals, our principles, our hopes and aspirations," would activists "rid the world of its misconceptions of homosexuality and homosexuals." By midcentury, Rowland and Hay had been forced to cede their positions of leadership, and Rieger's rhetoric was the standard. The *Mattachine Review* and the *Ladder,* respective mouthpieces for the Mattachine Society and the exclusively female but comparably conservative Daughters of Bilitis, urged readers to prove through their dress and activity that they were "average people in all other respects outside of our private sexual inclinations." The Daughters of Bilitis in particular cautioned lesbians against wearing pants, keeping their hair short, and frequenting bars, plaintively suggesting that they do "a little 'policing' on their own." [20]

Although this strategy faced significant challenges before Stonewall, especially in the 1960s, presented through contrasting models for political action offered by the civil rights movement,[21] this conservatism nevertheless remained pervasive in gay communities and their activism throughout the 1950s, when Lee was writing *To Kill a Mockingbird.* Indeed, she ultimately resolves the novel's negotiations of closetedness in a manner comparable to this political strategy. Like gay activists of the day, Lee condemns the closet as a site of darkness, death, and decay. "The house was low," Scout recalls of the Radleys' home, and "was once white with a deep front porch and green shutters, but had long ago darkened to the color of the slate-gray yard around it. Rain-rotted shingles drooped over the eaves of the veranda; oak trees kept the sun away. The remains of a picket drunkenly guarded the front yard—a 'swept' yard that was never swept—where johnson grass and rab-bit-tobacco grew in abundance" (13). Yet, when the cultural outsider who has been forced into this space decides to come out, he reveals himself to be no flamboyant Randolph or Folner but instead precisely what Marilyn Rieger expected of gays and lesbians: practically "no different from anyone else" and warmly embraced by an accepting community.

Like Rieger, however, Lee does not completely eradicate all differences in Boo. Although Scout may at first take his body to be that of an ordinary farmer, it nevertheless reveals subtle differences, most noticeably in its pale-ness. "His face was as white as his hands, but for a shadow on his jutting chin," Scout recalls from her one interaction with Boo. "His cheeks were thin to hollowness; his mouth was wide; there were shallow, almost delicate indentations at his temples, and his gray eyes were so colorless I thought he was blind. His hair was dead and thin, almost feathery on top of his head" (273). Moreover, Boo is painfully inept in navigating unfamiliar spaces. "Every move he made was uncertain, as if he were not sure his hands and feet could make proper contact with the things he touched" (279–80), Scout remembers.

As Lee figures these differences, though, they do not alienate Boo from others but rather endear him to them. Upon seeing Boo's understandable difficulties in negotiating crowds and strange environs, Scout derives satis-faction in both helping Boo and living out her imagination interactions: "'Won't you have a seat, Mr. Arthur? This rocking-chair's nice and com-fortable.' My small fantasy about him was alive again: he would be sitting on the porch . . . right pretty spell we're having, isn't it, Mr. Arthur? Yes, a right pretty spell. Feeling slightly unreal, I led him to the chair farthest from At-ticus and Mr. Tate. It was in deep shadow. Boo would feel more comfort-able in the dark" (274–75). As in the imaginations of Rieger and other con-servative gay activists of the 1950s, where mainstream culture would willingly help gays and lesbians function in society once they proved their normalcy was not forfeited by differing sexual desires, when Scout can as-cribe to Boo a sympathetic identity, she is more than generous in assisting him during his foray into public space.

Heart-tugging though Lee's final pages may be, they nevertheless pre-sent potentially disturbing images when Scout offers this assistance to Boo. He is cast almost as helpless, unable to negotiate even the simplest of actions, such as stroking Jem's hair or climbing steps. When one reads this help potentially to symbolize heterosexual society's response to uncloseted gays and lesbians, it suggests a disconcerting balance of power. Just as Boo is wholly reliant on Scout, in this reading, homosexuals are exclusively dependent on heterosexuals' acceptance to function outside the closet. Lee's plot even imagines this acceptance as so overwhelming that the closet may have to be reinstated as a haven from heterosexuals' attention. Heck Tate is adamant that Bob Ewell dies by accidentally falling on his knife so that Boo Radley can escape not so much being brought to trial but the communal adoration of him as a hero. Attuned to the fickleness of popular response, Tate realizes that the very people who have disseminated the rumors about Boo will, upon hearing of his exploits, disregard his heretofore emphasized differences and virtually smother him with acceptance. As a result, Tate thus effectively erases all traces of Boo's coming out, leaving them to exist only in Scout's memories.

With these final images Lee once again reveals how radically her novel differs from those of Capote and Smith if one entertains this specific reading of Boo's closetedness. Unlike *Other Voices, Other Rooms* and *Strange Fruit*, in which homosexuality is markedly at variance with cultural norms and gay or lesbian individuals face overwhelming forces of homophobia, *To Kill a Mockingbird* ultimately imagines southern community to be already queer and permeated with transgressions of gender and sexuality. The implications are that, within this community, so long as a transgressive person is not too excessively or multiply different from those around him or her, and thus in harmony with the general cultural queerness, an acknowledgment of sexual otherness brings exaggerated acceptance rather than communal disfavor. This acceptance is so pervasive that it threatens to eradicate the very elements of identity necessitating the closet in the first place and therefore indirectly bolsters this space as a site of refuge. Thus, like the gay activists organizing across the United States at precisely the moment that Lee was composing her novel, she presents a community in which, once difference has been dismissed as minor and similarity acknowledged as already existing, no more innocent mockingbirds need ever be killed, no more African Americans need ever face racism, and, if only figuratively, no more gays and lesbians need ever face homophobia.

6

Carson McCullers and Gay/Lesbian (Non) Representation

IN CONTRAST TO THE POSITIVE REVIEWS of *To Kill a Mockingbird*, its rapid adaptation into film, and its near omnipresence within national curricula, *Clock Without Hands*, Carson McCullers's last novel, published the following year, met with quicksilver popularity and subsequent neglect. Only recently, four decades after its initial appearance, has the novel been reprinted, and it remains the only one of McCullers's longer works unfilmed. Contemporary responses to *Clock* were at best mixed, and few reviewers lauded it. Rumer Godden deemed it a "marvel of a novel," one "powerful yet humble, dignified yet utterly unpretentious," and Charles Rolo held that it was "a strong contender" for the 1961 National Book Award for fiction. Gore Vidal, focusing on style and structure, offered that, unlike the "terrible gaseous prose" of Faulkner and Wolfe, there "is never a false note." McCullers's "genius for prose," Vidal sweepingly asserted, "remains one of the few satisfactory achievements of our second-rate culture." And yet, when reviewers tended toward kindness, it was often in deference to *Clock* having been written by a dying woman whose body had been wracked by a series of strokes and who weighed barely a hundred pounds. As Judith Giblin James notes, amplifying the work of Margaret McDowell, "The reviews, indeed, were haunted by the image of a wunderkind, now tragically disabled, working slowly and heroically in a battle against time."[1]

Others' criticisms were not tempered by McCullers's crisis in health. Irving Howe, who maintained that *The Ballad of the Sad Café* was "one of the finest novels ever written by an American," had nothing positive to say about *Clock Without Hands:* "[T]he book is so poorly constructed—one is troubled throughout by a disharmony between the sober realism of the Malone section and the grotesque capers of the section dealing with the Judge and Sherman Pew—that the symbolic scheme fails to carry strength or conviction. . . . What is most disturbing about *Clock Without Hands* is the lethargic flatness of the prose. The style . . . is that of a novelist mechanically going through the motions, and committing to paper not an integrated vision of life but an unadorned and scrappy scenario for a not-yet-written novel." Robert O. Bowen was even more dismissive, asserting that the novel was "Southern Gothic of an almost purely Partisan Review-New Yorker-Guggenheim Foundation basis" that consisted of "a dash of sympathy for homosexuals, a bit of the macabre, some basting with lavatory-wall vulgarisms and a garnish of pseudo-liberal canards on race and religion." Writing from below the Mason-Dixon Line, Louis Rubin was also disturbed by the novel that he would later call "an artistic disaster," and pronounced the project a "failure" because of the work's ostensibly simplistic political focus on race: "It is as if Miss McCullers determined to write a novel 'about' the segregation issues, and fashioned her people entirely with this issue in mind. The result is not a novel but a tract. The failure is exemplified in the failure of Sherman Pew as a character; sometimes he is a symbol, sometimes a human being, but never both at the same time." Flannery O'Connor privately stated that *Clock Without Hands* was "absolutely the worst novel" she had ever read. Even McCullers's friends voiced their dismay that the work was objectionable on any number of levels, and Tennessee Williams was so horrified upon reading an advance copy that he begged McCullers to postpone publication.[2]

It was in this informal arena, however, that Lillian Smith made some of the most insightful and balanced criticism of the novel, offering in a letter to Margaret Long what Will Brantley calls "perhaps the most provocative response to that novel now in print." "Carson McCullers's new book," Smith offered, "is funny and tender; good and full of a kind of cockeyed truth." Yet, sounding like the reviewers of her own *Strange Fruit,* Smith feared that *Clock Without Hands* intentionally includes all the necessary tokens of a bestseller: "But somehow it bothers me too: it has all the ingredients for a New York success: interracial sex: be sure to make it white woman having baby by black man; politics: be sure to make it exaggerated and stereotyped so that you can't take the old Congressman seriously; adolescence: be sure to make it vaguely homosexual and beatnik and 'full of compassion;' when people are killed or hurt, be sure it seems to happen without reason and sense or even evil." "Could she, perhaps, be so much a part of the intellectual and psychological climate of New York City," Smith echoed Bowen, "that she did this unconsciously—just following the New York line about southerners all being evil or fools or idiots, and the line about sex, and the line about having only absurd characters which no reader would ever need to identify with. I don't know. But I think it is the least real of any of her books." Smith also indicted McCullers of being less than original: "I stumbled across bits of *Strange Fruit* in it, bits of *One Hour*, bits of *Killers*, bits of Truman Capote's *Breakfast at Tiffany's*, bits of *Finian's Rainbow*—and others up here at Clayton say it is like in spots *To Kill A Mocking Bird* which I have not bothered to read, although I have a copy." Finally, just as many concluded of Wright when *The Long Dream* appeared three years earlier, Smith suggested that Mc-Cullers was too removed from the ever-changing South of the late 1950s and early 1960s to speak of it meaningfully and accurately, writing instead as "if from memory of her childhood in the 1930's and what she has picked up in New York about recent happenings in the South. And the two do not click."[3]

Smith's and others' criticisms notwithstanding, *Clock Without Hands* is important to an understanding of McCullers's overarching literary project, and the novel's general neglect, like that of Goyen's *The House of Breath* and Wright's *The Long Dream*, is unfortunate in that it removes from circulation significant representations of same-sex desire within southern literary production at midcentury. As recent work by Rachel Adams and others suggests, *Clock Without Hands* offers one of the most complex of the representations, both within McCullers's own corpus and within the period's broader southern literary production. Texts such as *The Long Dream, Strange Fruit,* and *To Kill a Mockingbird* simultaneously explore homoeroticism and interracial desire but isolate these desires from one another. *Other Voices, Other Rooms* addresses interracial and interethnic same-sex desire through Randolph's infatuations with Keg and Pepe Alvarez but does so cursorily. In contrast, *Clock Without Hands* attempts to centralize interracial desire between men and thus negotiates two of the most persisting concerns in mid-twentieth-century southern literary production: relations between European Americans and African Americans and the specter of deviant sexuality.

*   *   *

The centrality of male same-sex desire to *Clock Without Hands* is by no means unanticipated by McCullers's earlier work. To the contrary, just as her fiction and drama are famously preoccupied with recurring themes of rejection and unrequited love, so too does work from throughout her career repeatedly concern itself with male homoeroticism. Yet, until of late, critics have tended either not to interrogate the relationships between desire and love in McCullers's work or largely to dismiss its unfulfilled erotic desire—and especially deviant erotic desire, such as homoeroticism—as merely a symbol of isolation and loneliness and to emphasize McCullers's investment in asexual, platonic love. These primarily early critics insist that her work be read only through allegorical lenses. Oliver Evans asserts, "It is impossible to understand Mrs. McCullers's work unless one realizes that she conceives of fiction chiefly as parable. The reader who concerns himself exclusively with the realistic level of her stories will never fully appreciate them, though he may be momentarily diverted." In contrast to Evans's opinions, when one does not read through such lenses and thus does not valorize platonic love at the expense of eroticism, one finds McCullers's work consistently involved with impressively intricate representations of sexual desire, as Adams and Lori Kenschaft, among others, have established.[4]

McCullers begins this exploration of male homoeroticism in some of her earliest writing. "Sucker," written in the early 1930s but not published until the 1960s, presents the titular character's idolization of his older cousin Pete and the resulting homoeroticism that arises between the pubescent boys. "It seemed to me suddenly that I did like him more than anybody else I knew," Peter confesses in light of Sucker's devotion, "more than any other boy, more than my sisters, more in a certain way even than [Pete's girlfriend] Maybelle." As the two boys lie in bed together, Pete feels "good all over," and Sucker is ecstatic at Pete's closeness: "His voice was excited and he kept on talking fast like he could never get the words out in time. When I went to sleep he was still talking and I could still feel his breathing on my shoulder, warm and close." And yet, typical of McCullers's later plots in which mutual love is rarely, if ever, lasting, this bond soon breaks. Pete realizes the transgressiveness of their relationship and violently rejects Sucker, devastating him. "Don't you know a single thing?" Pete yells at Sucker. "Haven't you even been around at all? Why don't you get a girl friend instead of me? What kind of a sissy do you want to grow up to be anyway?" The story ends, however, with Maybelle's abandonment of Pete and his renewed awareness of the now disdainful Sucker's importance to him. "I don't care a flip for Maybelle or any particular girl any more," he concludes; "it's only this thing between Sucker and me that is the trouble now. . . . I miss the way Sucker and I were for a while in a funny, sad way that before this I never would have believed."[5]

If the homoerotic relation between Pete and Sucker may be dismissed as close friendship or one boy's youthful adoration of an older one, safely within the homosocial realm, McCullers forecloses such a dismissal in *The Heart Is a Lonely Hunter* (1940). Despite not including overt sexual interactions, the relationship between the novel's two deaf mutes, Spiros Antonapoulos and the ironically named John Singer, is not only homoerotically charged but also, in fact, seems a longtime companionship marked by compassion and devotion, especially on the part of Singer, and suggests that McCullers intends theirs to be types of homosexual identities. Singer centers his existence on Antonapoulos, working diligently to support the twosome and nursing his friend's precarious health. Tenderness pervades these actions, as Singer's daily leave-takings of Antonapoulos reveal. After walking "arm in arm" with him, Singer "nearly always put his hand on his friend's arm and looked for a second into his face before leaving him."[6] Upon their reunion, Singer abandons his customary public reticence and metamorphoses in Antonapoulos's private presence: "At home Singer was always talking to Antonapoulos. His hands shaped the words in a swift series of designs. His face was eager and his gray-green eyes sparkled brightly" (2).

Singer's investment in Antonapoulos is so great that his institutionalization is hardly bearable. This decision by Antonapoulos's cousin stuns Singer, and he responds with a heated scrawl on his notepad, *"You cannot do this. Antonapoulos must stay with me"* (6). The separation is, however, inevitable, and Singer tries desperately before Antonapoulos's departure to pour out "all the thoughts that had ever been in his mind and heart, but there was not time" (7). Singer remains preoccupied in Antonapoulos's absence, dreams about him incessantly, and concludes, "Nothing seemed real except the ten years with Antonapoulos. In his half-dreams he saw his friend very vividly, and when he awakened a great aching loneliness would be in him" (8). Despite periodic visits to Antonapoulos's asylum, Singer's dreams intensify as the separation persists: "Within Singer there was always the memory of his friend. At night when he closed his eyes the Greek's face was there in the darkness—round and oily, with a wise and gentle smile. In his dreams they were always together" (170). As McCullers writes in the outline of "The Mute," the novel's earliest form, "Singer's love for Antonapoulos threads through the whole book from the first page until the very end. No part of Singer is left untouched by this love and when they are separated his life is meaningless and he is only marking time until he can be with his friend again."[7]

Although the unmailed letters that Singer writes to Antonapoulos provide little escape from his loneliness, they nevertheless reveal Singer's unflagging devotion to and "love unchecked" (276) for his companion. Surrounded by a coterie of needy individuals who feel themselves close to Singer, he still addresses Antonapoulos as "My Only Friend" (181) and concludes his letter, "I am not meant to be alone and without you who understand" (185). When this absence becomes absolute rather than temporary upon Antonapoulos's death, Singer opts not to live without his companion and commits suicide by firing a bullet through his chest.

McCullers reinforces the couple's implied erotic and emotional investments in one another with symbolism and suggestive imagery that accrues around the two figures. Antonapoulos is significantly Greek, a national and/or ethnic identity frequently linked to same-sex acts—and anal sex in particular—because of the region's accepted pederastic relationships during antiquity. Unlike his cousin, who immediately Americanizes his name to Charles Parker, Antonapoulos retains the family's distinctively Greek surname and thus seems less anxious to distance himself from whatever connotations that national identity may have. His and Singer's muteness works similarly to imply homosexuality in that, because of their inability to talk, theirs is truly a love that dare not speak his name. With these identities, which are distanced from explicitly transgressive sexual ones but are nevertheless deviant, McCullers thus creates a scenario comparable to that which Harper Lee crafts in Boo Radley's reclusiveness: homosexuality is by no means overtly identified, and yet the situation is one that readers can meaningfully associate with such an identity.

In contrast to this symbolic or encoded representation of male homosexuality, *Reflections in a Golden Eye* (1941), McCullers's next novel, includes little such restraint in imagining male homoeroticism. She instead boldly offers among her six central characters Weldon Penderton, who, in the course of the novel, awakens to his desire for one of the soldiers stationed on the base. McCullers anticipates as much in the opening pages by destabilizing the heterosexuality suggested by Penderton's marriage. His sexual desire for women is minimal, as are his heterosexual acts within his union with Leonora. "When she married the Captain she had been a virgin," the narrative asserts. "Four nights after her wedding she was still a virgin, and on the fifth night her status was changed only enough to leave her somewhat puzzled."[8] Little suggests that these interactions change, and the marriage ultimately seems an arranged one of appearances.

Rather than Leonora's voluptuous figure, it is the male bodies surrounding Penderton on the post that fascinate and arouse him. Alienated from these men by his rank, he longs to integrate himself among them in the homosociality of the barracks, that which McCullers casts in Whitmanic terms: "the hubbub of young male voices, the genial loafing in the sun, the irresponsible shenanigans of camaraderie" (96). None of these male bodies, however, captivates like that of Ellgee Williams. When misfortune brings Penderton in contact with the young private naked in the woods, the older man cannot exorcise the vision from his thoughts. He repeatedly recalls the images in which Williams, neither disturbed nor embarrassed at having been caught naked, dutifully reigns Penderton's horse and returns it to the stables, all the while providing a provocative display of the "pure, curved outlines" (46) of his toned exposed body: "He was completely naked. His slim body glistened in the late sun. . . . The naked man did not bother to walk around his [Penderton's] outstretched body. He left his place by the tree and lightly stepped over the officer. The Captain had a close swift view of the young soldier's bare foot: it was slim and delicately built, with a high instep marked by blue veins" (62). Long after Williams leaves, Penderton dwells "on the pure-cut lines of the young man's body" and, as he ponders this form, at last realizes that he feels for Williams a "hatred, passionate as love, [that] would be with him all the remaining days of his life" (63).

Penderton is correct: this desire does not wane, and Williams becomes as much of an obsession for Penderton as Leonora is for Williams. Prompted by "an aching want for contact between them of some sort," Penderton visits the stables where Williams is assigned to work "as often as he could reasonably do so." Such visits prove exquisite torture for him: "When the Captain knew in advance that he would meet the soldier, he felt himself grow dizzy. During their brief, impersonal meetings he suffered a curious lapse of sensory impressions; when he was near the soldier he found himself unable to see or to hear properly, and it was only after he had ridden away and was alone again that the scene developed itself for the first time in his mind. The thought of the young man's face—the dumb eyes, the heavy sensual lips that were often wet, the childish page-boy bangs—this image was intolerable to him" (81–82). Intolerable though Williams may be, he is, like Antonapoulos for Singer, omnipresent in Penderton's thoughts, and he embarks on a series of desperate and often pathetic moves to interact with Williams beyond time at the stables. In the beginning the moves are innocuous, such as snatching up for a keepsake a candy wrapper that Williams discards. They culminate, however, in Penderton's deadly shooting of the private at the novel's close: "The Captain was a good marksman, and although he shot twice only one raw hole was left in the center of the soldier's chest" (111). Unable to gratify his sexual desire for Williams physically and jealous of the private's eroticized voyeurism directed at Leonora, Penderton opts—whether consciously or not—to gratify his desire symbolically with the shooting, this giving vent to his hatred while at the same time piercing Williams with all the ferocity that may be involved in sexual penetration.

It is presumably of this newly acknowledged deviant desire in himself that Penderton thinks when he launches his defense of Anacleto, the Langdons' effeminate house boy. In response to Morris Langdon's repeated assertions that Anacleto needs to be put through the army's rigors that "might have made a man out of him" and thus stop this "dancing around to music and messing with watercolors" (99), Penderton heatedly questions whether "any fulfillment obtained at the expense of normalcy is wrong, and should not be allowed to bring happiness. In short, it is better, because it is morally honorable, for the square peg to keep scraping about the round hole rather than to discover and use the unorthodox square that would fit it?" (99). Thus, much as Capote and Lee manipulate Randolph and Scout respectively to articulate calls for liberal social tolerance for transgressive identities, McCullers uses Penderton simultaneously to demand a relaxation of the strictures regulating the performance of gender and, given his own homoerotic desire, to promote a sympathetic understanding of homosexual activities.

This plea for the acceptance of nonnormative gender and desire is perhaps as forcefully made by McCullers's demonization of the novel's heterosexuals as stupid, animalistic, nymphomaniacal, and/or sadistic. These persons are largely of two sorts: one typified by Alison Langdon and the other by Ellgee Williams, Leonora Penderton, and Morris Langdon. McCullers presents in Alison a woman so invested in the results of her procreative heterosexuality that when her child dies, she mutilates those parts of her body simultaneously associated with erotic stimulation and the nurture of children. With horrific understatement, the narrative relates that they "found Mrs. Langdon unconscious and she had cut off the tender nipples of her breasts with the garden shears" (25). After this incident, she retreats to her bedroom, distances herself sexually and emotionally from her husband, and attempts to imagine Anacleto as something of a surrogate for the dead daughter.

In contrast to Alison, who, despite her penchant for self-mutilation, is delicate and refined in fulfillment of idealized southern womanhood, her husband and Leonora are coarse and stupid. Morris Langdon abhors opera and ballet, and Leonora is, so the narrative voice asserts as the "truth of the matter," "a little feebleminded." "She could not have multiplied twelve by thirteen under threat of the rack," readers learn. "If ever it was strictly necessary that she write a letter, such as a note to thank her uncle for a birthday check or a letter ordering a new bridle, it was a weighty enterprise for her" (14). Even a game of blackjack proves serious mental work for her— "Leonora had a studious, serious air, as she was trying to add fourteen and seven on her fingers underneath the table" (24)—and casual conversation after dinner is no less of a hurdle: "'They giveth it and then they taketh it away,' said Leonora, whose intentions were better than her command of Scripture" (100).

What Leonora and Langdon lack in culture, they make up for in sexual appetite. This desire for sex is as avid as theirs for food, and both Leonora and Major Langdon "were great eaters" (14). Like Scarlett O'Hara's, Leonora's eyes rarely fail to light up at a litany of southern foods: "After a hunt we'd come in to a table just loaded with fish roe, broiled ham, fried chicken, biscuits the size of your hand—" (55). Moreover, unlike Alison, neither Leonora nor Langdon is particularly anxious about her or his sexualized body. Leonora sleeps naked or "'in the raw,' as she called it" (43), and has few qualms about fondling Langdon in the presence of their spouses. Such displays prompt Alison to deem Leonora "nothing but an animal" (68) and her name therefore appropriate insofar as it connotes ferocious leonine femininity. Langdon too is figured as more beast than man, the hulking hirsute major being known around the stables as The Buffalo "because when in the saddle he slumped his great heavy shoulder and lowered his head" (19).

McCullers scripts the murderous Ellgee Williams in comparable terms, replicating in him the virile animalism of Goyen's Christy Ganchion. The private features eyes that have "a mute expression that is usually found in the eyes of animals," moves "with the silence and agility of a wild creature" (2), and sports "a sensual, savage smile" (47). Even after Penderton kills Williams, "in death the body of the soldier still had the look of warm, animal comfort" (111). As Penderton memorably learns, Williams also parallels Leonora in his tendency toward exhibitionistic nudity. Like Goyen and Hawthorne, McCullers configures the woods as a site of sexual freedom, and it is here that Williams escapes to tan his body, either sunning on rocks or, still without clothes, riding at a furious gallop.

Williams's sexual desires are no less consuming than those of Penderton, Leonora, and Langdon and lead to similar extremes. It is Penderton, however, whom Williams perhaps most directly parallels. Just as the novel delineates the captain's growing awareness of his forbidden desire for men, the work simultaneously charts Williams's nascent realizations of his heretofore forbidden desire for women. His vision of the naked Leonora instigates just as profound a reconsideration of childhood inculcations about sexuality as Penderton's glimpse of Williams's body does: "And never before in his life had this young soldier seen a naked woman. He had been brought up in household exclusively male. From his father, who ran a one-mule farm and preached on Sunday at a Holiness church, he had learned that women carried in them a deadly and catching disease which made men blind, crippled, and doomed to hell" (15–16). As a result of this misogynistic teaching, "Private Williams had never willingly touched, or looked at, or spoken to a female since he was eight years old" (16).

McCullers suggests that heteroeroticism has been as insistently latent in Williams as homoeroticism has been in Penderton. As a youth Williams engages in a tempered bestiality arising from what seems to be attempts to gratify his desire for women, whether in the role of a mother, a lover, or a conflation of the two. Recalling Faulkner's Jewel Bundren and the acquisition of his beloved horse in *As I Lay Dying*, Williams "accumulated a hundred dollars by plowing and picking cotton" to buy a cow. Once the beast is purchased, however, Williams seems more reminiscent of Ike Snopes than Jewel Bundren, for the cow becomes the feminine object of Williams's erotic desire: "On winter mornings the boy would get up before daylight and go out with a lantern to his cow's stall. He would press his forehead against her warm flank as he milked and talk to her in soft, urgent whispers. He put his cupped hands down into the pail of frothy milk and drank with lingering swallows" (22). Although McCullers does not have Williams engage in overt sexual acts with the cow, as Faulkner figures Ike to do, it nevertheless becomes clear that Williams's heterosexual desire for women is so insistent that he will improvise an eroticized relationship with a female animal to gratify this longing.

The actions manifesting from his desire are no less deviant when Williams finally encounters actual women's bodies. Leonora's nakedness so obsesses him that he returns repeatedly to gaze at it, eventually growing brave enough to force entries into the Pendertons' house and spend entire nights observing Leonora's bare sleeping body. His efforts and risks are rewarded, however, since at these moments the "young soldier felt in him a keen, strange sweetness that never before in his life had he known" (45). Stalking and voyeurism thus culminate a series of representations in which McCullers links heterosexual desire to exhibitionism, bestiality, and near idiocy and thereby darkly suggests that persons whose potential sexualities are centrally informed by same-sex desire should be tolerated since these people are no more repulsive and/or socially deviant than those who find erotic gratification in persons of the other sex.

McCullers returns to this logic in *The Ballad of the Sad Café* (1943), depicting with comparable detachment circulations of unreciprocated desire among three characters as grotesque as those of her earlier novels: the Amazonian Amelia Evans, the hunchbacked Lymon Willis, and the satanic Marvin Macy. Although the novella most centrally interrogates Amelia's emotional investment in Lymon, the second half of the work reintroduces Marvin Macy into the plot, establishes Lymon's inexplicable homoerotic investment in Marvin, and thus invites the comparison of these two loves. Just as Amelia dotes on Lymon despite his rebuffs, he uses all tricks in his repertoire to fawn on Marvin Macy. When wiggling his ears fails to arrest Marvin's attention, Lymon, "seeing that his accomplishment was getting him nowhere, added new efforts of persuasion. He fluttered his eyelids, so that they were like pale, trapped moths in his sockets. He scraped his feet around the ground, waved his hands about, and finally began doing a little trotlike dance."[9] Like Pepe Alvarez in his furious drunken reactions to Randolph's affections in *Other Voices, Other Rooms*, Marvin responds to Lymon with violence. The hunchback, however, only grows more infatuated with the ex-convict: "For since first setting eyes on Marvin Macy the hunchback was possessed by an unnatural spirit. Every minute he wanted to be following along behind this jailbird, and he was full of silly schemes to attract attention to himself. . . . Sometimes the hunchback would give up, perch himself on the banister of the front porch much as a sick bird huddles on a telephone wire, and grieve publicly." "'Oh, Marvin Macy,' groaned the hunchback, and the sound of the name was enough to upset the rhythm of his sobs so that he hiccuped" (52–53). Even though Lymon leaves with Marvin Macy after the decisive fight with Amelia, there is little sign that he returns Lymon's affections. Rather, if anything, Marvin seems to cultivate the relationship with the hunchback only to exact revenge on Amelia for not having returned his love and erotic overtures during her ten-day marriage to Marvin.

As with the emotional and erotic investments of *Reflections in a Golden Eye,* none of them in *The Ballad of the Sad Café*—a man's love of a woman, a woman's love of a man, and a man's love of a man—is particularly valorized. None of them, however, is dismissed as invalid or anymore freakish than the others. Rather, the images of these relationships parallel what the narrative voice makes overt concerning McCullers's understanding of love, desire, and sexuality. She is emphatic, in this famous passage, that the emotional and erotic investments of a lover for a beloved are not contingent upon differing sexes. Just as "this lover about whom we speak need not necessarily be a young man saving for a wedding ring—this lover can be man, woman, child, or indeed any human creature on this earth," so too "the beloved can also be of any description":

> The most outlandish people can be the stimulus for love. A man may be a doddering great-grandfather and still love only a strange girl he saw in the streets of Cheehaw one afternoon two decades past. The preacher may love a fallen woman. The beloved may be treacherous, greasy-headed, and given to evil habits. Yes, and the lover may see this as clearly as anyone else—but that does not affect the evolution of his love one whit. A most mediocre person can be the object of a love which is wild, extravagant, and beautiful as the poison lilies of the swamp. A good man may be the stimulus for a love both violent and debased, or a jabbering madman may bring about in the soul of someone a tender and simple idyll. Therefore, the value and quality of any love is determined solely by the lover himself. (26–27)

Thus, just as Captain Penderton's passionate comments about the square peg discovering the unorthodox square that will fit it can subtly refer to same-sex desire and its tolerance, this discourse on love includes a similar reference and, when contextualized with the various relations represented within the novella, suggests that for McCullers same-sex desire is structured no differently than that between any two persons.

Although McCullers's subsequent works, like her earlier ones, do not always reveal such a problematically ahistoricized and decontextualized understanding of desire, they nevertheless evince an ongoing preoccupation with same-sex attractions between men. Even texts in which such attractions are not central, such as *The Member of the Wedding* (1946), provide enough passing glimpses to keep readers reminded of alternatives to heterosexual desire. For instance, on her shopping trip for a dress to wear to her brother's wedding, Frankie Addams has much the same experience as Capote's Joel Knox does while wandering the streets of New Orleans. She sees—but does not understand—two men apparently kissing: "There in the alley were only two colored boys, one taller than the other and with his arm resting on the shorter boy's shoulder. That was all—but something about the angle or the way they stood, or the pose of their shapes, had reflected the sudden picture of her brother and the bride that had so shocked her." [10]

Such a vague and seemingly inconsequential image takes on importance a few pages later when Berenice offers her litany to Frankie and John Henry of the forms that love may assume. A mouthpiece for McCullers, who rehearses many of the sentiments expressed in the discourse on the lover and the beloved in *The Ballad of the Sad Café*, Berenice confirms—albeit in a slightly homophobic fashion—the existence of homoeroticism in the character McCullers designates in her outline of the novel as "an abandoned, waifish Negro homosexual" [11]:

> "I have heard of many a queer thing," said Berenice. "I have knew mens to fall in love with girls so ugly that you had to wonder if their eyes is straight. . . . I have knew womens to love veritable Satans and thank Jesus when they put their split hooves over the threshold. I have knew boys to take it into their heads to fall in love with other boys. You know Lily Mae Jenkins?"
>
> F. Jasmine thought a minute, and then answered: "I'm not sure."
>
> "Well, you either know him or you don't know him. He prisses around with a pink satin blouse and one arm akimbo. Now this Lily Mae fell in love with a man name Juney Jones. A man, mind you. And Lily Mae turned into a girl. He changed his nature and his sex and turned into a girl." (75–76)

Berenice's recital thus not only acknowledges the presence of a gay man but also, like Capote's Randolph and Goyen's Folner, reinscribes the mid-twentieth-century presumption of popular culture that same-sex desire, effeminacy, and transvestism are mutually constitutive of gayness.

This understanding of the relation between gender and sexuality as articulated by Berenice in *The Member of the Wedding* should not, however, be taken as that of McCullers herself. Instead of reifying the inseparability of gender transitivity, homoeroticism, and gayness and thus rehearsing an investment in Havelock Ellis's theories of sexual inversion, as Lori Kenschaft discusses in McCullers's work, she seeks to represent the complexity and mutability of gender's relation to desire and sexuality and the rarity with which "deviant" desire and sexuality may be validly conflated with "deviant" performances of gender. That is not to say, however, that McCullers forecloses that men negotiating same-sex desire may be effeminate or less than masculine, since, as Kenschaft shows, the representations of male homoeroticism delineated above often manifest in gender-transitive (inverted, in Ellis's terms) men other than Lily Mae Jenkins. Penderton, for instance, "had been brought up by five old-maid aunts" who "were constantly arranging picnics, fussy excursions, and Sunday dinners to which they invited other old maids" (61). As a result of his upbringing, McCullers suggests, he fails to internalize masculine performances at the exclusion of feminine ones, as his broader cultural moment demands, and thus "obtained within himself a delicate balance between the male and female elements, with the susceptibilities of both the sexes and the active powers of neither" (8). Penderton's body, typified by his "white, fattish hands" (4), is soft, and despite years in the army, he avoids physical activity. When pressured into it, he consistently displays ineptness and suffers the ridicule of others. His riding skills, for example, are so comically undeveloped, especially in contrast to those of his wife, that around the stables he earns the snickered nickname of "Captain Flap-Fanny" (20).

Penderton's interests tend away from that which is physical and therefore supposedly masculine and instead toward the aesthetic and therefore ostensibly feminine. The events of the novel are catalyzed by his ordering of Williams to trim an oak tree to retain the "way the boughs swept down and made a background shutting off the rest of the woods" (6). When Williams lops away these branches, Penderton is furious: "Private, the whole idea was in the big oak tree. . . . Now it is all ruined" (6). Penderton's appreciation for the subtle and delicate also extends to his tastes in foods: "The plain, heavy Southern meals that Leonora and Morris enjoyed were especially distasteful to him. . . . He appreciated the subtle cookery of New Orleans, and the delicate, balanced harmony of French food. Often in the old days he used to go into the kitchen when he was in the house alone and prepare for his own enjoyment some luscious tidbit. His favorite dish was fillet of beef à la Béarnaise" (98). In each case, Penderton valorizes artistic expression, damning what he considers less tasteful than what he can envision or supposedly create if only allowed to do so by his culture.

Lymon Willis is perhaps even more transgressive of normative gender than Penderton. The hunchback's wardrobe, for instance, is a disharmonious miscellany that includes items of women's clothing as well as others that are understood by his community not to be masculine: "Beneath this was a fresh red and black checkered shirt belonging to Miss Amelia. He did not wear trousers such as ordinary men are meant to wear, but a pair of tight-fitting little knee-length breeches. On his skinny legs he wore black stockings, and his shoes were of a special kind, being queerly shaped, laced up over his ankles, and newly cleaned and polished with wax. Around his neck, so that his large, pale ears were almost completely covered, he wore a shawl of lime-green wool, the fringes of which almost touched the floor" (18). Moreover, like both Penderton and Capote's Randolph, Lymon prefers to surround himself in his private spaces with plush comfort and lingering Victorian excesses. His bedroom "was furnished with a large chiffarobe, a bureau covered with a stiff white linen cloth crocheted at the edges, and a marble-topped table. The bed was immense, an old fourposter made of carved, dark rosewood." Tucked beneath the bed and thus "modestly out of view" is, perhaps most telling, Lymon's "china chamber-pot painted with pink roses" (35). Such surroundings seem all the more lavish and effeminate when contrasted to Amelia's "smaller and very simple" bedroom: "The bed was narrow and made of pine. There was a bureau for her breeches, shirts, and Sunday dress, and she had hammered two nails in the closet wall on which to hang her swamp boots. There were no curtains, rugs, or ornaments of any kind" (35).

In contrast to the effeminate Penderton and Lymon, McCullers also offers Singer and Antonapoulos in *The Heart Is a Lonely Hunter*. Although the men are by no means masculine to the extremes of Goyen's Christy, the two mutes are also not particularly feminine. True, Singer functions in the traditionally feminine role of homemaker and caretaker, but he seems to do so more out of necessity than by choice. Moreover, he retains a certain supposedly masculine austerity about his performances of these roles and the environment they create and thus leads a life as neatly organized and linear as the narrow iron cot on which he sleeps and the board on which he plays chess. McCullers comparably accounts for Antonapoulos's periodic breaches of masculine behavior, such as his pervading passivity. It arises not so much out of a conscious decision to transgress gender norms, such as that informing Lily Mae Jenkins's behavior, as it does out of an inability even to *understand* these norms. Handicapped by a pronounced lack of cognitive development—his "mental, sexual and spiritual development," McCullers offers, "is that of a child of about seven years old"—as well as his muteness, Antonapoulos must rely upon others at practically every turn to function in a world more complex than he can understand.[12] Thus, while such a reliance forces him into a stereotypical feminine role, he has little decision in assuming it.

Although McCullers is no doubt interested in exploring varying representations of the interplay of gender, same-sex desire, and, less frequently, gayness in characters such as Antonapoulos, Singer, Penderton, and Lymon, she seems equally—if not more so—concerned with representing deviant performances of gender in persons not necessarily attracted to others of the same sex. Her corpus includes a number of gender-transitive men who, although perhaps not invested in heterosexual desire, are also not presented as overtly homosexual. Consider, for instance, Anacleto, the Langdons' Filipino houseboy in *Reflections in a Golden Eye.* His effeminacy is so extreme that even Penderton seems masculine in comparison. Anacleto typically dresses in "sandals, soft gray trousers, and a blouse of aquamarine linen" (32); moreover, he meddles, gossips, paints, keeps up a stream of "soft and vivacious chattering to himself," laces his conversation with French, and, at unexpected moments, bursts into the moves of a ballet dancer, all of which prompts Morris Langdon to exclaim, "God! You're a rare bird" (33). Yet McCullers includes nothing in the novel to establish Anacleto's desire for other men. He seems to want only to be Alison's constant companion, since he "had been with Mrs. Langdon since he was seventeen years old" and "adored her" (27). This adoration culminates in his presumptions of Alison's perfection, and it "was common knowledge that he thought the Lord had blundered grossly in the making of everyone except himself and Madame Alison" (33). The resulting bond is largely desexualized, and little implies that Anacleto seeks erotic gratification outside the relationship, thus suggesting that the union is, although not heterosexual, at least one in which companionship between a man and a woman is self-sufficient for both of them.

Reflections in a Golden Eye also includes the effeminate Lieutenant Weincheck, who, as Leonora complains, talks without end "about highbrow things" (29), sews, listens to Mozart, and maintains an apartment "crowded [with] an accumulation of a lifetime, including a grand piano, a shelf of phonograph albums, many hundreds of books, a big Angora cat, and about a dozen potted plants" (30). As with Anacleto, however, McCullers does not confirm in Weincheck desire for other men, despite effeminate behavior. Indeed, she establishes little about his desire whatsoever, and readers thus face a dilemma similar to that posed by Harper Lee's Jack Finch. Given the era's relative intolerance of overt depictions of same-sex desire in mainstream literary production, McCullers, like many of her contemporaries, may be using gender transitivity as an understandable cultural shorthand for gayness. However, in consideration of her fairly forthright representations of same-sex desire elsewhere, as well as her images of gender-transitive men who are not gay, one wonders if Weincheck should not be taken at face value: he is effeminate, but McCullers's text simply does not establish for him a sexual identity. Although she may fully intend for Weincheck to be understood as gay, to assume such is both to risk an overreading of the novel and potentially to reduce McCullers's characters into a restrictive binarism of having either a heterosexual or a homosexual identity.

The space outside this hetero/homo binarism is precisely that occupied by Biff Brannon by the end of *The Heart Is a Lonely Hunter*. Yet, if one ascribes to effeminacy being an inescapable designation of male homosexuality, as Richard Cook does, Biff ought rightly to be considered gay, since he, like Anacleto and Weincheck, is not conventionally masculine.[13] The novel charts Biff's steady evolution away from such—to him—restrictive masculine performances and toward feminine ones in the aftermath of his wife's death. When Alice dies, he begins to put lemon rinse on his hair and to dab perfume beneath his armpits, adding these effeminizations of his body to the already-established habit of wearing his mother's wedding band. Recalling the pleasure he receives as a child from "the feel and colors of beautiful cloth" scraps he would play with for hours under the kitchen table, Biff directs comparable attention to his heretofore "tacky and flossy and drab" apartment:

> All of this he had changed. He traded the iron bed for a studio couch. There was a thick red rug on the floor, and he had bought a beautiful cloth of Chinese blue to hang on the side of the wall where the cracks were worst. He had unsealed the fireplace and kept it laid with pine logs. Over the mantel was a small photograph of Baby and a colored picture of a little boy in velvet holding a ball in his hands. A glassed case in the corner held the curios he had collected— specimens of butterflies, a rare arrowhead, a curious rock shaped like a human profile. Blue-silk cushions were on the studio couch, and he had borrowed Lucile's sewing-machine to make deep red curtains for the windows. He loved the room. It was both luxurious and sedate. On the table there was a little Japanese pagoda with glass pendants that tinkled with strange musical tones in a draught. (191–92)

In light of subsequent images by McCullers and her contemporaries, these surroundings seem not unlike the familiar ones of gay characters such as Lymon and Capote's Randolph.

Biff's artistic expression is not relegated, however, to his body and the privacy of his apartment. Just as Penderton seeks to beautify the space surrounding his house, Biff's latent penchant for design finds its way into the busy café. Repulsed at the display window, where the "gravy from the duck had run into the cranberry sauce and a fly was stuck in the dessert," Biff, "with an eye for color and design," replaces the distasteful food with an artful arrangement of fruit (195–96). The novel closes with him decorating the same window with flowers: "he stood in the street to regard his handiwork. The awkward stems of the flowers had been bent to just the right degree of restful looseness. The electric lights detracted, but when the sun rose the display would show at its best advantage." "Downright artistic," Biff notes to himself (303).

Striking though Biff's amateur interior decorating and flower arranging are, his feminine performances culminate in the caretaking of his niece. When she fretfully defies her rather inept mother, "Biff took the situation in charge. He soothed Baby with a ball of candy gum and eased the coat from her shoulders. Her dress had lost its set in the struggle with Lucile. He straightened it so that the yoke was in line across her chest. He retied her sash and crushed the bow in just the right shape with his fingers" (196).

Gratified with this knowledge about his parenting, Biff fantasizes about adopting children, in no small part so to secure an outlet for his creativity in designing and making girls' clothes: "And the clothes he would make for her—pink crêpe de Chine frocks with dainty smocking at the yokes and sleeves. Silk socks and white buckskin shoes. And a little red-velvet coat and cap and muff for winter" (201). During such daydreams, although Biff is usually careful to define himself as these imagined children's father, he at times so wants to perform these roles supposedly relegated only to women that he will transsexualize himself. He rationalizes, "By nature all people are of both sexes. So that marriage and the bed is not all by any means. The proof? Real youth and old age. Because often old men's voices grow high and reedy and they take on a mincing walk. And old women sometimes grow fat and their voices get rough and deep and they grow dark little mustaches" (112). "And even he proved it himself," Biff thinks, "the part of him that sometimes almost wished he was a mother and that Mick and Baby were his kids" (112–13).

For all of Biff's desire to behave in roles culturally scripted as appropriate only for women or, in the cases of interior designers and florists, stereotypically effeminate gay men, McCullers constantly balances this femininity with Biff's powerful masculinity. Although he may prefer much the same lavish surroundings as Randolph, Biff's body is the antithesis of the pale, smooth plumpness of Capote's character. More like Goyen's Christy, Biff is a "hard man of middle height, with a beard so dark and heavy that the lower part of his face looked as though it were molded of iron" (9). After only a day's growth, this beard is "black and heavy as though it had grown for three days" (11); his hands are large and callused. Moreover, although he may alter the smell of his body, he does not attempt to eradicate those bodily markers culturally understood to designate masculinity, such as his "dark, hairy armpits" (191). Biff thus emerges as a thoroughly ironic character so long as one retains traditional understandings of gender symmetry, those in which men's bodies perform masculinely and women's perform femininely. Insofar as inert bodies are already gendered on the basis of appearance, Biff's hard, hairy body epitomizes masculinity. His behavior, however, is anything by manly and thus disrupts normal expectations concerning the mapping of sex and gender.

This disruption is even greater because this masculine body that behaves femininely is not necessarily that of a man whose identity is structured around same-sex desire, as is perhaps the cultural expectation arising from the Foucaultian model. This is not to say, however, that Biff retains a coherent, satisfactory, and exclusively heterosexual identity. To the contrary, just as the novel delineates his move away from gender conformity, the work also charts Biff's waning desire to interact sexually with women. Just as the physical gratification he receives from Alice's body early in the marriage diminishes, so too, eventually, does the pleasure he receives from female prostitutes, and he ultimately abandons physically actualized heterosexuality altogether: "Through the first year when he was happy and when she [Alice] seemed happy even too. And when the bed came down with them twice in three months. And he didn't know that all the time her brain was busy with how she could save a nickel or squeeze out an extra dime. And then him with Rio and the girls at her place. Gyp and Madeline and Lou. And then later when suddenly he lost it. When he could lie with a woman no longer. Motherogod! So that at first it seemed everything was gone" (201). McCullers includes little, however, to indicate that Biff replaces these heterosexual acts with either homosexual ones or even the unfulfilled desire to engage in them. Identified by McCullers as impotent in an early outline of the novel, he mourns this loss and seems to resolve himself to a generic love of humankind, one that is largely desexualized and thus outside a hetero/homo binarism.[14] The novel's final pages underscore this resolution as Biff destroys the freakish multicolored zinnia with an impromptu game of "Loves Me, Loves Me Not": "He plucked the soft, bright petals and the last one came out on love. But who? Who would he be loving now? No one person. Anybody decent who came in out of the street to sit for an hour and have a drink. But no one person. He had known his loves and they were over. Alice, Madeline and Gyp. Finished" (304–5). This broad love presumably includes the love of other men, and one might argue that Singer is the first person to receive Biff's love after his reconceptualization of love, sex, gender, and sexuality. In accordance with these very reconfigurations, however, this relationship is consistently desexualized, and Biff—perhaps naively, much like McCullers herself, according to biographers—allows no space for any future relationships that include sexual components. Thus, as with Anacleto, McCullers presents in Biff Brannon a character who defies the cultural scripting of effeminate man as invariably gay or even homoerotically attracted to other men. With the sum of these characters—Lily Mae, Penderton, Lymon, Singer, Antonapoulos, Weincheck, Anacleto, Biff—McCullers offers a range of men who, as Rachel Adams asserts, "combine qualities of masculine and feminine to suggest a model of sexuality based on a continuum rather than strict binary oppositions."[15]

McCullers similarly removes men—and particularly effeminate ones—from a hetero/homo binarism by characterizing them as prepubescent and thus supposedly too young for crystallized sexualities of any sort. Although such is not the case, the majority of American society remains extraordinarily anxious regarding children's erotic desire and on the whole prefers to postpone presumptions and/or negotiations of eroticism until after childhood. McCullers herself seems to share this anxiety and, unlike Wright, desexualizes the children she represents, appearing content to explore in them only the mappings of sex and gender. Contrary to frequent critical presumptions, however, McCullers's corpus does not offer only stock images of children as either sissies or tomboys. These representations instead provide a range of characters not unlike that of her adults. Her fictional boys, for instance, almost always deviate in some way from gender norms, but these figures vary from Bubber Kelly's slight transgressions in *The Heart Is a Lonely Hunter* to John Henry West's blatant gender transitivity in *The Member of the Wedding*.

First consider Bubber. Like Biff Brannon, he nurses an artistic side and, despite cultural policing of such tendencies in boys, makes public his appreciation of the beauty that he finds in female fashion. When Bubber sees Baby Wilson parading through the neighborhood in her soirée costume of "a little pink-gauze skirt that stuck out short and stiff, a pink body waist, pink dancing shoes, and even a little pink pocketbook," he is enchanted, crooning, "That sure is a cute little pink pocketbook" (139–40). She is so provocative that he confesses his desire to dress similarly: "I sure to wish I had a costume . . . A real cool costume. A real pretty one made out of all different colors. Like a butterfly" (140). And yet, as with Biff, McCullers establishes Bubber as simultaneously masculine. He carries a rifle throughout this scene, taking aim at various targets even as he continues his observations regarding Baby's costume. His compulsion to perform masculinely eventually dominates in that the scene culminates with his violent shooting of the girl, leading Mick to conclude that Bubber "wasn't a sissy" but instead "just loved pretty things" (141). Indeed, his fracturing of Baby's skull as he imagines himself in a similar costume ironically earns him the butch nickname of

"Baby-Killer Kelly" (153), which irrevocably replaces the more effeminate one of "Bubber."

In contrast stands the six-year-old John Henry West, whom Adams deems "the queerest of all," the "best a freak can be."[16] Although on first appearance he seems largely a resurrection of the earlier-discussed character, John Henry displays none of Bubber's masculinity and instead more closely resembles Lee's effeminate Dill, performing almost without exception as young girls his age ought according to the day's cultural scriptings of gender. Largely because of his age, John Henry's body is hardly masculine: "His chest was white and wet and naked, and he wore around his neck a tiny lead donkey tied by a string. . . . He was small to be six years old, but he had the largest knees that Frankie had ever seen, and on one of them was always a scab or a bandage where he had fallen down and skinned himself. John Henry had a little screwed white face and he wore tiny gold-rimmed glasses" (3). Moreover, his actions are those of a stereotypical sissy. He, like Anacleto, is prone to meddle and, like Biff Brannon, willingly assumes roles of mothering inculcated in girls during childhood. John Henry treasures Frankie's rejected doll, for instance, rocking it as he hurries to name it: "He pulled up the doll's dress and fingered the real panties and body-waist. 'I will name her Belle'" (15).

McCullers reinforces this lack of conventional masculinity by establishing in John Henry an appreciation of aesthetics reminiscent of that nursed by Penderton and Biff Brannon. When John Henry sculpts his biscuit man, for instance, he does so with acute sensitivity to form and detail:

> John Henry did not play with the dough; he worked on the biscuit man as though it were a very serious business. Now and then he stopped off, settled his glasses with his little hand, and studied what he had done. He was like a tiny watchmaker, and he drew up a chair and knelt on it so that he could get directly over the work. . . . When he had finished, he wiped his hands on the seat of his shorts, and there was a little biscuit man with separate fingers, a hat on, and even walking stick. John Henry had worked so hard that the dough was now gray and wet. But it was a perfect little biscuit man, and, as a matter of fact, it reminded Frankie of John Henry himself. (7–8)

He is comparably sensitive to the beauty he perceives in the moths—for him, the "beautiful butterflies" (11)—drawn to the window screens at night and in the freakish little Pin Head he sees at the fair. Despite Frankie's and Berenice's protests, John Henry is adamant about the Pin Head's attractiveness, asserting that she is "the cutest little girl I ever saw. I never saw anything so cute in my whole life" (18), and thus sounding much like Bubber in his appreciation of Baby's costume.

John Henry is equally fascinated by Lily Mae Jenkins, the gay man in Berenice's recital of the various "queer" loves she has known. Yet John Henry is not so much intrigued by the sexual practices implied by Lily Mae's love of Juney Jones as by Lily Mae's transgressions of normative gender. "How?" John Henry suddenly asks. "How did that boy change into a girl?" (77). This transsexualization so captivates his imagination that, when it is his turn to play Holy Lord God, he offers that "people ought to be half boy and half girl" (92) and thus supposedly escape the gender restrictions that so distress Frankie. Indeed, within the privacy of the Addamses' kitchen, John Henry approximates such a transsexualization by cross-dressing so that he appears "a little old woman dwarf, wearing the pink hat with the plume, and the high-heel shoes" (117).

Despite John Henry's cross-dressing and his and Bubber's fascination with "pretty things," it remains constant that, although cultural assumptions about effeminate boys may call these characters' adult heterosexualities into question, McCullers's texts rarely, if ever, do. In contrast to the bond between Pete and Sucker in the early short story, little homoeroticism circulates within the relationships respectively formed by John Henry and Bubber. To speculate of the boys' eventual homosexualities is thus as problematic as to guess about Lieutenant Weincheck's. Yet critics such as Mab Segrest have indulged in precisely these presumptions. So far as McCullers's text definitively establishes, John Henry is hardly Frankie's "little faggot cousin," as Segrest terms him.[17] He and Bubber are instead largely desexualized, gender-transitive boys whose adult sexualities remain unrepresented. Male characters such as Penderton and Lymon Willis suggest that McCullers acknowledges how she understands same-sex desire and effeminacy may simultaneously structure identity. Other male characters, however, such as Anacleto and Biff Brannon, check that this structuring is not always a given. To the contrary, effeminate men in McCullers's imagination need not desire other men. Thus, to presume an adult gay identity for John Henry and Bubber seems a risky endeavor.

* * *

In contrast to the diversity of McCullers's male characters, her images of women are fewer and less varied. Some texts are conspicuously male centered, such as *The Heart Is a Lonely Hunter*, which offers only Mick Kelly among a range of male protagonists. When McCullers does depict women, their sexualities are often, as noted earlier, emphatically hetero-sexual or asexual, as with Leonora Penderton and Alison Langdon. *The Member of the Wedding*, McCullers's text perhaps most concerned with women, continues this focus on female heterosexuality with Sadie Berenice Brown. The Addamses' cook, whom Barbara White labels "a completely man-oriented woman" and Thadious Davis characterizes as thoroughly "secure in her sexual identity," remarries three times and plans an eventual fourth wedding in hopes of replicating the bond she has with her beloved first husband.[18] She does so in part because she understands heterosexual intimacy as something of a panacea for the world's ills. Perhaps foremost of these concerns for her as an African American living in McCullers's imag-ined midcentury South is racism, as Berenice attempts to explain: "Because I am colored. Everybody is caught one way or another. But they done drawn completely extra bounds around all colored people. They done squeezed us off in one corner by ourself. So we caught that firstway I was telling you, as all human beings is caught. And we caught as colored people also" (113–14). The anxiety of being thus doubly "caught" and alienated from oth-ers prompts Berenice to find a surrogate for her idealized first husband: "And we try in one way or another to widen ourself free. For instance, me and Ludie. When I was with Ludie, I didn't feel so caught" (114). "My in-tention," she tells Frankie of the subsequent marriages, "was to repeat me and Ludie" (101). Although these efforts largely fail, Berenice remains con-vinced of heterosexuality's curative powers, counseling that Frankie needs only to find herself a "nice little white boy beau" (77) to stave off depression and anxiety.

These overtly heterosexual female characters are not, however, those who have prompted the most critical interest. Instead, McCullers's tomboys— "those boy-girl adolescents," as Leslie Fiedler terms them—and the Ama-zonian Amelia Evans have captured more attention than McCullers's other female characters, perhaps because of their autobiographical bases. Interro-gations of these characters remain problematic, however, because any num-ber of critics, often with markedly different agendas, set up an artificial bi-narism in which Mick, Amelia, Frankie, and McCullers herself emerge as either lesbians or proto-lesbians and thus directly antithetical to McCullers's heterosexual female characters. Segrest's groundbreaking efforts to queer southern literature—those that reduce John Henry West to a "little faggot"—have, for instance, led her to deem Amelia a "dyke" and Frankie a "twelve-year-old baby-dyke." Although overstated and oversimplified, Segrest's characterizations are nevertheless understandable, since, as Lori Kenschaft offers, Segrest, like others, shifts the emphasis from author and text to reader and approaches McCullers's "coded descriptions" as a lesbian "in the context of a historically grounded and historically changing interpretive community of lesbians." And yet Segrest seems too willing in her search for lesbian representation to reduce "McCullers's portrayal of multiplicitous, shifting, and often obsessive desires" to homosexuality.[19]

Even critics who do not work from homophilic positions, as Segrest and Kenschaft do, have often argued for characters' lesbian identities. Louis Rubin flatly deems McCullers a lesbian and, insofar as he holds Mick and Frankie to be McCullers's self-representations, reads them as proto-lesbian. He confesses he cannot separate McCullers from her fictional characters: "These young girls, both with masculine names, remain fixed in preadolescence; when they have to become women, as they must, they are, as characters, all but destroyed. Mick seduces Harry Minowitz; her initiation accomplished, she wants nothing whatever to do with him, and gladly lets him run away. Frankie, more innocent, smashes the vase over the head of a soldier, . . . then becomes Frances and is Frankie no more. I think of those photographs in Mrs. Carr's biography, of Carson at Yaddo looking like a boyish preadolescent girl, and of what she did to poor Reeves McCullers."[20] Rubin's biases seem clear: those girls who cannot "become women" pathetically assume lesbian identities, as he holds McCullers to have done. These women are to be pitied in that they are "all but destroyed," but even greater sympathy should be accorded Harry Minowitz in *The Heart Is a Lonely Hunter,* the soldier of *The Member of the Wedding,* and "poor Reeves McCullers," the men who are physically and emotionally abused as these women come to accept their lesbianism.

Other early critics, such as Chester Eisinger and Ihab Hassan, resemble Rubin in rehearsing these presumptions of lesbianism, but few have been as dogmatic as Leslie Fiedler. In a discussion of what he calls the "Good Bad Small Girl," he asserts: "The lesbian implications of this image were not apparent to the great audience of the past, which would have found in any hint of female homosexuality the really unforgivable blasphemy against the conventions of womanhood. But Carson McCullers has taken full advantage of those implications, projecting in her neo-tomboys, ambiguous and epicene, the homosexual's sense of exclusion from the family and his uneasiness before heterosexual passion." And yet, as White argues, Fiedler interrogates these characters' sexualities no further: "We never learn what a 'homosexual sensibility' might be and how it is 'abnormal,' what the 'tomboy image' has to do with lesbianism." Fiedler instead lets these sexualities stand insofar as they neatly exemplify a lesbian parallel to the "innocent" interracial male homosexuality he posits as structuring "classic" American literature. Although he comes close to dismissing Frankie as "a sentimental parody" of Mick, "a child victim, to be wept over condescendingly," he nevertheless retains Frankie as a metamorphosed Huck, yearning for "the arms of her black mammy" just as Twain's hero hankers for Jim's comfort. Indeed, Fiedler ends his brief discussion of McCullers's work by nodding to this parallel, asserting that Frankie, despite her differences from Huck, ultimately "comes, oddly, back to the raft."[21]

Segrest, Rubin, and Fiedler all problematically accept McCullers's exclusive investment in models of inversion and thus presume deviancy within a character's performances of gender to designate her sexual deviancy and thus largely disregard the absences of sexuality that McCullers includes with these figures, absences much like those in her characterizations of John Henry West and Bubber Kelly. Moreover, these and similar critics rarely address these girls' complex negotiations of sexuality when they do finally reach puberty. Consider Mick Kelly, one of McCullers's earliest depictions of a girl poised at adolescence. Like Capote's Idabel and Lee's Scout, Mick defies social norms of femininity and instead both appears and acts like a boy. Biff Brannon characterizes her as a "gangling, towheaded youngster, a girl of about twelve," who "dressed in khaki shorts, a blue shirt, and tennis shoes—so that at first glance she was like a very young boy" (14). She has a "hoarse, boyish voice" and a "habit of hitching up her khaki shorts and swaggering like a cowboy in the picture show" (17). Moreover, like McCullers herself, Mick repeatedly wishes to change her sex, raging at her condescending feminine sisters, "I'd rather be a boy any day" (35). It is thus perhaps not surprising that Mick fills her days with the preoccupations of the era's stereotypical boy: writing profane graffiti on the walls of an uncompleted house, taking mechanical shop in school, vowing to fight Nazism.

With the onset of puberty, Mick begins a series of intense emotional investments, many of which are in other girls and older women and thus replete with the "lesbian implications" that Fiedler notes. The first of these unacted-upon crushes occurs several years before the novel's setting: "Celeste never talked to her and she never talked to Celeste. Although that was what she wanted more than anything else. At night she would lie awake and think about Celeste. She would plan that they were best friends and think about the time when Celeste could come home with her to eat supper and spend the night" (206–7). These feelings extend to other women, such as "the lady who sold lottery tickets for a turkey raffle. And Miss Anglin who taught the seventh grade. And Carole Lombard in the movies. All of them" (207). And yet these crushes are not exclusively on women. McCullers anticipates her notions about the inexplicability of the beloved in *The Ballad of the Sad Café* when she has Mick recall her infatuation with the repulsive Buck. "He was big and had pimples on his face. When she stood by him in line to march in at eight-thirty he smelled bad—like his britches needed airing," she recalls. "When he laughed he lifted his upper lip and shook all over. She thought about him like she had thought about Celeste" (207). Moreover, Mick grows to love Singer and even senses a depth to these feelings previously unknown. Thus, even if one accords a sexual element to these emotional investments, they seem to establish Mick not as lesbian but as more appropriately akin to Wright's adolescent Fishbelly Tucker, since both willingly seek to bond with persons of the same and the other sex.

When Mick does decide to act physically upon these desires, she does so within a heterosexual context. It is she who is overcome with sexual excitement and suggests that she and Harry Minowitz swim naked. The subsequent loss of her virginity, however, is less than pleasurable: "They both turned at the same time. They were close against each other. She felt him trembling and her fists were tight enough to crack. 'O, God,' he kept saying over and over. It was like her head was broke off from her body and thrown away. And her eyes looked up straight into the blinding sun while she counted something in her mind. And then this was the way. This was how it was" (235). McCullers's imagery is inescapably violent, equating Mick's experience during intercourse with both blindness and decapitation. Afterwards she vows, "I didn't like that. I never will marry with any boy" (236). Yet, as with Biff Brannon, who comparably repudiates heterosexual interactions, McCullers does not suggest in Mick a nascent homosexual identity free to emerge after ostensibly normative sexuality has been rejected. Her crushes on girls remain relegated to her past, since, whereas Biff expands his capacity for desexualized love to whatever random strangers may now enter his life, Mick throws herself into the financial and emotional support of her family, rejecting love on every front after Singer's death. Thus, insofar as it is possible, Mick assumes an asexual identity and, like Biff, escapes—if only momentarily—the anxieties of a hetero/homo binarism.

McCullers's return to this autobiographical tomboy in *The Member of the Wedding* is even more tenuously charged with same-sex desire between women, despite Frankie's violations of normative gender so closely replicating those of Mick. Also hovering at puberty, Frankie has rejected or, by her rapid growth, been forced out of communally expected performances of femininity: "This summer she was grown so tall that she was almost a big freak, and her shoulders were narrow, her legs too long. She wore a pair of blue black shorts, a B.V.D. undervest, and she was barefooted. Her hair had been cut like a boy's, but it had not been cut for a long time and was now not even parted" (2). Her behavior is no more feminine than her appearances. She curses, angrily threatens Berenice with a knife, and shamelessly abuses John Henry. A lack of delicacy pervades almost all these interactions, as symbolized when she attempts to extract a splinter from her foot with a butcher knife rather than a needle, as Berenice urges. But, instead of being distraught at this indelicacy, Frankie takes pleasure in the resulting callousness that allows her to withstand what "would hurt other people" (26).

Frankie experiences much the same social policing of these transgressions that Scout does in *To Kill a Mockingbird* and is forcefully reminded of the consequences of such deviancy when the girls' club repeatedly rejects Frankie for her nonconformity. Her early response, however, is closer to Mick's than Scout's: to fantasize about a transsexualization into a male body that *can* legitimately behave as Frankie wishes. Awash with patriotism as World War II closes, she dreams of participating in the war effort as a boy, "flying aeroplanes and winning gold medals for bravery" (21). The Holy Lord God Frankie's decrees are thus not far from those of the Holy Lord God John Henry. In her ideal world, "people could instantly change back and forth from boys to girls, which ever way they felt like and wanted" (92). Even in her less fantastical dreams, she imagines herself performing with heroism that is inappropriate to and/or supposedly not achievable by her sex. When she decides to donate blood, she imagines "the army doctors saying that the blood of Frankie Addams was the reddest and the strongest blood they had ever known" (21).

Frankie opts at other times for the same strategy to negotiate gender that Scout uses at her aunt's missionary tea, attempting to allay anxieties by performing exactly as her community expects. The image that results when Frankie purchases her wedding dress and shoes is, however, no less comical to those around her than the figure Scout poses. "It just looks peculiar," Berenice explains. "You had all your hair shaved off like a convict, and now you tie a silver ribbon around this head without any hair." "Here you got on this grown woman's evening dress. Orange satin. And that brown crust on your elbows. The two things just don't mix," she concludes, snorting, "I'm not accustomed to human Christmas trees in August" (84–85). As with Scout's, Frankie's masculinized body masquerading in feminine attire reaffirms that her gender-transitive performances have become so routinized that any deviations from them—even in displays of normative gender—are just as disruptive as her everyday performances, if not more so. Thus, rather than allaying Frankie's anxieties, her attempts at gender conformity only augment her sense of freakishness.

Such negotiations of gender do not, however, mark Frankie's identity as any more centrally structured by lesbian desire than they do Scout's, prompting White to assert flatly, "In fact, there is no evidence in *The Member of the Wedding* that Frankie is homosexual."[22] Quite the contrary, even as McCullers insistently establishes Frankie's multiple transgressions of normative gender, she simultaneously emphasizes Frankie's thorough naiveté regarding sexuality, both others' and her own. She does not understand the implications of Berenice's comment that her current beau, T. T. Williams, "don't make me shiver none" (89), nor does Frankie comprehend the sexual activity she witnesses in the boarders' room, that which, "after a single glance, sent her running to the kitchen: Mr. Marlowe is having a fit!" (37). Even when such activity is broadly explained to her, she refuses to accept its usual role within marriage, characterizing the older girls' discussion of sex as "nasty lies" (11). Thus, by midnovel Frankie faces the anxious self-created scenario of desperately trying to master adult performances of gender but rejecting all knowledge of adult sexuality culturally mapping onto these enactments of gender.

Frankie's own sexual activity has been little and so marked with guilt that it is largely unenjoyable. When she commits "a secret and unknown sin" with Barney MacKean, she presumes it to be horrific, although "how bad it was she did not know. The sin made a shriveling sickness in her stomach, and she dreaded the eyes of everyone" (23). Given this naiveté, relative lack of experience, and pronounced guilt, Frankie's later sexual activities are not surprisingly motivated more by the wish to appear adult than the desire to give and/or receive erotic pleasure. She seems largely unaware of the sexual element when she accepts the date with the nameless soldier, doing so only because it affirms her maturity: "The very word, *date*, was a grown word used by older girls" (69). Even when the soldier begins his advances on Frankie in the hotel room, she does not understand that she risks being raped. She only vaguely senses danger and responds by ironically victimizing the solider with her own series of violent and degrading acts: biting his tongue, smashing a pitcher over his head, and leaving him "still, with the amazed expression on his freckled face that was now pale, and a froth of blood showed on his mouth. But his head was not broken, or even cracked, and whether he was dead or not she did not know" (130).

Frankie's rejection of sexualized relations does not, however, indicate a comparable dismissal of human connectedness. To the contrary, *The Member of the Wedding* centers on Frankie's desperate attempts to find a *"we of me"* (39) and her ironic distancing of the very persons who can and do provide this connection: John Henry and Berenice. Frankie initially thrills, for instance, at the closeness and comfort that John Henry provides as the two lie in bed together: "She heard him breathe in the darkness, and now she had what she wanted so many nights that summer; there was somebody sleeping in the bed with her." Her pleasure is so great that she cannot resist touching her cousin, providing a simultaneously innocent and provocatively erotic image: "Carefully she put her hand on his stomach and moved closer; it felt as though a little clock was ticking inside him and he smelled of sweat and Sweet Serenade. He smelled like a sour little rose. Frankie leaned down and licked him behind the ear. Then she breathed deeply, settled herself with her chin on his sharp damp should, and closed her eyes: for now, with somebody sleeping in the dark with her, she was not so much afraid" (13). Despite this comfort, however, she rejects him because of his youth as an unacceptable companion for the supposedly more mature girl. "He's a child!" she screams in a fit of anger. "It is hopeless! Hopeless! Hopeless!" (14).

Frankie similarly dismisses Berenice not because of her age but rather because of her race. Reflecting in fiction much the same argument that Lillian Smith posits as structuring the relations between a certain class of white southern children and their black mammies in the early twentieth century, the care that Berenice shows Frankie is, in the girl's racist understanding, always somewhat illegitimate because it comes from an African American. Indeed, race is consistently the defining factor of Berenice's identity for Frankie. When she thinks of the groups to which various persons belong, she can only imagine Berenice's membership as being contingent upon her blackness. "When Berenice said *we,*" Frankie thinks, "she meant Honey and Big Mama, her lodge, or her church" (39). And yet Frankie's interpretation of Berenice's assertions is not necessarily incorrect, since midcentury southern segregation did, for the most part, foreclose "legitimate" personal relations that crossed lines of color. As a result of these factors—John Henry's age and Berenice's race—"Frankie had had no *we* to claim, unless it would be the terrible summer *we* of her and John Henry and Berenice—and that was the last *we* in the world she wanted" (39).

Frankie's desire to form a—to her mind—legitimate *we* leads her to scheme of figuratively marrying both her brother and his fiancée. "I'm going with them," Frankie declares upon her epiphany. "After the wedding at Winter Hill, I'm going off with the two of them to whatever place that they will ever go" (43). Such a plan, if executed, would perhaps establish a degree of same-sex desire within Frankie, since the marriage's presumed sexual component would allow for the contours of a lesbian relationship between her and Janice. This union would also, however, introduce at least two other sexually transgressive elements: the incest between Frankie and Jarvis and the lack of monogamy for all three persons. It is perhaps the latter that is most disconcerting. "Remember back to the time of the flood? Remember Noah and the ark?" Berenice asks Frankie. "He admitted them creatures two by two" (73). Yet, as established, Frankie has little or no perception of the intricacies of sexuality and thus fails to understand any of the transgressive implications of her scheme. In her thinking such a union is as innocuous as becoming *Jasmine* so that her name alliterates with Janice's and Jarvis's.

The third and most excessively masculine of McCullers's triumvirate of gender-transitive female characters is Amelia of *The Ballad of the Sad Café*. She is "a dark, tall women with bones and muscle like a man" (4) and "strong, hairy thigh[s]" (60). Moreover, she wears her hair "cut short and brushed back from the forehead, and there was about her sunburned face a tense, haggard quality" (4). Her actions are no less transgressive than her body. A "powerful blunderbuss of a person" (25), she cherishes her pipe and is "forever trying out her strength, lifting up heavy objects, or poking her tough biceps with her finger" (45). McCullers even goes so far as to establish Amelia's masculinity by figuring her as thoroughly inept at negotiating the processes of specifically female bodies: "If a patient came in with a female complaint she could do nothing. Indeed at the mere mention of the words her face would slowly darken with shame, and she would stand there craning her neck against the collar of her shirt, or rubbing her swamp boots together, for all the world like a great, shamed, dumb-tongued child" (17). Only in this arena does Amelia's otherwise curative hand fail her.

To deem Amelia lesbian on the basis of this gender transitivity, as Segrest does, seems, however, misguided. When one considers Amelia's sexuality, especially in conjunction with her sociality, she emerges as a figure not unlike Anacleto in *Reflections in a Golden Eye:* a gender-transitive person who is largely divested of an overt sexual identity yet leads a life centered on a person of the differing sex. Much like Mick, Amelia has attempted — or, in her case, more accurately, stumbled into — physically actualized heterosexuality and is so repulsed by it that she utterly repudiates those acts. When Marvin Macy presumably attempts to consummate his ill-fated marriage, Amelia storms out of the bedroom, preferring to spend the night typing. Marvin remains "in a sorry fix" (31) throughout the ten-day marriage, and Amelia emerges from the experience firmly convinced that she "cared nothing for the love of men" (4).

As with Mick, however, this rejection of heterosexuality does not allow a crystallizing lesbian identity to develop within Amelia. She too instead becomes "a solitary person" (4), generally relegating herself outside both hetero- and homosocial arenas, much less hetero- and homosexual ones. Moreover, when she does eventually love, she chooses a man as her beloved. "The time has come to speak about love," the narrative voice asserts. "For Miss Amelia loved Cousin Lymon. So much was clear to everyone. They lived in the same house together and were never seen apart" (25). But, as with the love shared by Anacleto and Alison Langdon, these feelings of Amelia for Lymon seem not to include erotic desire but rather to constitute, according to Louise Westling, a maternal investment "without any threat of sexuality." [23] Thus, rather than reducing the complexities of Amelia's sexed, sexualized, and gendered identity to that of a butch lesbian, one might more rightly acknowledge this identity to be one most centrally structured by violations of gender norms and rejections of sexuality, while being all too briefly punctuated by a potentially heterosocial bond with Lymon.

With female figures such as Amelia, Mick, and Frankie, McCullers's corpus thus reveals its imaginings of same-sex desire to be something of the inverse of Lillian Smith's representations. Whereas Smith's writing privileges lesbian presences while including virtually no images of gay men, McCullers's fiction before *Clock Without Hands* repeatedly represents men negotiating same-sex desire while offering no overt lesbians. Whenever McCullers seems to approach such a representation, as with the triumvirate of gender-transitive women, she carefully divorces the figure of an overt sexual identity. McCullers's anxious negotiations of gender and sexuality in her own embodied experiences were no doubt factors in this divorce, and one wonders whether she would have offered a fictional interrogation of lesbianism had she not died at fifty. And yet, if *Clock Without Hands* is any indication, such seems unlikely, for although McCullers attempts to negotiate new complexities of same-sex desire in her last novel, she once again does so to the exclusion of same-sex desire between women.

In many ways, as Smith's candid, informal review of *Clock Without Hands* implies, the novel includes all the elements expected in a McCullers text: a southern setting, adolescents struggling with sexual and gendered identities, a largely sympathetic portrayal of Jews and African Americans, and, of course, loneliness and unrequited love. As in McCullers's earlier fiction, isolated persons starved for human connectedness fill *Clock Without Hands*. Diagnosed with leukemia, the rather autobiographical J. T. Malone becomes "surrounded by a zone of loneliness" as he faces inevitable death, and John Jester Clane wants as desperately as Frankie Addams to confess "*I've been very lonely*, but he could not bring himself to admit this truth aloud."[24] The omnipresence of this loneliness as perpetuated by unrequited love has even prompted Oliver Evans to reduce *Clock Without Hands* to its plot of misdirected erotic investments: "Malone's daughter, Ellen, loves Jester, who is scarcely aware of her existence; Jester is secretly in love with Sherman, who constantly mistreats him; and Sherman worships another Negro, Zippo, whose 'house guest' he is and who mistreats *him*."[25]

Of these seemingly standard elements in McCullers's work, her handling of same-sex desire in particular seems—if only initially—in keeping with earlier representations. As noted, lesbianism remains conspicuously absent. (The novel generally lacks women; the judge's wife and daughter-in-law are both dead, and Malone's wife and daughter have, at best, marginal presences.) It is, as Evans's summary offers, exclusively men who negotiate same-sex desire. Yet, in her depictions of Jester and Sherman, McCullers reveals a striking difference from the representations of her previous fiction. Because both boys—and only they within the novel—are effeminate, *Clock Without Hands* seems more akin to Capote's *Other Voices, Other Rooms* than much of McCullers's earlier work and threatens to reify cultural understandings that male homoeroticism and gender transitivity are mutually constitutive of gayness, those same understandings that allow the majority of McCullers's female characters to be so easily and consistently read as lesbian. Jester, for example, is "a slight limber boy of seventeen with auburn hair and a complexion so fair that the freckles on his upturned nose were like cinnamon sprinkled over cream" (21). Neither sports nor other rough-and-tumble homosocial activities interest him, and he prefers to nurture his musical talents, spending long hours playing classical works by Bach and Schubert. As a result of this effeminate appearance and behavior, Jester "had never been like a Milan boy," and the town regards him suspiciously. As the narrative, focalized through Malone, offers, Jester "was arrogant and at the same time overpolite. There was something hidden about the boy and his softness, his brightness seemed somehow dangerous—it was as though he resembled a silk-sheathed knife" (23).

Although Sherman's muscular body is not nearly as delicate as Jester's, the ostensibly black boy's actions mark him as potentially even more effeminate than his white counterpart. Like Jester, Sherman is a musician, a gifted singer. More telling, however, he is as persnickety about his surroundings as Biff Brannon and Weldon Penderton are. When Jester first visits the apartment Sherman shares with his beloved Zippo Mullins, the queenish Sherman insists on giving a tour of the space, elaborating with unintended humor on the supposedly impressive and tasteful touches but ignoring those that are not:

> With pride he pointed out each piece in the crowded, fancy, dreary room, "This rug is pure Wilton and the hide-a-bed sofa cost one hundred and eight dollars secondhand. It can sleep four if necessary." Jester eyed the three-quarter-size sofa, wondering how four people could sleep in it. . . . "The end tables are genuine antique as you can see. The plant was a birthday gift for Zippo." Sherman did not point out the red lamp with ragged fringes, two obviously broken

chairs and other pieces of sad-looking furniture. "I wouldn't have anything to happen to this apt" (he said the abbreviation). "You haven't seen the rest of the apt . . . just gorgeous." (71)

A foray into the kitchenette reveals an equally dreary reality that Sherman's lies cannot eradicate. The refrigerator that he assures Jester usually holds caviar and champagne features only "a head of wilted lettuce" and "a dish of cold back-eyed peas jelled in their own grease." Sherman's display of all "the most modern conveniences" does not change Jester's opinion of the "cramped dingy kitchenette" (71–72) but instead vaguely amuses and then bores him.

These effeminate concerns with the aesthetics and display of one's material surroundings also suggest a conflation on McCullers's part of specifically male homosexuality and either elevated class or the anxious performance of it. Despite—or perhaps because of—a tremendous loss of wealth during the Civil War, the Clanes are among Milan's most prestigious families. Although Sherman, the mulatto orphan of sharecroppers, is not wealthy, he is so acutely self-conscious of his lower-class status that, albeit with stereotypical camp, he tries desperately to compensate for his perceived inadequacies. He stresses, "I don't serve rotgut to my guests" but instead "Lord Calvert's, bottled in bond, ninety-eight per cent proof." Although perhaps implied, Sherman does not say that "he had bought this whiskey for the year he had been drinking because of the advertisement, 'The Man of Distinction'" and has repeatedly—though unsuccessfully—attempted to replicate the "negligent care of the man in the ad" (68). He becomes so invested in establishing this image of carefree wealth that he eventually leases a house in a white neighborhood, fills the space with antique furniture and a baby grand piano, and refuses to leave even when informed of bomb threats: "'Leave my furniture?' With one of the wild swings of mood that Jester knew so well, Sherman began to talk about the furniture. 'And you haven't even seen the bedroom suit, with the pink sheets and boudoir pillows. Or my clothes.' He opened the closet door. 'Four brand new Hart, Schaffner & Marx suits.' Wheeling wildly to the kitchen, he said, 'And the kitchen, with all modern conveniences. And all my own.' In an ecstasy of ownership, Sherman seemed to have forgotten all about the fear" (227). Such representations suggest that McCullers either holds as valid or seeks to expose a popular gay self-perception that assumes gay men must maintain at least the appearance of affluence. Moreover, these images hint that, within these perceptions, gay men, regardless of socioeconomic backgrounds, hold themselves to have the inherent tastes necessary to perpetuate such an illusion.

Rachel Adams furthers this analysis and provocatively argues that conspicuous consumption is a sign of queerness and cultural alienation. The accumulated material possessions are "always inappropriate luxury items that indicate a desire in excess of respectable, family-oriented modes of mass consumption. Rather than guaranteeing entry into the comfortable anonymity of consumer culture, the ownership of frivolous things instead draws attention to the irreconcilable differences of the freak's body, which provide the visible evidence of queer desires that cannot be domesticated." In the case of the mulatto Sherman, this "fetishization of material things as compensation for racial inequality, the death of his parents, his lack of education, and the absence of erotically satisfying relationships bring about his violent death."[26]

In many ways, the performances that Sherman provides in the hopes of establishing his elevated class and cultivated tastes are unnecessary to impress Jester. It is simply Sherman's male body that captivates him. Perhaps the most overt of McCullers's characters negotiating male homoeroticism, Jester almost exclusively desires men, even though he anxiously dissociates himself from a homosexual identity: "If it turned out he was homosexual like men in the *Kinsey Report*, Jester had vowed that he would kill himself" (94). Nonetheless, he repeatedly masturbates to images of other boys' masculine bodies. "His hard boy's hands unzipped his fly and touched his genitals for solace," McCullers writes. "No, he had no passion, but he had had love. Sometimes for a day, a week, a month, once for a whole year. The one year's love was for Ted Hopkins who was the best all-around athlete in school" (42). Even when Jester's crushes are for women, they are conspicuously masculine ones: "He loved, too, Miss Pafford who taught English and wore bangs but put on no lipstick. Lipstick was repulsive to Jester, and he could not understand how anyone could kiss a woman who wore gummy smeary lipstick. But since nearly all girls and women wore lipstick, Jester's loves were severely limited" (43). Sherman thus seems a fitting beloved for Jester, and he so invests his desire in Sherman that, when he is ultimately killed by a Klansman, Jester vows to avenge the death and only at the last minute fails to kill Sammy Lank, the poor white who fatally bombs Sherman's house.

Despite the intensity of this love for Sherman, however, Jester ultimately receives little gratification from sexual contact with this body. When, after having diligently policed his impulses, Jester finally succumbs and kisses Sherman, he slaps him "so hard that Jester sat down on the floor," and "Sherman's voice was strangled with rage" (145). Jester must therefore seek gratification in continued masturbation or the heterosexual intimacies at Reba's whorehouse. Even here, however, Sherman's body haunts Jester, and, since he "had never felt the normal sexual urge" (93), this body seems *a*—if not *the*—crucial factor in allowing his sexual interactions with women: "he lay in bed with a woman with orange hair and gold in her teeth. He closed his eyes, and having in mind a dark face with blue flickering eyes, he was able to become a man" (84).

As this emphasis on Sherman's "dark face" suggests, the color of his body is perhaps the single most attractive feature to Jester, and he repeatedly eroticizes this darkness. On his first visit to Sherman's apartment, for instance, Jester "knew he ought to go home, but it was as though he was hypnotized by the blue eyes set in the dark face. Then without a word, Sherman began to sing and play. It was the song Jester had heard in his own room and he felt that he had never been so moved. Sherman's strong fingers seemed very dark against the ivory keyboard and his strong neck was thrown back as he sang" (67). These images of homoeroticized black male bodies do not, however, replicate the more stereotypical ones scripted by Capote in Randolph's figurings of the dark-skinned Keg. Rather than perpetuate the figure of the hypersexual, hypermasculine black man of Randolph's fantasies, McCullers tempers Sherman's masculinity and sexual aggressiveness to suggest that his desirability is not necessarily contingent upon these excesses. This tempering in turn also helps to deflate the stereotype of the passive gay man whose sexual gratification is contingent upon masochistic abuse at the hands of the virile male rapist.

More problematically, however, McCullers also tempers Sherman's blackness as it is supposedly signified by his body. This "hybridity," which Adams reads as such a powerful draw to the perplexed Jester who is negotiating and seeking parallels to his queerness, seems much more vexed.[27] As a mulatto, Sherman's skin is dark but not black as Keg's is, and his eyes, his inheritance from his white mother, are piercingly blue. As the cited passages reveal, only when Sherman's dark skin is considered *along with* these blue eyes does Jester feel the attraction to this body. This infatuation, like Tracy Deen's miscegenistic desire for the light-skinned Nonnie Anderson in *Strange Fruit*, suggests that, at least in Smith's and McCullers's understandings of the South's racialized sexual interactions at midcentury, white men—regardless if they act out of homoerotic or heteroerotic desire—often choose "black" partners whose bodies exhibit some feature or features culturally understood to designate the mediation by "whiteness" of "blackness" and all that it pejoratively connotes in a racist society. That is, although white women such as Sherman's mother can enter into a valued sexual and emotional relationship with a black man, it remains a near impossibility within these fictional representations for white men—any more than the black men of Wright's understandings—to make significant erotic and/or emotional investments in racially unmixed and therefore culturally devalued African Americans.

If this reading of Jester's desire for Sherman implies a certain degree of white racism, it is countered—but not necessarily discredited—by another, perhaps even more important element to this infatuation, one in which Sherman's blackness rather than its mediation is crucial. Jester's desire for Sherman may possibly arise not so much out of the attractiveness of Sherman's specific identity as differentiated from those of other African Americans but out of Jester's impulse to punish his grandfather for his provincial conservatism, racism, and, to a lesser extent, homophobia. To desire a black man both emotionally and physically gives Jester a means to vent his increasing impatience with Clane and, should such a desire ever be made public, allows the boy a degree of power over the old man that rivals his son's when he commits suicide. Just as Johnny Clane's self-inflicted death in protest to his father's conviction of an innocent black man for murder strikes a harsh punitive blow to Clane, Jester's desire for Sherman—or any other African American—has the potential to do the same.

Although the 1954 setting of *Clock Without Hands* and its inclusions of black nationalism, racially motivated hate bombings, and murders not unlike Emmett Till's reveal McCullers's contribution to midcentury discourses condemning white southern racism, especially in light of increased tensions following *Brown v. Board of Education,* her political activism within the novel does little to hone her artistic subtlety. As Smith rightly argues, McCullers creates in Clane a symbol—or, perhaps more correctly, a parodic personification—of the aristocratic white South that is so "exaggerated and stereotyped" that it is difficult to take him seriously. And yet, if one does, McCullers's South makes abundantly clear why Jester and other comparable liberals of his age figuratively seek to exact revenge on previous generations of southerners. The judge's rants reveal a litany of issues that *were* historical concerns for many conservative white southerners of the 1950s: the ever-increasing role of federal government, the abolition of the poll tax so that "every ignorant Nigra can vote" (13), the payment of income tax, the inflation of the minimum wage, the continued presence of the NAACP, the decline of the Ku Klux Klan, and the legacy of "TVA, FHA, and FDR, all those muckery-muck letters" (192).

Clane's rhetoric is not that different from the Agrarians', nor are the two sets of sentiments radically divergent. Andrew Lytle or Donald Davidson might well have responded as Clane does in the novel when publicly deemed a reactionary; he is nothing short of elated. "It's nothing to be sorry about," he tells his grandson. "A reactionary is a citizen who *reacts* when the age-long standards of the South are threatened. When States' rights are trampled on by the Federal Government, then the Southern patriot is duty-bound to react. Otherwise the noble standards of the South will be betrayed. . . . The noble standards of our way of life, the traditional institutions of the South" (27–28). Only when Clane reveals his outrageous scheme for the federal government to redeem Confederate currency and make reparations for freed slaves does his devotion to the South become truly questionable in light of historical realities.

Like the conservatism of so many white southerners of the 1950s, however, Clane's manifests itself foremost in a stance against desegregation. A strikingly different man than John Taylor, his more racially enlightened counterpart in *To Kill a Mockingbird,* Clane has few qualms in sentencing at least two innocent black men to death and even rankles when his son, a less well-drawn Atticus Finch, attempts to defend one of them: "Self-defense or no, the Nigra was doomed to die and Johnny knew it as well as anybody else. Why then did he persist in taking the case, which was a lost cause from the beginning?" (182). "My son was trying to break an axiom," Clane tells Malone, "about something inconsequential" (19). Other moves to overturn this axiom incite comparable anger in the judge. "Equal rights in education will be the next thing," he grumbles to Malone. "Imagine a future where delicate little white girls must share their desks with coal-black niggers in order to learn to read and write" (13).

McCullers leaves little doubt that readers are to respond to this figuring of white southern patriarchy as obscene, unhealthy, and grotesque. Clane's body has bloated to well over three hundred pounds and has been partially paralyzed by a stroke, leaving his left hand inert and "slightly puffy from disuse" (12). Perhaps most damning, however, the judge has lost control of his bowels and is now prone to "sudden bathroom accidents, bathroom accidents which he knew were unbecoming to a magistrate . . . especially if it occurred in the courthouse office as it had two times" (86). Ironically, the judge takes immense pleasure in defecation, savoring the smells that his body produces: "When the odor in the bathroom rose, he was not annoyed by this; on the contrary, since he was pleased by anything that belonged to him, and his feces were no exception, the smell rather soothed him. So he sat there, relaxed and meditative, pleased with himself" (89). These images of Clane culminate in the novel's final page, where, on learning of the Supreme Court's decision supporting integration, he lapses into incoherent babbling and pathetic pleading after illogically citing the Gettysburg Address.

In contrast to Clane, Jester despises reactionary politics and particularly its stance toward race, and the novel is as much about Jester's divestment of his grandfather's political views as it is about the boy's exploration of sexuality. "All my life I've seen things like you and the family wanted me to see them," Jester tells Clane. "And now this summer I don't see things as I used to—and I have different feelings, different thoughts. . . . For one thing, I question the justice of white supremacy" (30–31). When Clane poses his question about integrated classrooms to Jester, he retorts, "How about a hulking white girl sharing a desk with a delicate little Negro boy?" (28). As the judge continues his racist tirade, he only grows more offensive to his grandson, who eventually—and cruelly—blurts out, "Sometimes I wonder if I'm not beginning to suspect why my father—did what he did" (32). This confrontation significantly comes *before* Jester meets Sherman, so that Jester's sentiments therefore seem to arise from either genuine concern for racial equality or general defiance of his grandfather but not out of a specific defense of Sherman that has been broadened to include all African Americans.

If McCullers's representation of Jester's desire for Sherman is thus a vexed one, intricately structured by homoerotic desire, the eroticization of racial otherness, the fear of this racial otherness being too significant, the wish to exact revenge or punishment through social transgression, or some configuration of all these factors, she nevertheless does allow such a representation of interracial same-sex desire in white men for black ones.[28] In contrast, just as the absences in *Clock Without Hands* suggest a foreclosure of same-sex desire between women, they include no imaginings of interracial same-sex desire in black men for white ones. When McCullers offers African American men's desire for sexual contact with other men or their less clearly sexual infatuations with other men, she keeps those objects of desire invariably within the race. When Sherman is sexually molested— "boogered" (79), he tells Jester—at the age of eleven, it is by the married black man with whom Sherman is boarding. Moreover, although his investment in Zippo is never established as having an overt sexual component, it is nevertheless the willing subjugation of one black man to another. Sherman "admired and feared Zippo," although he "was always insulting him, never washed a dish even when Sherman did the cooking, and treated him very much as he now treated Jester" (168). Thus, despite McCullers's apparent interest in exploring various manifestations of male homoeroticism, both *Clock Without Hands* and the sum of her literary production end without significant space allowed for either desire of a black man for a white one or an interracial same-sex relation structured by mutual desire between men.

Epilogue
Other Voices, Other Rooms

IN THE FOUR DECADES SINCE Carson McCullers published *Clock Without Hands,* southern literary production, like that of the broader nation, has witnessed a proliferation of texts openly concerned with same-sex desire. Southern fiction in particular has given close attention to these representations, as suggested by the work of an extensive list of authors: Dorothy Allison, Lisa Alther, Raymond Andrews, Blanche McCrary Boyd, Rita Mae Brown, Pat Conroy, James Dickey, Clyde Edgerton, Fannie Flagg, Richard Ford, Harlan Greene, Jim Grimsley, Allan Gurganus, Bertha Harris, Randall Kenan, Jill McCorkle, Reynolds Price, Anne Rice, Christopher Rice, Edward Swift, John Kennedy Toole, Alice Walker, Peter Weltner, and James Wilcox. As texts ranging from Allison's *Bastard out of Carolina* to Wilcox's *Plain and Normal* attest, same-sex desire has quite simply become as inescapable in southern fiction as it has in other modes of southern literary production and southern culture. But, perhaps even more importantly, this partial catalogue also suggests the variety of persons preoccupied with representing this desire. The sexes, classes, races, ethnicities, and regional affiliations of these writers are amazingly diverse, as are their own sexualities, and indeed some contemporary straight writers seem as engaged in depicting the cultural circulations of same-sex desire as do gay, lesbian, and bisexual ones.[1]

Given these forty years and the social and literary evolutions—or even revolutions—spanned by these decades, it is not surprising that this recent work shows dramatic shifts in theme and form from the fiction of the 1940s,

1950s, and early 1960s. These shifts have arisen for multiple reasons, of course, not least of which is the increased influence of postmodern techniques of narrative on southern literary production. Moreover, gay liberation, contemporary feminism, and the politics of queerness have allowed for—and even demanded—less closetedness in gay/lesbian fiction and, in fact, have destabilized the very term *gay/lesbian,* if it was ever stable at all. The so-called sexual revolution has also dramatically affected this subgenre, perhaps most directly in gay and lesbian fiction's increased use of sexual explicitness, a strategy that has complicated the distinctions between pornography and nonpornography, as well as injected deliciously frank humor into these novels. (One can scarcely imagine Lillian Smith or Richard Wright, for instance, penning the prologue of Allan Gurganus's *Plays Well with Others,* that featuring a broom closet full of thirty dildoes, "weak-eyed rats, startled by daylight," that gape "like an open-mouthed choir of retarded children, looking heavenward.")[2] Finally, since the mid-1980s, the AIDS pandemic has altered many of the central narratives of gay men's lives and fictions, and preoccupations with initial sexual experiences and coming out have often shifted to negotiating sexual contact, HIV status, and AIDS on daily bases.

The work of virtually any of the cited writers showcases the differences between the midcentury and the late-century representations of southernness and same-sex desire, but the novels of Harlan Greene seem particularly rich sites of interrogation, since so many of these factors coalesce in his fiction and throw the earlier texts into sharp relief. Consider first his award-winning but critically neglected 1991 novel *What the Dead Remember,* a text noteworthy for its investments in multiple postmodern strategies to represent gayness and AIDS within southern history and culture. In contrast to the obsessively present-focused texts of midcentury, Greene's novel, like his earlier *Why We Never Danced the Charleston* (1984), revises dominant historical narratives, critiques atrophied social monoliths, and offers relentless parodies to indict the region and its literary production as distressingly and even lethally ignoring same-sex desire between men. And yet, because Greene makes this indictment through these particularly postmodern strategies, he also allows components of canonical southern literary history, ranging from Henry Timrod's poems to Harper Lee's novel, meaningfully to re-signify in provocative and even shocking ways for contemporary readers.

That Greene's fiction consistently concerns itself with public history and cultural otherness is perhaps expected given his personal past. Born and raised in Charleston, he grew up in an environment permeated with physical and psychic intrusions from the eighteenth and nineteenth centuries. These presences, he writes, drew him to the formal study of history during college, and he soon "became one of Charleston's handmaidens" as a state archivist and "was taken up into the cult of the city." But, while his hometown viewed him as simply "that nice young man at the Historical Society," the openly gay, Jewish Greene was immersing himself in the city's and the region's archives and arriving at a postmodern critique of history, that based in Foucaultian skepticism of any totalizing master narrative. Greene in particular attuned himself to the deprived play of available discourses in the construction of the city's history, its flatly coercive and omission-prone public narratives, and the systems of power these narratives seek to reify. Like others concerned with the "history of intimacy," to use Martin Duberman's phrase, Greene soon realized that sexual otherness permeates archival documents but is routinely excised from public circulation. The reasons for this suppression are multiple but frequently arise from an impulse, Duberman offers, to protect and preserve "traditional moral values in general and . . . a given family's 'good name' in particular," such as that of noted antebellum South Carolinian and "writhing bedfellow" James Henry Hammond. These are but two of the presumable suppressions Linda Hutcheon alludes to when she asserts, "If the archive is composed of texts, it is open to all kinds of use and abuse. The archive has always been a site of a lot of activity, but rarely of such self-consciously totalizing activity as it is today." Drawing similar conclusions to Duberman and Hutcheon, Greene maintains that the past "is a subversive place, really; for within it lies not the pleasant fictions or lies that most people believe. Walled up is the truth, seething." His commitment to a recoverable finite "truth" no doubt reflects the limits of his postmodern investments, but these sentiments nevertheless reveal a radically different understanding of history from most Charlestonians, and it is from this position that Greene says he "understood why that rich conservative in pancake makeup and pink tennis shoes refused to give money to the Historical Society, calling it a hotbed of liberality."[3]

To combat this erasure of disruptive gay desire, Greene has used his fiction to assert counternarratives to Charleston's—and, by extension, the South's—conservative provincial accounts that, whether from benign neglect, antiquated codes of propriety, or outright homophobia, have omitted gayness. He uses much the same tactic as Gurganus, who, echoing Whitman, imagines Confederate soldiers' wartime existences to be crucially organized by intensely homoerotic bonds in *The Oldest Living Confederate Widow Tells All.* Greene comparably creates in *Why We Never Danced the Charleston* a variant Roaring Twenties, an era in which the city's men shun St. Cecilia Balls and instead savor midnight gay orgies at houses on the Battery. Likewise, he envisions in *What the Dead Remember* a Charleston of the 1950s that has, lurking beneath a drowsy heteronormativity, young boys who masturbate to men's underwear advertisements and excitedly witness the same-sex promiscuity of well-endowed rednecks.

Within these revisionist scriptings, however, Greene does retain that well-worn trope of the region's writing: the burden of southern history and culture upon the individual. Characters such as his nameless gay narrators are almost invariably frustrated at not sensing a past that speaks to and includes them. Rather, these figures instead detect the pressures of disconnection that link them to the likes of Quentin Compson, Jack Burden, and Tate's visitor of the Confederate dead. "Everywhere we went, the past rose up around us," the narrator of *What the Dead Remember* recalls, inflecting his assessment with disconcerting violence. "History rumbled like thunder in the distance and worked up from underneath, like tree roots splitting the concrete."[4] Similarly, the narrator of *Why We Never Danced* offers that "[h]istory haunted us all, especially those of us born in a sleepy old southern town that had Fort Sumter for a legacy. It rose up from the harbor to stain the sky."[5]

But Greene crucially differs from canonical midcentury writers in at least two ways here. He both posits the key source of alienation for his narrators to be their sexualities and allows no momentary easing of this burden, no points of entry in which the individual *can* insert himself into these otherwise oppressive narratives, as, say, Faulkner does when he casts the Civil War in terms that are as gratifyingly identity-granting as identity-thwarting. Consider, for instance, his oft-cited valorization of Gettysburg in *Intruder in the Dust* (1948):

> For every Southern boy fourteen years old, not once but whenever he wants it, there is the instant when it's still not yet two oclock on that July afternoon in 1863, the brigades are in position behind the rail fence, the guns are laid and ready in the woods and the furled flags are already loosened to break out and

Pickett himself with his long oiled ringlets and his hat in one hand probably and
his sword in the other looking up the hill waiting for Longstreet to give the word
and it's all in the balance, it hasn't happened yet, it hasn't even begun yet . . . [6]

Greene's novels dare to imply that for a fourteen-year-old *gay* boy of either
the 1920s or 1950s, this ostensibly liberating moment—full of possibility and
"whenever he wants it"—licenses only an anxious performance of normative
gender and sexuality. For the adolescent "transfixed" by "a black-and-white
picture of men and boys advertising Hanes or BVDs" (18) in *What the Dead
Remember,* the only appealing element of Faulkner's fantasy is perhaps Pickett's eroticized ringlets. And when Greene's characters do play Faulkner's
game in *Why We Never Danced the Charleston,* it is one not of endless possibility but rather of mindless repetition and flat stock characters—"Spoons
Butler, Lincoln, or Sherman; I always won, being the good and saintly Robert E. Lee" (16)—that merely amuse onlooking senile Confederate spinsters.

For Greene's narrators, virtually the only moments of reassurance are
contingent upon a destruction of the past. Like so many of Josephine
Humphreys's characters, the narrator of *What the Dead Remember* finds particular comfort in the demolition of Charleston's landmarks: "I pressed
through the crowd and saw a row of columns, . . . two stories high and
Greek. When the ball hit one, it toppled into another, dissolving instantly,
like sugar in tea. Dust rose up like a roar or a cheer. . . . The crash and clat-
ter delighted me" (16–17). The narrator immediately leaves for the "mod-
ernized" drugstore, complete with its "sleek facade" (17); palms the tempting
Saturday Evening Post; and then retreats to his bedroom to masturbate, even
as the throb of demolition continues: "Naked I lay in front of it; it was a
balm—as if I had taken the cool from the drugstore with me. I dreamed,
and a tremor shook the city. Summer was finally starting for me" (20). Thus
the boy's homoerotically fired orgasm coincides precisely with the erasure of
physical southern history.

Of these landmarks, it is those associated with the Civil War that
Greene most centrally seeks to erase, reveal as culturally spent, or defuse
through parody. He dismisses Fort Sumter as sky-staining and has his gay
characters lampoon patriotic southern organizations through their forming
of "The Sons of Wisteria Society" (32) in *Why We Never Danced the Charleston.* Moreover, he reduces the Confederate Home of the 1920s to "an almost
underwater world in which . . . a damp and moist atmosphere . . . mildewed

and moldered everything" (10) and populates it with "gaunt gray" (10) ghosts, sexless in their long-arrested heterosexuality, "eternal Miss Havershams" (11). Although material antebellum mementos fair slightly better than these ladies for Charleston's gay men, their parents' attics do not hold sacred relics of the Lost Cause but instead "hoopskirts, Confederate uniforms, old silk sashes, fantastic hats, and fabric" (137) that allow for flamboyant drag shows. The only other way that the war becomes meaningful to this group is through its campy commodification in and through *Gone with the Wind*. In both Margaret Mitchell's novel and David Selznick's film, Greene's narrator at last finds a viable southern lens for self-assessment. "[L]ike Scarlett O'Hara," he confesses, "who never had a handkerchief, I am never quite prepared for crises," adding in an immediate aside, "When *Gone with the Wind* was published, Hilary and I would weep over it, ruining 10,000 hankies" (134–35).

And yet Greene by no means concedes that official historical narratives and their valorized artifacts can ever be fully eradicated or even significantly challenged. He may, along the lines of Gurganus, violate a heterosexualized Confederate past when the narrator and Ned Grimke tire of predictable Civil War reenactments and have their first sexualized physical contact within the bounds of the Confederate Home, yet the Home remains an ominous symbolic trap, escapable only in Quentinesque suicide. But even more troubling for Greene is that this arresting of time forecloses serious consideration of issues that are more pressing to the city's contemporary gay communities. His gloss of *What the Dead Remember* with excerpts of Henry Timrod's 1863 poem "Charleston" seems simultaneously his critique of this foreclosure and a perfect example of the double-coded postmodern parody discussed by Hutcheon, a strategy that "both legitimizes and subverts that which it parodies."[7] When Greene cites the poem's largely metaphoric lines fretting over northern military aggression during the Civil War, such as the first stanza—"Calm as that second summer which precedes / The first fall of the snow / In the broad sunlight of heroic deeds, / The City bides the foe"—he brings back into circulation a once central but now almost forgotten southern literary hero in Timrod and, by wrenching the poem into the new context of an AIDS novel, uses the lines to critique the region's continued fetishizing of the Civil War. At the end of the twentieth century, Greene implies, the uncertain "foe" that most threatens Charleston with the "triumph or the tomb" is not northern conquest but rather HIV, which has indeed proven as fatal (especially when Greene was writing in the late 1980s and early 1990s) or at very least life-altering to large populaces of southern men as the Civil War did.

This gloss from Timrod also suggests that Greene is as concerned with revising and playing off existing southern literary texts as with attempting to reimagine southern history. His tactics are partially those of the later Reynolds Price and Randall Kenan, whose intertextual, multigenerational fictions revise Faulkner's mythic Yoknapatawpha to allow for acknowledged circulations of same-sex desire, and partially those of, say, the earlier Price, Bobbie Ann Mason, and Barry Hannah, who parody their midcentury forebears to burlesque, strategically recontextualize, or metaphorically kill off these forebears or their characters. *What the Dead Remember* particularly parodies texts by Eudora Welty, Truman Capote, Tennessee Williams, and Harper Lee, those midcentury southern writers whose works repeatedly— if also, as I hope I have suggested earlier, momentarily, cryptically, and/or problematically—feature same-sex desire and broader sexual difference. As with the citation of Timrod, Greene's parodies here simultaneously pay homage to these texts' value—that, seemingly for him, implicit in their introduction of same-sex desire into southern literary production—and demolish them, comparable to the Charleston landmarks within his novels, to clear space for new expressions and concerns, such as graphic sexuality and AIDS, that were unimaginable to earlier writers. Consider, for instance, the names of the narrator's aging aunt and uncle who nurture the boy, impose constricting modes of behavior on him, and, perhaps most significantly, die within the course of the novel. These names—Violet and Reynaldo—resonate with those of earlier writers and their characters. The malevolent, daiquiri-sipping Violet Venable, who refuses to acknowledge her son's deviant desires in *Suddenly Last Summer*, lingers behind Greene's indomitable aunt, just as Uncle Reynaldo, tucked within "dark, varnished shelves and the Gothic-arched doors" of his library, among "mounted moths and butterflies" (9), cites the campy Randolph from *Other Voices, Other Rooms*, the kimono-wearing Uncle Rondo in Welty's "Why I Live at the P.O.," and even Reynolds Price himself. Similarly Violet and Reynaldo's house, "one sunk in summer, stagnant and green" (3), revises these texts, echoing Sebastian's savage garden and Capote's Gothic Skully's Landing.

In contrast to these figures, symbolic of the parodied older order of limited and limiting gay southern literary production, the narrator, a compilation of Joel Knox, Dill Harris, Allan Grey, and Sebastian Venable, is allowed to live and love, even if not necessarily happily. Greene does not arrest his narrator's gayness at ambiguous adolescence, as do Capote, Lee, and, at least with her female characters, McCullers. Nor does Greene fate his narrator to suicide, institutionalization, or cannibalistic ingestion, the disconcerting fates of Williams's midcentury characters negotiating same-sex desire. Rather, the HIV-positive narrator of *What the Dead Remember* survives, like Ishmael, to tell his tale and, even more importantly, to struggle with the all-too-real issues of the contemporary South: "As I got sick, I saw faces fly by and I woke up drenched in sweat and stuck to the sheets like something washed up on the beach. . . . I got better, though Charleston has no use for people like me. They treat us like we don't exist, as if we are beyond help, dead already" (179).

But the work of Greene's parodies exceeds that identified by Hutcheon as simultaneous critique of and homage to earlier texts. By directing such pointed focus on these midcentury works, Greene's novels prompt readers to recall the virtual absence of parody in the earlier fiction at least as far as citations of preexisting texts. That is, his allusions to these works remind readers just how unallusive the earlier texts in turn are. Indeed, as with the comic sexual explicitness, one can hardly imagine any of the six writers who have been discussed structuring their fiction around parodic citations. Even Harper Lee, with her spoofing of normative gender and heterosexuality in *To Kill a Mockingbird,* parodies social performances rather than literary representations of these performances. This absence of parodic citation seems not necessarily a limitation, however, but rather a testimony to the freshness of the representations offered by Capote, McCullers, and the like. Quite simply, when depicting southern negotiations of same-sex desire at midcentury, these writers had few or no antecedents to address.

And yet, especially when yoked with the conflicting demands within the literary marketplace and the other mechanisms of canonization discussed in chapter 1, the absence of these antecedents was hardly less anxiety inducing for these writers than the presence of later antecedents has been for Greene. The relatively clean slate—or blank screen—is often more frightening than the one already filled. What emerges from the representations of these writers is a pronounced tentativeness in filling these absences. Even as all six sought to include same-sex desire in depictions of southern social matrices, these writers again and again deployed strategies of indirection: Capote's and Goyen's obfuscatory lyricism, Wright's brevity, Smith's and Lee's marginalization of desire to race, McCullers's displacement of one form of homoeroticism onto another. In each case, the negotiation of same-sex desire is hesitant, encoded, deferred.

But, as I hope has become clear, these representations persist despite this tentativeness, emerging sufficiently to document that southern fiction at midcentury was indeed, as Sedgwick has suspected, preoccupied with "gay desires, peoples, discourses, prohibitions, and energies." Even more importantly, these images suggest just how complicated and even contradictory understandings of same-sex desire in the American South were during the 1940s and 1950s. Always limited theoretical models attempting to meaningfully relate desire, sexuality, gender, and race to one another competed and even confused the very persons most deeply invested in them, as the representations arising out of these models reflect. Nonetheless, these literary negotiations stand, powerful depictions that simultaneously showcase the centrality of southern fiction to American discourses of sexuality long before the current contributions of Greene and his contemporaries, and suggest the equally absolute centrality of sexual otherness to southern literary production at midcentury.

Notes

INTRODUCTION

1. Eve Kosofsky Sedgwick, *Epistemology of the Closet* (Berkeley: Univ. of California Press, 1990), 58–59.

2. Rachel Adams, "'A Mixture of Delicious and Freak': The Queer Fiction of Carson McCullers," *American Literature* 71 (September 1999): 552, 556, 553, 556.

3. See Roger Austen, *Playing the Game: The Homosexual Novel in America* (Indianapolis: Bobbs-Merrill, 1977), 59–62; George Chauncey, Jr., *Gay New York* (New York: HarperCollins, 1994), 17, 191, 242; and James Levin, *The Gay Novel in America* (New York: Garland, 1991), 36–38.

4. See Lillian Faderman, *Odd Girls and Twilight Lovers* (1991; reprint, New York: Penguin, 1992), 146–48; Lillian Faderman, *Surpassing the Love of Men* (New York: William Morrow, 1981), 392–410; and John Howard, *Men Like That: A Southern Queer History* (Chicago: Univ. of Chicago Press, 1999), 188–220.

5. On the homoeroticism of Faulkner's texts, see Joseph Allen Boone, *Libidinal Currents* (Chicago: Univ. of Chicago Press, 1998), 298–322; Cleanth Brooks, *William Faulkner: The Yoknapatawpha Country* (1963; reprint, Baton Rouge: Louisiana State Univ. Press, 1990), 57; Leslie Fiedler, *Love and Death in the American Novel* (1960; reprint, with an afterword by Fiedler, New York: Anchor Books, 1992), 411–14; Don Merrick Liles, "William Faulkner's *Absalom, Absalom!* An Exegesis of the Homoerotic Configurations in the Novel," in *Literary Visions of Homosexuality*, ed. Stuart Kellogg (New York: Haworth, 1983), 99–111; and Georges-Michel Sarotte, *Like a Brother, Like a Lover*, trans. Richard Miller (Garden City, N.Y.: Doubleday, 1978), 39–40.

6. Sedgwick, *Epistemology of the Closet*, 53.

7. See Mab Segrest, "Southern Women Writing: Toward a Literature of Wholeness," in *My Mama's Dead Squirrel* (Ithaca, N.Y.: Firebrand Books, 1985), 19–42; and Mab Segrest, "'Lines I Dare': Southern Lesbian Writing," in *My Mama's Dead Squirrel*, 100–145.

8. Truman Capote, *Music for Chameleons* (1980; reprint, New York: Random House, 1981),

264. See also Gerald Clarke, *Capote: A Biography* (New York: Simon & Schuster, 1988), 44–46, 62–64, 276; Lawrence Grobel, *Conversations with Capote* (New York: New American Library, 1985), 59–79; and George Plimpton, *Truman Capote* (1997; reprint, New York: Anchor Books, 1998), 95–99, 391–95.

9. See Margaret Rose Gladney, "Personalizing the Political, Politicizing the Personal: Reflections on Editing the Letters of Lillian Smith," in *Carryin' On in the Lesbian and Gay South*, ed. John Howard (New York: New York Univ. Press, 1997), 93–103; Margaret Rose Gladney, preface to *How Am I to Be Heard?* by Lillian Smith, ed. Margaret Rose Gladney (Chapel Hill: Univ. of North Carolina Press, 1993), xvi; Anne C. Loveland, *Lillian Smith* (Baton Rouge: Louisiana State Univ. Press, 1986), 200–204; and Smith, *How Am I to Be Heard?*

10. See Virginia Spencer Carr, *The Lonely Hunter: A Biography of Carson McCullers* (1975; reprint, New York: Carroll & Graf, 1989); Carlos L. Dews, introduction to *Illumination and Night Glare*, by Carson McCullers, ed. Carlos L. Dews (Madison: Univ. of Wisconsin Press, 1999), xix–xxi; Oliver Evans, *The Ballad of Carson McCullers* (New York: Coward-McCann, 1966), 86–87; McCullers, *Illumination and Night Glare*; and Josyane Savigneau, *Carson McCullers: A Life*, trans. Joan E. Howard (Boston: Houghton Mifflin, 2001), 53–54, 70–74, 90, 181–82.

11. See William Goyen, *William Goyen: Selected Letters from a Writer's Life*, ed. Robert Phillips (Austin: Univ. of Texas Press, 1995); and Stephen Spender, afterword to *William Goyen: Selected Letters*, 411–13.

CHAPTER 1

1. H. L. Mencken, "The Sahara of the Bozart," in *Prejudices: Second Series* (New York: Knopf, 1920), 136, 138–39.

2. W. J. Cash, *The Mind of the South* (1941; reprint, New York: Random House, 1969), 333.

3. Donald Davidson, "A Mirror for Artists," in *I'll Take My Stand* (1930; reprint, with an introduction by Louis D. Rubin, Jr., Baton Rouge: Louisiana State Univ. Press, 1977), 58–59; and John Crowe Ransom, "Introduction: A Statement of Principles," in *I'll Take My Stand*, xlvii. See Allen Tate, "The New Provincialism," in *Essays of Four Decades* (Chicago: Swallow Press, 1968), 535–46.

4. Michael Kreyling, "Race and Southern Literature: 'The Problem' in the Work of Louis D. Rubin, Jr.," in *The South as an American Problem*, ed. Larry J. Griffin and Don H. Doyle (Athens: Univ. of Georgia Press, 1995), 242; Louis D. Rubin, Jr., introduction to *The History of Southern Literature*, ed. Louis D. Rubin, Jr., et al. (Baton Rouge: Louisiana State Univ. Press, 1985), 3, 4.

5. Rubin, introduction, 1, 2.

6. Davidson, "A Mirror for Artists," 58, 59; John Edward Hardy, "Ellen Glasgow," in *Southern Renascence*, ed. Louis D. Rubin, Jr., and Robert D. Jacobs (Baltimore, Md.: Johns Hopkins Press, 1953), 237; Robert Hazel, "Notes on Erskine Caldwell," in *Southern Renascence*, 316; and Thomas Daniel Young, introduction to part 3 of *History of Southern Literature*, 262.

7. Sedgwick, *Epistemology of the Closet*, 53. For a more extensive discussion of such dismissals, see Sedgwick, *Epistemology of the Closet*, 48–59.

8. John Crowe Ransom, "Criticism, Inc.," in *Selected Essays of John Crowe Ransom*, ed.

Thomas Daniel Young and John Hindle (Baton Rouge: Louisiana State Univ. Press, 1984), 94, 105–6; Terry Eagleton, *Literary Theory: An Introduction* (1983; reprint, Minneapolis: Univ. of Minnesota Press, 1989), 47.

9. Tate to Jean Toomer, 7 November 1923, in *Cane*, ed. Darwin T. Turner (New York: W. W. Norton, 1988), 161; and Brooks, *William Faulkner*, 57.

10. See Nancylee Novell Jonza, *The Underground Stream: The Life and Art of Caroline Gordon* (Athens: Univ. of Georgia Press, 1995), 46–47, 49–51, 66–67.

11. Allen Tate, "Remarks on the Southern Religion," in *I'll Take My Stand*, 168; Ransom, "Introduction," xlii; Richard Weaver, "Aspects of the Southern Philosophy," in *Southern Renascence*, 15; and Andrew Nelson Lytle, *Bedford Forrest and His Critter Company* (1931; reprint, with a preface by Walter Sullivan, Nashville, Tenn.: J. S. Saunders, 1992), xxvi.

12. Lyle Lanier, "A Critique of the Philosophy of Progress," in *I'll Take My Stand*, 146–47.

13. Andrew Nelson Lytle, "The Hind Tit," in *I'll Take My Stand*, 236; Walter Sullivan, preface to *Bedford Forrest and His Critter Company*, xiv; and Richard M. Weaver, *The Southern Tradition at Bay: A History of Postbellum Thought*, ed. George Core and M. E. Bradford (New Rochelle, N.Y.: Arlington House, 1986), 392, quoted in Richard Gray, *Writing the South: Ideas of an American Region* (Cambridge: Cambridge Univ. Press, 1986), 280.

14. See Robert Penn Warren, *At Heaven's Gate* (1942; reprint, New York: New Directions, 1985), 252, 256.

15. Robert B. Heilman, "The Southern Temper," in *Southern Renascence*, 3.

16. Ray B. West, Jr., "Katherine Anne Porter and 'Historic Memory,'" in *Southern Renascence*, 283.

17. John Farrelly, review of *Other Voices, Other Rooms*, by Truman Capote, and *The Circus in the Attic*, by Robert Penn Warren, *New Republic* (26 January 1948): 31–32. For a comparable configuration of McCullers's relation to the Renaissance, see Lawrence Graver, *Carson McCullers* (Minneapolis: Univ. of Minnesota Press, 1969), 45.

18. Richard H. King, *A Southern Renaissance: The Cultural Awakening of the American South, 1930–1955* (New York: Oxford Univ. Press, 1980), 3.

19. Ibid., 3–4.

20. Thomas Bonner, Jr., "Truman Capote," in *History of Southern Literature*, 484; Joseph R. Millichap, "Carson McCullers," in *History of Southern Literature*, 487; Martha E. Cook, "Old Ways and New Ways," in *History of Southern Literature*, 532. See also James Mellard, "The Fiction of Social Commitment," in *History of Southern Literature*, 351–55; and Michael Kreyling, "Reynolds Price," in *History of Southern Literature*, 519–22.

21. King, *Southern Renaissance*, 188, 96. See Fred Hobson, foreword to *Strange Fruit*, by Lillian Smith (Athens: Univ. of Georgia Press, 1985), vii–xviii; and Fred Hobson, *Tell About the South* (Baton Rouge: Louisiana State Univ. Press, 1983), 312.

22. See Bertram Wyatt-Brown, *The House of Percy: Honor, Melancholy, and Imagination in a Southern Family* (New York: Oxford Univ. Press, 1994), 196–99, 204–9, 218–23; William Armstrong Percy III, "William Alexander Percy (1885–1942): His Homosexuality and Why It Matters," in *Carryin' On in the Lesbian and Gay South*, 75–92; and Fred Hobson, *But Now I See: The White Southern Racial Conversion Narrative* (Baton Rouge: Louisiana State Univ. Press, 1999), 21–22.

23. See Gary Richards, "Moving beyond Mississippi: Beth Henley and the Anxieties of Postsouthernness," in *Beth Henley: A Casebook,* ed. Julia A. Fesmire (New York: Routledge, 2002), 45–46.

24. Barbara Smith, "Homophobia: Why Bring It Up?" in *The Lesbian and Gay Studies Reader,* ed. Henry Abelove, Michèle Aina Barale, and David M. Halperin (New York: Routledge, 1993), 101.

25. See Chauncey, *Gay New York,* 244–67; and Eric Garber, "A Spectacle of Color: The Lesbian and Gay Subculture of Jazz Age Harlem," in *Hidden from History: Reclaiming the Gay and Lesbian Past,* ed. Martin Duberman, Martha Vicinus, and George Chauncey, Jr. (New York: Penguin, 1989), 318–31.

26. Chauncey, *Gay New York,* 74, 132.

27. Ernest Hemingway, *Death in the Afternoon* (New York: Charles Scribner's Sons, 1932), 179.

28. Ibid., 180, 182. For assessments of Hemingway's anxieties regarding male homosexuality in this passage and elsewhere, as well as the literary competition supposedly offered by Faulkner, see Truman Capote, "Truman Capote Talks, Talks, Talks," interview by C. Robert Jennings, *Truman Capote: Conversations,* ed. M. Thomas Inge (Jackson: Univ. Press of Mississippi, 1987), 164–70; Nancy R. Comley and Robert Scholes, *Hemingway's Genders: Rereading the Hemingway Text* (New Haven: Yale Univ. Press, 1994), 123–31; and Sarotte, *Like a Brother,* 262–79.

29. Fiedler, *Love and Death,* 25, 12.

30. Ibid., 12, 368, 290.

31. Ibid., 474.

32. Ibid., 475–76, 490.

33. Gray, *Writing the South,* 230; and Flannery O'Connor, "Some Aspects of the Grotesque in Southern Fiction," in *Mystery and Manners,* ed. Sally Fitzgerald and Robert Fitzgerald (New York: Farrar, Straus & Giroux, 1962), 40.

34. Sara Suleri, "Woman Skin Deep: Feminism and the Postcolonial Condition," in *Colonial Discourse and Post-Colonial Theory,* ed. Patrick Williams and Laura Chrisman (New York: Columbia Univ. Press, 1994), 245.

CHAPTER 2

1. Sedgwick, *Epistemology of the Closet,* 44–45.

2. Ibid., 44, 45–46; and Michel Foucault, *The History of Sexuality. volume 1: An Introduction,* trans. Robert Hurley (New York: Random House, 1978), 43.

3. David M. Halperin, *One Hundred Years of Homosexuality and Other Essays on Greek Love* (New York: Routledge, 1990), 9.

4. Sedgwick, *Epistemology of the Closet,* 47–48.

5. See Truman Capote, "Truman Capote," interview by Roy Newquist, *Truman Capote: Conversations,* 39–40; and Truman Capote, "Playboy Interview: Truman Capote," interview by Eric Norden, *Truman Capote: Conversations,* 115.

6. Truman Capote, "A Visit with Truman Capote," interview by Gloria Steinem, *Truman*

Capote: Conversations, 74; Capote, "Playboy Interview," 112; and Truman Capote, "Checking in with Truman Capote," interview by Gerald Clarke, *Truman Capote: Conversations,* 196.

7. Truman Capote, *Other Voices, Other Rooms* (1948; reprint, New York: Random House, 1994), 147, hereafter cited by page number in the text.

8. Florence King, *Southern Ladies and Gentlemen* (1975; reprint, New York: St. Martin's Press, 1993), 148.

9. Richard McLaughlin, "A Dixieland Stew," review of *Other Voices, Other Rooms,* by Truman Capote, *Saturday Review* (14 February 1948): 13.

10. For a rare positive review, see Lloyd Morris, "A Vivid, Inner, Secret World: Truman Capote's First Novel Fulfills High Expectations," review of *Other Voices, Other Rooms,* by Truman Capote, *New York Herald Tribune Weekly Book Review* (18 January 1948): 2.

11. Charles J. Rolo, review of *Other Voices, Other Rooms,* by Truman Capote, *Atlantic* 181 (March 1948): 109; Review of *Other Voices, Other Rooms,* by Truman Capote, *New Yorker* (24 January 1948): 80; and "Spare the Laurels," review of *Other Voices, Other Rooms,* by Truman Capote, *Time* (26 January 1948): 102.

12. Farrelly, review of *Other Voices, Other Rooms* and *The Circus in the Attic,* 31; W. E. Harriss, review of *Other Voices, Other Rooms,* by Truman Capote, *Commonweal* (27 February 1948): 500; and Jesse E. Cross, review of *Other Voices, Other Rooms,* by Truman Capote, *Library Journal* (1 December 1947): 1685.

13. Diana Trilling, review of *Other Voices, Other Rooms,* by Truman Capote, *Nation* (31 January 1948): 133–34.

14. Clarke, *Capote: A Biography,* 158.

15. William Goyen, *The House of Breath* (1950; reprint, New York: Random House, 1975), 141, 147, 135–36, 148, hereafter cited by page number in the text.

16. See Levin, *Gay Novel in America,* 90–91; and Robert Phillips, *William Goyen* (Boston: G. K. Hall, 1979), 42–43.

17. Phillips, *William Goyen,* 39.

18. Ibid., 43.

19. See Sarotte, *Like a Brother,* 49.

20. See Goyen, *William Goyen: Selected Letters,* 12–20.

21. For a contrasting analysis, see Phillips, *William Goyen,* 43–44.

CHAPTER 3

1. Adrienne Rich, "Compulsory Heterosexuality and Lesbian Existence," in *Blood, Bread, and Poetry: Selected Prose 1979–1985* (New York: W. W. Norton, 1986), 24, 36.

2. Mary Helen Washington, "'The Darkened Eye Restored': Notes Toward a Literary History of Black Women," in *Reading Black, Reading Feminist,* ed. Henry Louis Gates, Jr. (New York: Penguin, 1990), 38.

3. Michel Fabre, *Richard Wright: Books and Writers* (Jackson: Univ. Press of Mississippi, 1990), 9.

4. Margaret Walker, *Richard Wright, Daemonic Genius* (New York: Warner Books, 1988), 88.

For a critique of Walker, her relationship to Wright, and its impact on her biography, see Hazel Rowley, *Richard Wright: The Life and Times* (New York: Henry Holt, 2001), 168–72.

5. Walker, *Richard Wright, Daemonic Genius,* 87–88. For radically different discussions of punks and punk-hunting, see Chauncey, *Gay New York,* 88–96; and Eldridge Cleaver, *Soul on Ice* (1968; reprint, New York: Dell, 1992), 103.

6. Walker, *Richard Wright, Daemonic Genius,* 88; and Carr, *The Lonely Hunter,* 119.

7. Fabre, *Richard Wright: Books and Writers,* 88, 134, 167, 57, 89, 156, 170.

8. Addison Gayle, *Richard Wright: Ordeal of a Native Son* (Garden City, N.Y.: Doubleday, 1980), 236; and Walker, *Richard Wright, Daemonic Genius,* 310.

9. Walker, *Richard Wright, Daemonic Genius,* 88, 90–91; Constance Webb, *Richard Wright: A Biography* (New York: Putnam's Sons, 1968), 181; and Rowley, *Richard Wright,* 429.

10. Richard Wright, *The Long Dream* (1958; reprint, New York: Harper & Row, 1987), 35, 36, hereafter cited in the text by page number.

11. Smith, "Homophobia," 101; and Rich, "Compulsory Heterosexuality," 58.

12. LeRoi Jones, quoted in Sarotte, *Like a Brother,* 94; and Cleaver, *Soul on Ice,* 106.

13. Sedgwick, *Epistemology of the Closet,* 33. For other readings of this scene, see Robert Felgar, *Richard Wright* (Boston: Twayne, 1980), 128; and Katherine Sprandel, "*The Long Dream,*" in *Richard Wright: Impressions and Perspectives,* ed. David Ray and Robert M. Farnsworth (Ann Arbor: Univ. of Michigan Press, 1971), 176.

14. Sigmund Freud, *Leonardo da Vinci and a Memory of His Childhood,* trans. Alan Tyson (New York: W. W. Norton, 1964), 54–55.

15. Ibid., 50, 62–63. For critiques of Freudian theories of male homosexuality, see, for instance, Henry Abelove, "Freud, Male Homosexuality, and the Americans," in *The Lesbian and Gay Studies Reader,* 381–93; and Michael Warner, "Homo-Narcissism; or, Heterosexuality," in *Engendering Men: The Question of Male Feminist Criticism,* ed. Joseph A. Boone and Michael Cadden (New York: Routledge, 1990), 190–206.

16. Zora Neale Hurston, *Their Eyes Were Watching God* (1937; reprint, Urbana: Univ. of Illinois Press, 1978), 29; Alice Walker, *The Color Purple* (New York: Simon & Schuster, 1982), 213; and Hazel V. Carby, "'On the Threshold of Woman's Era': Lynching, Empire, and Sexuality in Black Feminist Theory," in *"Race," Writing, and Difference,* ed. Henry Louis Gates, Jr. (Chicago: Univ. of Chicago Press, 1986), 308–9.

17. See Earle V. Bryant, "Sexual Initiation and Survival in Richard Wright's *The Long Dream,*" *Southern Quarterly* 21, no. 3 (Spring 1983): 59.

18. Katherine Fishburn, *Richard Wright's Hero: The Faces of a Rebel-Victim* (Metuchen, N.J.: Scarecrow Press, 1977), 19.

19. Neil R. McMillen, *Dark Journey: Black Mississippians in the Age of Jim Crow* (Urbana: Univ. of Illinois Press, 1990), xiii, 14, 15, 229.

20. Trudier Harris, *Exorcising Blackness: Historical and Literary Lynching and Burning Rituals* (Bloomington: Indiana Univ. Press, 1984), 2. See also McMillen, *Dark Journey,* 234.

21. McMillen, *Dark Journey,* 235–36.

22. For a theorization of white men's homosexual desire for black ones, see Lee Edelman, "The Part for the (W)hole: Baldwin, Homophobia, and the Fantasmatics of 'Race,'" in *Homographesis: Essays in Gay Literary and Cultural Theory* (New York: Routledge, 1994), 42–75.

23. Bryant, "Sexual Initiation," 57.

24. William Faulkner, *Absalom, Absalom!* (1936; reprint, New York: Random House, 1987), 471.

25. James Baldwin, *Giovanni's Room* (1956; reprint, New York: Bantam Doubleday Dell, 1988), 35.

26. See Fishburn, *Richard Wright's Hero*, 2, 14–15; Keneth Kinnamon, *The Emergence of Richard Wright* (Urbana: Univ. of Illinois Press, 1972), 85; and David Bakish, *Richard Wright* (New York: Ungar, 1973), 90.

27. Richard Wright, "Big Boy Leaves Home," in *Uncle Tom's Children* (1940; reprint, New York: HarperCollins, 1992), 27, hereafter cited in the text by page number.

CHAPTER 4

1. Mellard, "The Fiction of Social Commitment," 351; and Hobson, *Tell About the South*, 297. For additional discussion of southern liberalism, especially as negotiated by southern women writers, see Will Brantley, *Feminine Sense in Southern Memoir: Smith, Glasgow, Welty, Hellman, Porter, and Hurston* (Jackson: Univ. Press of Mississippi, 1993), 3–37.

2. Smith to George Brockway, June 1949, in *How Am I to Be Heard?* 125–26.

3. Smith to Jerome Bick, 9 September 1961, in *How Am I to Be Heard?* 278–79; and Smith to Wilma Dykeman Stokeley [*sic*], 30 October 1965, in *How Am I to Be Heard?* 333–34.

4. Hobson, *Tell About the South*, 319; Hobson, foreword to *Strange Fruit*, vii; and Gladney, preface to *How Am I to be Heard?* xiv. See also Louise Blackwell and Frances Clay, *Lillian Smith* (New York: Twayne, 1971), 127–31; and Hobson, *But Now I See*, 18–36.

5. Smith to Lawrence Kubie, 10 October 1957, in *How Am I to Be Heard?* 219; Smith to Jerome Bick, 9 September 1961, in *How Am I to Be Heard?* 278; and Smith to Jerome Bick, 27 October 1961, in *How Am I to Be Heard?* 288.

6. Smith to Jerome Bick, 27 October 1961, in *How Am I to Be Heard?* 289; Smith to Jerome Bick, 9 September 1961, in *How Am I to Be Heard?* 278; and Smith to George Brockway, 3 July 1965, in *How Am I to Be Heard?* 323.

7. Francis Downing, review of *Strange Fruit*, by Lillian Smith, *Commonweal* (7 April 1944): 626; Diana Trilling, review of *Strange Fruit*, by Lillian Smith, *Nation* (18 March 1944): 342; Edward Weeks, review of *Strange Fruit*, by Lillian Smith, *Atlantic* 173 (May 1944): 124; and Malcolm Cowley, "Southways," review of *Strange Fruit*, by Lillian Smith, *New Republic* (6 March 1944): 320, 321.

8. Lillian Smith, *Strange Fruit* (1944; reprint, with a foreword by Fred Hobson, Athens: Univ. of Georgia Press, 1985), 225–26, hereafter cited by page number in the text.

9. Joseph McSorley, review of *Strange Fruit*, by Lillian Smith, *Catholic World* 159 (May 1944): 182; and Weeks, review of *Strange Fruit*, 124.

10. Blackwell and Clay, *Lillian Smith*, 20, 6, 21.

11. Ibid., 51; and Sedgwick, *Epistemology of the Closet*, 52–53.

12. Mellard, "The Fiction of Social Commitment," 355; and Hobson, *Tell About the South*, 322, 314.

13. Will Brantley, "Missives from Macedonia," review of *How Am I to Be Heard? Letters of*

Lillian Smith, by Lillian Smith, ed. Margaret Rose Gladney, *Mississippi Quarterly* 97 (Fall 1994): 662; and Gladney, preface to *How Am I to Be Heard?* xvi.

14. Gladney, preface to *How Am I to Be Heard?* xvi; Smith to Paula Snelling, 21 January 1946, in *How Am I to Be Heard?* 96, 97; and Smith to Paula Snelling, 6 February 1946, in *How Am I to Be Heard?* 101.

15. Smith to Paula Snelling, 20 June 1961, in *How Am I to Be Heard?* 275–76, 277.

16. Gladney, preface to *How Am I to Be Heard?* xiii.

17. For a critique of Smith's presentations of an essentialized white southern childhood based on her own economically privileged one, see Hobson, *Tell About the South,* 316–17.

18. Lillian Smith, *Killers of the Dream* (1949; reprint, New York: W. W. Norton, 1978), 27, 202, 28, hereafter cited by page number in the text.

19. Anne Goodwyn Jones, *Tomorrow Is Another Day: The Woman Writer in the South, 1859–1936* (Baton Rouge: Louisiana State Univ. Press, 1981), 4, 5, 9–10.

20. Ibid., 9.

21. Smith to Jerome Bick, 9 September 1961, in *How Am I to Be Heard?* 279; Smith to Rochelle Girson, 5 March 1962, in *How Am I to Be Heard?* 295; and Gladney, *How Am I to Be Heard?* 10.

22. Lillian Smith, *One Hour* (1959; reprint, with an introduction by Margaret Rose Gladney, Chapel Hill: Univ. of North Carolina Press, 1994), 352–53, 212.

23. Gladney, *How Am I to Be Heard?* 6, 4.

CHAPTER 5

1. Review of *To Kill a Mockingbird,* by Harper Lee, *Commonweal* 9 (December 1960): 289; Robert W. Henderson, review of *To Kill a Mockingbird,* by Harper Lee, *Library Journal* (15 May 1960): 1937; Granville Hicks, "Three at the Outset," review of *To Kill a Mockingbird,* by Harper Lee, *Saturday Review* 23 (July 1960): 15; Keith Waterhouse, review of *To Kill a Mockingbird,* by Harper Lee, *New Statesman* (15 October 1960): 580; Frank H. Lyell, "One-Taxi Town," review of *To Kill a Mockingbird,* by Harper Lee, *New York Times Book Review* (10 July 1960): 5; and "About Life and Little Girls," review of *To Kill a Mockingbird,* by Harper Lee, *Time* (1 August 1960): 70–71.

2. Hicks, "Three at the Outset," 15; "Summer Reading," review of *To Kill a Mockingbird,* by Harper Lee, *Atlantic Monthly* 206 (August 1960): 98; review of *To Kill a Mockingbird,* by Harper Lee, *Booklist* 57 (1 September 1960): 23; and "About Life and Little Girls," 70; review of *To Kill a Mockingbird, Commonweal,* 289.

3. Eric J. Sundquist, "Blues for Atticus Finch: Scottsboro, *Brown,* and Harper Lee," in *The South as an American Problem,* 182, 183, 186, 187.

4. Cook, "Old Ways," 529. See Sundquist, "Blues for Atticus Finch," 181–209; Claudia Durst Johnson, "The Secret Courts of Men's Hearts: Code and Law in Harper Lee's *To Kill a Mockingbird,*" *Studies in American Fiction* 19 (Autumn 1991): 129–39; and Claudia Durst Johnson, *To Kill a Mockingbird: Threatening Boundaries* (New York: Twayne, 1994).

5. Harper Lee, *To Kill a Mockingbird* (1960; reprint, New York: Fawcett, 1962), 11, hereafter cited in the text by page number.

6. Grobel, *Conversations with Capote,* 53; and Clarke, *Capote: A Biography,* 42.

7. Clarke, *Capote: A Biography,* 389. See also Amy Fine Collins, "A Night to Remember," *Vanity Fair* 431 (July 1996): 120–39.

8. Kenneth T. Reed, *Truman Capote* (Boston: Twayne, 1981), 15–16. See also Clarke, *Capote: A Biography,* 410–15.

9. See Johnson, "The Secret Courts of Men's Hearts," 131, 134–38.

10. Ibid., 136.

11. Judith Butler, *Gender Trouble: Feminism and the Subversion of Identity* (New York: Routledge, 1990), 140–41.

12. Ibid., 137–38, 139, 141.

13. Ibid., 137.

14. For a discussion of Lee's conservative representations of racial equality, see Sundquist, "Blues for Atticus Finch," 181–209.

15. Sedgwick, *Epistemology of the Closet,* 33.

16. For a brief discussion of closetedness not specific to gayness, see Sedgwick, *Epistemology of the Closet,* 72.

17. See Allan Bérubé, *Coming Out under Fire: The History of Gay Men and Women in World War Two* (1990; reprint, New York: Penguin, 1991), 8–33, 149–74.

18. Eve Kosofsky Sedgwick, *Tendencies* (Durham, N.C.: Duke Univ. Press, 1993), 2.

19. Sedgwick, *Epistemology of the Closet,* 67.

20. John D'Emilio, *Sexual Politics, Sexual Communities: The Making of a Homosexual Minority in the United States, 1940–1970* (Chicago: Univ. of Chicago Press, 1983), 79, 113. See also Martin Duberman, *Stonewall* (New York: Plume, 1983), 174.

21. See D'Emilio, *Sexual Politics, Sexual Communities,* 129–249; and Duberman, *Stonewall,* 73–166.

CHAPTER 6

1. Rumer Godden, "Death and Life in a Small Southern Town," review of *Clock Without Hands,* by Carson McCullers, *New York Herald Tribune Books* (17 September 1961): 5; Charles Rolo, "A Southern Drama," review of *Clock Without Hands,* by Carson McCullers, *Atlantic* 208 (October 1961): 126–27; Gore Vidal, "Carson McCullers's *Clock Without Hands,*" in *Carson McCullers,* ed. Harold Bloom (New York: Chelsea House, 1986), 18–19; and Judith Giblin James, *Wunderkind: The Reputation of Carson McCullers, 1940–1990* (Columbia, S.C.: Camden House, 1995), 143. See also Margaret McDowell, *Carson McCullers* (Boston: Twayne, 1980), 96–97.

2. Irving Howe, "In the Shadow of Death," review of *Clock Without Hands,* by Carson McCullers, *New York Times Book Review* (17 September 1961): 5; Robert O. Bowen, review of *Clock Without Hands,* by Carson McCullers, *Catholic World* 194 (December 1961), 186; Louis D. Rubin, Jr., "Carson McCullers: The Aesthetic of Pain," in *A Gallery of Southerners* (Baton Rouge: Louisiana State Univ. Press, 1982), 138; Louis D. Rubin, Jr., "Six Novels and S. Levin," review of *Clock Without Hands,* by Carson McCullers, *Sewanee Review* 70 (Summer 1962): 509; and Flannery O'Connor, quoted in Carr, *The Lonely Hunter,* 433. For a fuller review of the critical reception of *Clock Without Hands,* see James, *Wunderkind,* 143–64.

3. Brantley, "Missives from Macedonia," 667; and Smith to Margaret Long, 10 September 1961, in *How Am I to Be Heard?* 283–84.

4. Oliver Evans, "The Achievement of Carson McCullers," in *Carson McCullers,* ed. Bloom, 22. For a catalogue of those critics deploying this allegorical approach, see Adams, "'A Mixture of Delicious and Freak,'" 577; Frank Baldanza, "Plato in Dixie," *Georgia Review* 12 (Summer 1958): 151–67; Donna Bauerly, "Themes of Eros and Agape in the Major Fiction of Carson Mc-Cullers," *Pembroke Magazine* 20 (1988): 72–76; and Evans, *The Ballad of Carson McCullers.* See Lori J. Kenschaft, "Homoerotics and Human Connections: Reading Carson McCullers 'As a Lesbian,'" in *Critical Essays on Carson McCullers,* ed. Beverly Lyon Clark and Melvin J. Fried-man (New York: G. K. Hall, 1996), 220–33.

5. Carson McCullers, *Collected Stories of Carson McCullers* (Boston: Houghton Mifflin, 1987), 4, 5, 8, 9–10.

6. Carson McCullers, *The Heart Is a Lonely Hunter* (1940; reprint, New York: Bantam, 1981), 1, hereafter cited by page number in the text.

7. Carson McCullers, *The Mortgaged Heart,* ed. Margarita B. Smith (Boston: Houghton Mifflin, 1971), 125.

8. Carson McCullers, *Reflections in a Golden Eye* (1941; reprint, New York: Bantam, 1966), 13, hereafter cited by page number in the text.

9. Carson McCullers, *The Ballad of the Sad Café and Other Stories* (1951; reprint, New York: Bantam, 1991), 49–50, hereafter cited by page number in the text.

10. Carson McCullers, *The Member of the Wedding* (1946; reprint, New York: Bantam, 1958), 70, hereafter cited by page number in the text.

11. McCullers, *The Mortgaged Heart,* 140.

12. Ibid., 138.

13. See Richard M. Cook, *Carson McCullers* (New York: Ungar, 1975), 35, 146.

14. McCullers, *The Mortgaged Heart,* 135.

15. Adams, "'A Mixture of Delicious and Freak,'" 559.

16. Ibid., 574, 575.

17. Segrest, "'Lines I Dare,'" 141.

18. Barbara A. White, "Loss of Self in *The Member of the Wedding,*" in *Carson McCullers,* ed. Bloom, 192; and Thadious M. Davis, "Erasing the 'We of Me' and Rewriting the Racial Script: Carson McCullers's Two *Member[s] of the Wedding,*" in *Critical Essays on Carson McCullers,* 209.

19. Fiedler, *Love and Death,* 478; Segrest, "Southern Women Writing," 22; Segrest, "'Lines I Dare,'" 107; and Kenschaft, "Homoerotics and Human Connections," 220, 224, 226.

20. Rubin, "Carson McCullers," 145, 147–48.

21. Fiedler, *Love and Death,* 333; White, "Loss of Self," 134; and Fiedler, *Love and Death,* 479.

22. White, "Loss of Self," 136.

23. Louise Westling, "Carson McCullers' Amazon Nightmare," in *Carson McCullers,* ed. Bloom, 113.

24. Carson McCullers, *Clock Without Hands* (1961; reprint, Boston: Houghton Mifflin, 1998), 8, 31, hereafter cited by page number in the text.

25. Evans, *The Ballad of Carson McCullers,* 175.

26. Adams, "'A Mixture of Delicious and Freak,'" 553, 571.

27. Ibid., 569.

28. For representative minimizations of this complexity, see Cook, *Carson McCullers,* 115; Graver, *Carson McCullers,* 43; and Virginia Spencer Carr, *Understanding Carson McCullers* (Columbia: Univ. of South Carolina Press, 1990), 119–22.

EPILOGUE

1. For a general discussion of this literary production, see Rebecca Mark, "Lesbian Literature," in *The Companion to Southern Literature,* ed. Joseph M. Flora and Lucinda H. Mac Kethan (Baton Rouge: Louisiana State Univ. Press, 2002), 427–30; and J. Randal Woodland, "Gay Literature," in *Companion to Southern Literature,* 289–92.

2. Allan Gurganus, *Plays Well with Others* (New York: Knopf, 1997), 9.

3. Harlan Greene, "Charleston, South Carolina," in *Hometowns: Gay Men Write about Where They Belong,* ed. John Preston (New York: Dutton, 1991), 59, 64; Martin Duberman, *About Time: Exploring the Gay Past* (1986; reprint, with a note to revised edition, New York: Meridian, 1991), 14; Linda Hutcheon, *The Politics of Postmodernism,* (New York: Routledge, 1989), 80; and Greene, "Charleston," 64.

4. Harlan Greene, *What the Dead Remember* (1991; reprint, New York: Plume, 1992), 5, hereafter cited by page number in the text.

5. Harlan Greene, *Why We Never Danced the Charleston* (1984; reprint, New York: Penguin, 1985), 4, hereafter cited by page number in the text.

6. William Faulkner, *Intruder in the Dust* (1948; reprint, New York: Vintage, 1991), 190.

7. Hutcheon, *Politics of Postmodernism,* 101.

Bibliography

Abelove, Henry. "Freud, Male Homosexuality, and the Americans." In *The Lesbian and Gay Studies Reader,* edited by Henry Abelove, Michèle Aina Barale, and David M. Halperin. New York: Routledge, 1993.

"About Life and Little Girls." Review of *To Kill a Mockingbird,* by Harper Lee. *Time* (1 August 1960): 70–71.

Adams, Rachel. "'A Mixture of Delicious and Freak': The Queer Fiction of Carson McCullers." *American Literature* 71 (September 1999): 551–83.

Andrews, William L. et al., eds. *The Literature of the American South.* New York: W. W. Norton, 1998.

Austen, Roger. *Playing the Game: The Homosexual Novel in America.* Indianapolis: Bobbs-Merrill, 1977.

Bakish, David. *Richard Wright.* New York: Ungar, 1973.

Baldanza, Frank. "Plato in Dixie." *Georgia Review* 12 (Summer 1958): 151–67.

Baldwin, James. *Giovanni's Room.* 1956. Reprint. New York: Bantam Doubleday Dell, 1988.

Bauerly, Donna. "Themes of Eros and Agape in the Major Fiction of Carson McCullers." *Pembroke Magazine* 20 (1988): 72–76.

Bérubé, Allan. *Coming Out under Fire: The History of Gay Men and Women in World War Two.* 1990. Reprint. New York: Penguin, 1991.

Blackwell, Louise, and Frances Clay. *Lillian Smith.* New York: Twayne, 1971.

Bonner, Thomas, Jr. "Truman Capote." In *The History of Southern Literature,* edited by Louis D. Rubin, Jr., et al. Baton Rouge: Louisiana State Univ. Press, 1985.

Boone, Joseph Allen. *Libidinal Currents: Sexuality and the Shaping of Modernism.* Chicago: Univ. of Chicago Press, 1998.

Bowen, Robert O. Review of *Clock Without Hands,* by Carson McCullers. *Catholic World* 194 (December 1961): 186–88.

Brantley, Will. *Feminine Sense in Southern Memoir: Smith, Glasgow, Welty, Hellman, Porter, and Hurston.* Jackson: Univ. Press of Mississippi, 1993.

———. "Missives from Macedonia." Review of *How Am I to Be Heard? Letters of Lillian Smith,* by Lillian Smith, edited by Margaret Rose Gladney. *Mississippi Quarterly* 97 (Fall 1994): 661–68.

Brooks, Cleanth. *William Faulkner: The Yoknapatawpha Country.* 1963. Reprint. Baton Rouge: Louisiana State Univ. Press, 1990.

Bryant, Earle V. "Sexual Initiation and Survival in Richard Wright's *The Long Dream.*" *Southern Quarterly* 21, no. 3 (Spring 1983): 57–66.

Butler, Judith. *Gender Trouble: Feminism and the Subversion of Identity.* New York: Routledge, 1990.

Capote, Truman. "Checking in with Truman Capote." By Gerald Clarke. In *Truman Capote: Conversations,* edited by M. Thomas Inge. Jackson: Univ. Press of Mississippi, 1987.

———. *Music for Chameleons.* 1980. Reprint. New York: Random House, 1981.

———. *Other Voices, Other Rooms.* 1948. Reprint. New York: Random House, 1994.

———. "Playboy Interview: Truman Capote." By Eric Norden. In *Truman Capote: Conversations,* edited by M. Thomas Inge. Jackson: Univ. Press of Mississippi, 1987.

———. "Truman Capote." By Roy Newquist. In *Truman Capote: Conversations,* edited by M. Thomas Inge. Jackson: Univ. Press of Mississippi, 1987.

———. "Truman Capote Talks, Talks, Talks." By C. Robert Jennings. In *Truman Capote: Conversations,* edited by M. Thomas Inge. Jackson: Univ. Press of Mississippi, 1987.

———. "A Visit with Truman Capote." By Gloria Steinem. In *Truman Capote: Conversations,* edited by M. Thomas Inge. Jackson: Univ. Press of Mississippi, 1987.

Carby, Hazel V. "'On the Threshold of Woman's Era': Lynching, Empire, and Sexuality in Black Feminist Theory." In *"Race," Writing, and Difference,* edited by Henry Louis Gates, Jr. Chicago: Univ. of Chicago Press, 1986.

Carr, Virginia Spencer. *The Lonely Hunter: A Biography of Carson McCullers.* 1975. Reprint. New York: Carroll & Graf, 1989.

———. *Understanding Carson McCullers.* Columbia: Univ. of South Carolina Press, 1990.

Cash, W. J. *The Mind of the South.* 1941. Reprint. New York: Random House, 1969.

Chauncey, George, Jr. *Gay New York: Gender, Urban Culture, and the Making of the Gay Male World, 1890–1940.* New York: HarperCollins, 1994.

Clarke, Gerald. *Capote: A Biography.* New York: Simon & Schuster, 1988.

Cleaver, Eldridge. *Soul on Ice.* 1968. Reprint. New York: Dell, 1992.

Collins, Amy Fine. "A Night to Remember." *Vanity Fair* 431 (July 1996): 120–39.

Comley, Nancy R., and Robert Scholes. *Hemingway's Genders: Rereading the Hemingway Text.* New Haven: Yale Univ. Press, 1994.

Cook, Martha E. "Old Ways and New Ways." In *The History of Southern Literature,* edited by Louis D. Rubin, Jr., et al. Baton Rouge: Louisiana State Univ. Press, 1985.

Cook, Richard M. *Carson McCullers.* New York: Ungar, 1975.

Cowley, Malcolm. "Southways." Review of *Strange Fruit,* by Lillian Smith. *New Republic* (6 March 1944): 320–21.

Cross, Jesse E. Review of *Other Voices, Other Rooms,* by Truman Capote. *Library Journal* (1 December 1947): 1685.

Davidson, Donald. "A Mirror for Artists." In *I'll Take My Stand: The South and the Agrarian Tradition.* 1930. Reprint, with an introduction by Louis D. Rubin, Jr. Baton Rouge: Louisiana State Univ. Press, 1977.

Davis, Thadious M. "Erasing the 'We of Me' and Rewriting the Racial Script: Carson McCullers's Two *Member[s] of the Wedding.*" In *Critical Essays on Carson McCullers,* edited by Beverly Lyon Clark and Melvin J. Friedman. New York: G. K. Hall, 1996.

D'Emilio, John. *Sexual Politics, Sexual Communities: The Making of a Homosexual Minority in the United States, 1940–1970.* Chicago: Univ. of Chicago Press, 1983.

Dews, Carlos L. Introduction to *Illumination and Night Glare: The Unfinished Autobiography of Carson McCullers,* by Carson McCullers, edited by Carlos L. Dews. Madison: Univ. of Wisconsin Press, 1999.

Downing, Francis. Review of *Strange Fruit,* by Lillian Smith. *Commonweal* (7 April 1944): 626.

Duberman, Martin. *About Time: Exploring the Gay Past.* 1986. Reprint, with a note to revised edition. New York: Meridian, 1991.

———. *Stonewall.* New York: Plume, 1993.

Eagleton, Terry. *Literary Theory: An Introduction.* 1983. Reprint. Minneapolis: Univ. of Minnesota Press, 1989.

Edelman, Lee. "The Part for the (W)hole: Baldwin, Homophobia, and the Fantasmatics of 'Race.'" In *Homographesis: Essays in Gay Literary and Cultural Theory.* New York: Routledge, 1994.

Evans, Oliver. "The Achievement of Carson McCullers." In *Carson McCullers,* edited by Harold Bloom. New York: Chelsea House, 1986.

———. *The Ballad of Carson McCullers: A Biography.* New York: Coward-McCann, 1966.

Fabre, Michel. *Richard Wright: Books and Writers.* Jackson: Univ. Press of Mississippi, 1990.

Faderman, Lillian. *Odd Girls and Twilight Lovers: A History of Lesbian Life in Twentieth-Century America.* 1991. Reprint. New York: Penguin, 1992.

——. *Surpassing the Love of Men: Romantic Friendship and Love between Women from the Renaissance to the Present.* New York: William Morrow, 1981.

Farrelly, John. Review of *Other Voices, Other Rooms,* by Truman Capote, and *The Circus in the Attic,* by Robert Penn Warren. *New Republic* (26 January 1948): 31–32.

Faulkner, William. *Absalom, Absalom!* 1936. Reprint. New York: Random House, 1987.

——. *Intruder in the Dust.* 1948. Reprint. New York: Vintage, 1991.

Felgar, Robert. *Richard Wright.* Boston: Twayne, 1980.

Fiedler, Leslie. *Love and Death in the American Novel.* 1960. Reprint, with an afterword by Fiedler. New York: Anchor Books, 1992.

Fishburn, Katherine. *Richard Wright's Hero: The Faces of a Rebel-Victim.* Metuchen, N.J.: Scarecrow Press, 1977.

Foucault, Michel. *The History of Sexuality. volume 1: An Introduction.* Translated by Robert Hurley. New York: Random House, 1978.

Freud, Sigmund. *Leonardo da Vinci and a Memory of His Childhood.* Translated by Alan Tyson. New York: W. W. Norton, 1964.

Garber, Eric. "A Spectacle of Color: The Lesbian and Gay Subculture of Jazz Age Harlem." In *Hidden from History: Reclaiming the Gay and Lesbian Past,* edited by Martin Duberman, Martha Vicinus, and George Chauncey, Jr. New York: Penguin, 1989.

Gayle, Addison. *Richard Wright: Ordeal of a Native Son.* Garden City, N.Y.: Doubleday, 1980.

Gladney, Margaret Rose. "Personalizing the Political, Politicizing the Personal: Reflections on Editing the Letters of Lillian Smith." In *Carryin' On in the Lesbian and Gay South,* edited by John Howard. New York: New York Univ. Press, 1997.

——. Preface to *How Am I to Be Heard? Letters of Lillian Smith,* by Lillian Smith, edited by Margaret Rose Gladney. Chapel Hill: Univ. of North Carolina Press, 1993.

Godden, Rumer. "Death and Life in a Small Southern Town." Review of *Clock Without Hands,* by Carson McCullers. *New York Herald Tribune Books* (17 September 1961): 5.

Goyen, William. *The House of Breath.* 1950. Reprint. New York: Random House, 1975.

——. *William Goyen: Selected Letters from a Writer's Life.* Edited by Robert Phillips. Austin: Univ. of Texas Press, 1995.

Graver, Lawrence. *Carson McCullers.* Minneapolis: Univ. of Minnesota Press, 1969.

Gray, Richard. *Writing the South: Ideas of an American Region.* Cambridge, N.Y.: Cambridge Univ. Press, 1986.

Greene, Harlan. "Charleston, South Carolina." In *Hometowns: Gay Men Write about Where They Belong,* edited by John Preston. New York: Dutton, 1991.

————. *What the Dead Remember.* 1991. Reprint. New York: Plume, 1992.

————. *Why We Never Danced the Charleston.* 1984. Reprint. New York: Penguin, 1985.

Grobel, Lawrence. *Conversations with Capote.* New York: New American Library, 1985.

Gurganus, Allan. *Plays Well with Others.* New York: Knopf, 1997.

Halperin, David M. *One Hundred Years of Homosexuality and Other Essays on Greek Love.* New York: Routledge, 1990.

Hardy, John Edward. "Ellen Glasgow." In *Southern Renascence: The Literature of the Modern South,* edited by Louis D. Rubin, Jr., and Robert D. Jacobs. Baltimore, Md.: Johns Hopkins Press, 1953.

Harris, Trudier. *Exorcising Blackness: Historical and Literary Lynching and Burning Rituals.* Bloomington: Indiana Univ. Press, 1984.

Harriss, W. E. Review of *Other Voices, Other Rooms,* by Truman Capote. *Commonweal* (27 February 1948): 500.

Hazel, Robert. "Notes on Erskine Caldwell." In *Southern Renascence: The Literature of the Modern South,* edited by Louis D. Rubin, Jr., and Robert D. Jacobs. Baltimore, Md.: Johns Hopkins Press, 1953.

Heilman, Robert B. "The Southern Temper." In *Southern Renascence: The Literature of the Modern South,* edited by Louis D. Rubin, Jr., and Robert D. Jacobs. Baltimore, Md.: Johns Hopkins Press, 1953.

Hemingway, Ernest. *Death in the Afternoon.* New York: Charles Scribner's Sons, 1932.

Henderson, Robert W. Review of *To Kill a Mockingbird,* by Harper Lee. *Library Journal* (15 May 1960): 1937.

Hicks, Granville. "Three at the Outset." Review of *To Kill a Mockingbird,* by Harper Lee. *Saturday Review* (23 July 1960): 15.

Hobson, Fred. *But Now I See: The White Southern Racial Conversion Narrative.* Baton Rouge: Louisiana State Univ. Press, 1999.

————. Foreword to *Strange Fruit,* by Lillian Smith. Athens: Univ. of Georgia Press, 1985.

————. *Tell About the South: The Southern Rage to Explain.* Baton Rouge: Louisiana State Univ. Press, 1983.

Holy Bible. Revised Standard Version. Teaneck, N.J.: World Publishing, 1962.

Howard, John. *Men Like That: A Southern Queer History.* Chicago: Univ. of Chicago Press, 1999.

Howe, Irving. "In the Shadow of Death." Review of *Clock Without Hands,* by Carson McCullers. *New York Times Book Review* (17 September 1961): 5.

Hurston, Zora Neale. *Their Eyes Were Watching God.* 1937. Reprint. Urbana: Univ. of Illinois Press, 1978.

Hutcheon, Linda. *The Politics of Postmodernism.* New York: Routledge, 1989.

James, Judith Giblin. *Wunderkind: The Reputation of Carson McCullers, 1940–1990.* Columbia, S.C.: Camden House, 1995.

Johnson, Claudia Durst. *To Kill a Mockingbird: Threatening Boundaries.* New York: Twayne, 1994.

———. "The Secret Courts of Men's Hearts: Code and Law in Harper Lee's *To Kill a Mockingbird.*" *Studies in American Fiction* 19 (Autumn 1991): 129–39.

Jones, Anne Goodwyn. *Tomorrow Is Another Day: The Woman Writer in the South, 1859–1936.* Baton Rouge: Louisiana State Univ. Press, 1981.

Jonza, Nancylee Novell. *The Underground Stream: The Life and Art of Caroline Gordon.* Athens: Univ. of Georgia Press, 1995.

Kenschaft, Lori J. "Homoerotics and Human Connections: Reading Carson McCullers 'As a Lesbian.'" In *Critical Essays on Carson McCullers,* edited by Beverly Lyon Clark and Melvin J. Friedman. New York: G. K. Hall, 1996.

King, Florence. *Southern Ladies and Gentlemen.* 1975. Reprint. New York: St. Martin's Press, 1993.

King, Richard H. *A Southern Renaissance: The Cultural Awakening of the American South, 1930–1955.* New York: Oxford Univ. Press, 1980.

Kinnamon, Keneth. *The Emergence of Richard Wright.* Urbana: Univ. of Illinois Press, 1972.

Kreyling, Michael. "Race and Southern Literature: 'The Problem' in the Work of Louis D. Rubin, Jr." In *The South as an American Problem,* edited by Larry J. Griffin and Don H. Doyle. Athens: Univ. of Georgia Press, 1995.

———. "Reynolds Price." In *The History of Southern Literature,* edited by Louis D. Rubin, Jr., et al. Baton Rouge: Louisiana State Univ. Press, 1985.

Lanier, Lyle H. "A Critique of the Philosophy of Progress." In *I'll Take My Stand: The South and the Agrarian Tradition.* 1930. Reprint, with an introduction by Louis D. Rubin, Jr. Baton Rouge: Louisiana State Univ. Press, 1977.

Lee, Harper. *To Kill a Mockingbird.* 1960. Reprint. New York: Fawcett, 1962.

Levin, James. *The Gay Novel in America.* New York: Garland, 1991.

Liles, Don Merrick. "William Faulkner's *Absalom, Absalom!* An Exegesis of the Homoerotic Configurations in the Novel." In *Literary Visions of Homosexuality,* edited by Stuart Kellogg. New York: Haworth, 1983.

Loveland, Anne C. *Lillian Smith: A Southerner Confronting the South.* Baton Rouge: Louisiana State Univ. Press, 1986.

Lyell, Frank H. "One-Taxi Town." Review of *To Kill a Mockingbird,* by Harper Lee. *New York Times Book Review* (10 July 1960): 5, 18.

Lytle, Andrew Nelson. *Bedford Forrest and His Critter Company.* 1931. Reprint, with a preface by Walter Sullivan. Nashville, Tenn.: J. S. Saunders, 1992.

———. "The Hind Tit." In *I'll Take My Stand: The South and the Agrarian Tradition.* 1930. Reprint, with an introduction by Louis D. Rubin, Jr. Baton Rouge: Louisiana State Univ. Press, 1977.

Mark, Rebecca. "Lesbian Literature." In *The Companion to Southern Literature,* edited by Joseph M. Flora and Lucinda H. MacKethan. Baton Rouge: Louisiana State Univ. Press, 2002.

McCullers, Carson. *The Ballad of the Sad Café and Other Stories.* 1951. Reprint. New York: Bantam, 1991.

———. *Clock Without Hands.* 1961. Reprint. Boston: Houghton Mifflin, 1998.

———. *Collected Stories of Carson McCullers.* Boston: Houghton Mifflin, 1987.

———. *The Heart Is a Lonely Hunter.* 1940. Reprint. New York: Bantam, 1981.

———. *Illumination and Night Glare: The Unfinished Autobiography of Carson McCullers.* Edited by Carlos L. Dews. Madison: Univ. of Wisconsin Press, 1999.

———. *The Member of the Wedding.* 1946. Reprint. New York: Bantam, 1958.

———. *The Mortgaged Heart.* Edited by Margarita G. Smith. Boston: Houghton Mifflin, 1971.

———. *Reflections in a Golden Eye.* 1941. Reprint. New York: Bantam, 1966.

McDowell, Margaret B. *Carson McCullers.* Boston: Twayne, 1980.

McLaughlin, Richard. "A Dixieland Stew." Review of *Other Voices, Other Rooms,* by Truman Capote. *Saturday Review* (14 February 1948): 12–13.

McMillen, Neil R. *Dark Journey: Black Mississippians in the Age of Jim Crow.* Urbana: Univ. of Illinois Press, 1990.

McSorley, Joseph. Review of *Strange Fruit,* by Lillian Smith. *Catholic World* 159 (May 1944): 182.

Mellard, James. "The Fiction of Social Commitment." In *The History of Southern Literature,* edited by Louis D. Rubin, Jr., et al. Baton Rouge: Louisiana State Univ. Press, 1985.

Mencken, H. L. "The Sahara of the Bozart." In *Prejudices: Second Series.* New York: Knopf, 1920.

Millichap, Joseph R. "Carson McCullers." In *The History of Southern Literature,* edited by Louis D. Rubin, Jr., et al. Baton Rouge: Louisiana State Univ. Press, 1985.

Morris, Lloyd. "A Vivid, Inner, Secret World: Truman Capote's First Novel Fulfills

High Expectations." Review of *Other Voices, Other Rooms,* by Truman Capote. *New York Herald Tribune Weekly Book Review* (18 January 1948): 2.

O'Connor, Flannery. "Some Aspects of the Grotesque in Southern Fiction." In *Mystery and Manners,* edited by Sally Fitzgerald and Robert Fitzgerald. New York: Farrar, Straus & Giroux, 1962.

Percy, William Armstrong, III. "William Alexander Percy (1885–1942): His Homosexuality and Why It Matters." In *Carryin' On in the Lesbian and Gay South,* edited by John Howard. New York: New York Univ. Press, 1997.

Phillips, Robert. *William Goyen.* Boston: G. K. Hall, 1979.

Plimpton, George. *Truman Capote.* 1997. Reprint. New York: Anchor Books, 1998.

Ransom, John Crowe. "Criticism, Inc." In *Selected Essays of John Crowe Ransom,* edited by Thomas Daniel Young and John Hindle. Baton Rouge: Louisiana State Univ. Press, 1984.

———. "Introduction: A Statement of Principles." In *I'll Take My Stand: The South and the Agrarian Tradition.* 1930. Reprint, with an introduction by Louis D. Rubin, Jr. Baton Rouge: Louisiana State Univ. Press, 1977.

Reed, Kenneth T. *Truman Capote.* Boston: Twayne, 1981.

Review of *Other Voices, Other Rooms,* by Truman Capote. *New Yorker* (24 January 1948): 80.

Review of *To Kill a Mockingbird,* by Harper Lee. *Booklist* 57 (1 September 1960): 23.

Review of *To Kill a Mockingbird,* by Harper Lee. *Commonweal* (9 December 1960): 289.

Rich, Adrienne. "Compulsory Heterosexuality and Lesbian Existence." In *Blood, Bread, and Poetry: Selected Prose 1979–1985.* New York: W. W. Norton, 1986.

Richards, Gary. "Moving beyond Mississippi: Beth Henley and the Anxieties of Postsouthernness." In *Beth Henley: A Casebook,* edited by Julia A. Fesmire. New York: Routledge, 2002.

Rolo, Charles J. Review of *Other Voices, Other Rooms,* by Truman Capote. *Atlantic* 181 (March 1948): 109.

———. "A Southern Drama." Review of *Clock Without Hands,* by Carson McCullers. *Atlantic* 208 (October 1961): 126–27.

Rowley, Hazel. *Richard Wright: The Life and Times.* New York: Henry Holt, 2001.

Rubin, Louis D., Jr. "Carson McCullers: The Aesthetic of Pain." In *A Gallery of Southerners.* Baton Rouge: Louisiana State Univ. Press, 1982.

———. Introduction to *The History of Southern Literature,* edited by Louis D. Rubin, Jr., et al. Baton Rouge: Louisiana State Univ. Press, 1985.

———. "Six Novels and S. Levin." Review of *Clock Without Hands,* by Carson McCullers. *Sewanee Review* 70 (Summer 1962): 504–14.

Sarotte, Georges-Michel. *Like a Brother, Like a Lover: Male Homosexuality in the*

American Novel and Theater from Herman Melville to James Baldwin. Translated by Richard Miller. Garden City, N.Y.: Doubleday, 1978.

Savigneau, Josyane. *Carson McCullers: A Life.* Translated by Joan E. Howard. Boston: Houghton Mifflin, 2001.

Sedgwick, Eve Kosofsky. *Epistemology of the Closet.* Berkeley: Univ. of California Press, 1990.

———. *Tendencies.* Durham, N.C.: Duke Univ. Press, 1993.

Segrest, Mab. "'Lines I Dare': Southern Lesbian Writing." In *My Mama's Dead Squirrel: Lesbian Essays on Southern Culture.* Ithaca, N.Y.: Firebrand Books, 1985.

———. "Southern Women Writing: Toward a Literature of Wholeness." In *My Mama's Dead Squirrel: Lesbian Essays on Southern Culture.* Ithaca, N.Y.: Firebrand Books, 1985.

Smith, Barbara. "Homophobia: Why Bring It Up?" In *The Lesbian and Gay Studies Reader,* edited by Henry Abelove, Michèle Aina Barale, and David M. Halperin. New York: Routledge, 1993.

Smith, Lillian. *How Am I to Be Heard? Letters of Lillian Smith.* Edited by Margaret Rose Gladney. Chapel Hill: Univ. of North Carolina Press, 1993.

———. *Killers of the Dream.* 1949. Reprint. New York: W. W. Norton, 1978.

———. *One Hour.* 1959. Reprint, with an introduction by Margaret Rose Gladney. Chapel Hill: Univ. of North Carolina Press, 1994.

———. *Strange Fruit.* 1944. Reprint, with a foreword by Fred Hobson. Athens: Univ. of Georgia Press, 1985.

"Spare the Laurels." Review of *Other Voices, Other Rooms,* by Truman Capote. *Time* (26 January 1948): 102.

Spender, Stephen. Afterword to *William Goyen: Selected Letters from a Writer's Life,* edited by Robert Phillips. Austin: Univ. of Texas Press, 1995.

Sprandel, Katherine. "*The Long Dream.*" In *Richard Wright: Impressions and Perspectives,* edited by David Ray and Robert M. Farnsworth. Ann Arbor: Univ. of Michigan Press, 1971.

Suleri, Sara. "Woman Skin Deep: Feminism and the Postcolonial Condition." In *Colonial Discourse and Post-Colonial Theory,* edited by Patrick Williams and Laura Chrisman. New York: Columbia Univ. Press, 1994.

Sullivan, Walter. Preface to *Bedford Forrest and His Critter Company,* by Andrew Nelson Lytle. Nashville, Tenn.: J. S. Saunders, 1992.

"Summer Reading." Review of *To Kill a Mockingbird,* by Harper Lee. *Atlantic Monthly* 206 (August 1960): 98.

Sundquist, Eric J. "Blues for Atticus Finch: Scottsboro, *Brown,* and Harper Lee." In *The South as an American Problem,* edited by Larry J. Griffin and Don H. Doyle. Athens: Univ. of Georgia Press, 1995.

Tate, Allen. Allen Tate to Jean Toomer, 7 November 1923. In *Cane,* ed. Darwin T. Turner. New York: W. W. Norton, 1988.

———. "The New Provincialism." In *Essays of Four Decades.* Chicago: Swallow Press, 1968.

———. "Remarks on the Southern Religion." In *I'll Take My Stand: The South and the Agrarian Tradition.* 1930. Reprint, with an introduction by Louis D. Rubin, Jr. Baton Rouge: Louisiana State Univ. Press, 1977.

Trilling, Diana. Review of *Other Voices, Other Rooms,* by Truman Capote. *Nation* (31 January 1948): 133–34.

———. Review of *Strange Fruit,* by Lillian Smith. *Nation* (18 March 1944): 342.

Vidal, Gore. "Carson McCullers's *Clock Without Hands.*" In *Carson McCullers,* edited by Harold Bloom. New York: Chelsea House, 1986.

Walker, Alice. *The Color Purple.* New York: Simon & Schuster, 1982.

Walker, Margaret. *Richard Wright, Daemonic Genius: A Portrait of the Man, a Critical Look at His Work.* New York: Warner Books, 1988.

Warner, Michael. "Homo-Narcissism; or, Heterosexuality." In *Engendering Men: The Question of Male Feminist Criticism,* edited by Joseph A. Boone and Michael Cadden. New York: Routledge, 1990.

Warren, Robert Penn. *At Heaven's Gate.* 1942. Reprint. New York: New Directions, 1985.

Washington, Mary Helen. "'The Darkened Eye Restored': Notes Toward a Literary History of Black Women." In *Reading Black, Reading Feminist,* edited by Henry Louis Gates, Jr. New York: Penguin, 1990.

Waterhouse, Keith. Review of *To Kill a Mockingbird,* by Harper Lee. *New Statesman* (15 October 1960): 580.

Weaver, Richard M. "Aspects of the Southern Philosophy." In *Southern Renascence: The Literature of the Modern South,* edited by Louis D. Rubin, Jr., and Robert D. Jacobs. Baltimore, Md.: Johns Hopkins Press, 1953.

———. *The Southern Tradition at Bay: A History of Postbellum Thought,* edited by George Core and M. E. Bradford. New Rochelle, N.Y.: Arlington House, 1986. Quoted in Richard Gray, *Writing the South: Ideas of an American Region* (Cambridge, N.Y.: Cambridge Univ. Press, 1986), 280.

Webb, Constance. *Richard Wright: A Biography.* New York: Putnam's Sons, 1968.

Weeks, Edward. Review of *Strange Fruit,* by Lillian Smith. *Atlantic* 173 (May 1944): 123–24.

West, Ray B., Jr. "Katherine Anne Porter and 'Historic Memory.'" In *Southern Renascence: The Literature of the Modern South,* edited by Louis D. Rubin, Jr., and Robert D. Jacobs. Baltimore, Md.: Johns Hopkins Press, 1953.

Westling, Louise. "Carson McCullers' Amazon Nightmare." In *Carson McCullers,* edited by Harold Bloom. New York: Chelsea House, 1986.

White, Barbara A. "Loss of Self in *The Member of the Wedding*." In *Carson McCullers*, edited by Harold Bloom. New York: Chelsea House, 1986.

Woodland, J. Randal. "Gay Literature." In *The Companion to Southern Literature*, edited by Joseph M. Flora and Lucinda H. MacKethan. Baton Rouge: Louisiana State Univ. Press, 2002.

Wright, Richard. "Big Boy Leaves Home." In *Uncle Tom's Children*. 1940. Reprint. New York: HarperCollins, 1992.

————. *The Long Dream*. 1957. Reprint. New York: Harper & Row, 1987.

Wyatt-Brown, Bertram. *The House of Percy: Honor, Melancholy, and Imagination in a Southern Family*. New York: Oxford Univ. Press, 1994.

Young, Thomas Daniel. Introduction to part 3 of *The History of Southern Literature*, edited by Louis D. Rubin, et al. Baton Rouge: Louisiana State Univ. Press, 1985.

Index